TEACHING
IN THE EARLY
YEARS

Third Edition

TEACHING
IN THE EARLY
YEARS

BERNARD SPODEK
University of Illinois

PRENTICE-HALL, INC.
Englewood Cliffs, New Jersey 07632

Library of Congress Cataloging in Publication Data

Spodek, Bernard.
   Teaching in the early years.

   Bibliography: p.
   Includes index.
   1. Education, Primary. I. Title.
LB1523.S66 1985   372'.21   84–14376
ISBN 0–13–892613–1

Editorial/production supervision and
   interior design: Sylvia Moore
Cover design: Wanda Lubelska
Manufacturing buyer: Ron Chapman

Printed in the United States of America

10 9 8 7 6 5 4 3 2 1

ISBN 0-13-892613-1 01

Prentice-Hall International, Inc., *London*
Prentice-Hall of Australia Pty. Limited, *Sydney*
Editora Prentice-Hall do Brasil, Ltda., *Rio de Janeiro*
Prentice-Hall Canada Inc., *Toronto*
Prentice-Hall of India Private Limited, *New Delhi*
Prentice-Hall of Japan, Inc., *Tokyo*
Prentice-Hall of Southeast Asia Pte. Ltd., *Singapore*
Whitehall Books Limited, *Wellington, New Zealand*

Contents

v

Preface

A great deal of change has taken place in the field of early childhood education since the first edition of *Teaching in the Early Years* was written. Kindergarten, which just two decades ago provided education for less than half the five-year-olds, is now an almost universal part of public education. In addition, most children today have been in some program before entering kindergarten, often in a full-day program reflecting the increased use of day care services for children.

There has been a growing acceptance of the field of early childhood education. Parents are not considered suspect if they enroll their children in preschool classes. We have come to know that good day care does not have negative effects on young children. In fact, enrollment in preschool programs can have persistent, long-range, positive effects. Special programs have also evolved for gifted, handicapped, and bilingual children, and a greater concern is being shown for multicultural education, reflecting a concern for the diversity of the American population.

This period has also been productive of research related to early childhood education. Some of this research has been policy oriented, supporting the establishment of educational programs for young children, especially children from poor families and those with educational or developmental problems. A considerable amount of research has also been done in the area of the play of young children, as well as in relation to reading and prereading activities. Another important thread of research that is influencing the field, though less directly, relates to teaching. Researchers have begun to look at teachers' thought processes as well as teachers' behaviors. This suggests that what teachers think and what they know is as important as how they act in a classroom.

While there have been changes throughout the years, there has also been a considerable amount of stability in the field. The basic values that underlie the field of early childhood education have remained constant. Educators continue to believe in the importance of the early years for educating children. They remain concerned with providing basic developmental support and protection for young children. Early childhood teachers continue to nurture children's basic physical, social, and intellectual competence along with the development of skills in self-expression and creativity. They continue to value the individual child, selecting from among program alternatives and modifying curriculum within the class to be responsive to each individual.

Early childhood education is a unified field, encompassing the nursery, kindergarten, and primary years. Although levels may be separated administratively, children do not change from year to year to fit the expectations of educational grade levels. Change that does occur is gradual and developmental, with differences in rates of change among individual children. This change is one of the assumptions upon which this book is based. Other assumptions relate to the nature of early childhood curriculum and the role of the teacher.

Curriculum comes from many sources. Values are an important base of curriculum, as is understanding how children grow and learn. The conceptions of knowledge which underlie various subject areas provide yet another source. The state of the art of education must also be recognized as an important source, determining both possibilities for and limitations of education for young children. Finally, the traditions of the field become an important source of classroom practice.

This book is addressed to teachers and to those who are preparing to be teachers of young children. Although eclectic in its foundation, the approach suggested here is not a conglomerate of all the approaches available in early childhood education today. Rather it is based upon a judgment of what can be done with children, selecting from educational points of view that fit within a consistent framework. Teachers are viewed here as more than just participants in classroom activities. They are decision makers whose actions—even prior to their entrance into the classroom—help determine what children will learn.

The book is divided into three parts. The first three chapters provide the foundation for a look at curriculum and teaching in the early years. The first chapter presents a view of teaching related to the multidimensional role of the teacher. The second chapter reviews the various educational institutions provided for young children and outlines the traditions from which they developed. The third chapter addresses issues of curriculum for young children.

The second section, chapters 4 through 10, deals with the specific subject areas that make up the school program. Each chapter consists of two sections, one reviewing what we know about the particular area of the curriculum and one suggesting the content for school programs and the ways this might be approached. Play is treated as a legitimate part of the school program.

The final portion of the book deals with the teacher's other educational concerns: classroom organization, techniques of working with parents and children, and the evaluation of education.

One chapter relates to children with special educational needs. The concern for identifying and educating children with handicapping conditions as early as possible, and for providing this education in the least restrictive environment, has led to an increased emphasis on this area. In many cases, teachers of normal children will have to accommodate mildly and moderately handicapped children in their classes.

I wish to acknowledge my debt to the many teachers, undergraduate and graduate students, and children with whom I have worked over the past two decades. The ideas expressed here have grown out of interaction with many people who have influenced me as I hope that I have been an influence upon them. I owe a special debt to my colleagues at Beth Hayeled School, where I first began teaching. I continually reflect on my early experiences there as a source of ideas and inspiration.

Finally, and most important, I want to acknowledge not only her contribution to chapter eight, but especially the encouragement, love, and support I have received and continue to receive from my wife, Prudence.

1

Teaching

Whether standing in front of the classroom commanding the attention of all the children or sitting quietly in a corner working with a small group, teachers are central to all activity. Directly or indirectly, they control much of the activity and are responsible for all that occurs to children during school. They must respond to their many needs as they become apparent during the day. They must assure purposeful activities that produce educational benefit for the children.

Teachers perform many different tasks. They function as lecturers, storytellers, group discussion leaders, traffic directors, mediators of conflicts, psychological diagnosticians, custodians, assigners of academic work, and file clerks. Most important are the times when they directly interact with children verbally, as in a discussion, or behaviorally, as when placing an arm around a child's shoulders. The interactions may be gross, like redirecting a child from one part of the room to another, or subtle, such as giving a child a "knowing look."

Many things determine what teachers do in classrooms. Even with the limited age range of early childhood education—between three and eight years as defined in this book—different ages demand different responses from the teacher. Teaching in a day care center requires a greater degree of concern for the physical well-being of children than teaching in a half-day nursery school. In addition, institutional requirements often involve teachers in activities that have nothing directly to do with children's learning. Thus, teachers' duties vary according to place and time, because of the nature of the educational institution and its educational program.

READINESS FOR TEACHING

What does it take to become a teacher of young children? Few people are born with a desire to teach young children or with the necessary competencies. Yet both desire and competencies are requirements for successful teaching. There are other important requisites to teaching as well.

Over the years early childhood educators have stressed different requirements for teachers of young children. Millie Almy and Agnes Snyder (1947) suggested that early childhood teachers need physical stamina, world-mindedness, an understanding of human development, a respect for personality, and a scientific spirit. Others, like Sarah Lou Leeper (1968), have focused on personal qualities such as patience, warmth, kindness, security, and a love of children.

Recently, educators have attempted to specify requirements for early childhood personnel in terms of competencies. The Child Development Associate Consortium has developed a set of six general areas of competence as follows:

1. Establishes and maintains a safe and healthy learning environment
2. Advances physical and intellectual competence
3. Builds positive self-concept and individual strength
4. Promotes positive functioning of children and adults in a group
5. Brings about optimal coordination of home and center child-rearing practices and expectations
6. Carries out supplementary responsibilities related to children's programs (Ward, 1976).

Determining whether an individual possesses these competencies is a complex process requiring a team to judge teaching performance through direct observation as well as through assessment of a portfolio of professional materials.

All states certify primary teachers, often with an elementary school teaching certificate. Forty-nine states offer certificates for kindergarten teachers, while fewer states certify teachers of three-year-olds and four-year-olds (Goldsmith, 1975). In many states certification is required only for teachers who work within public school systems. Since the majority of nursery schools and day care centers are not within these systems, other criteria for assessing teacher competence might prevail. In most states, an agency other than the Office of Education licenses nursery schools and day care centers. Staff requirements are embedded within these licensing standards. Presently, a great range of requirements exist from state to state. Some require a college degree in early childhood education and a teaching certificate, only graduation from high school, or some limited amount of post high school education and early childhood teacher training. Presently, twenty-six states plus the District of Columbia require the Child Development Associate (CDA) Credential for at least one category of day care center staff. There is presently a trend toward the increased use of this credential in day care (Collins, 1983).

Teachers of young children are prepared in colleges and universities, often in early childhood education or child development programs, sometimes related to elementary education programs. Junior colleges also offer associate degrees or one-year programs in child development or early childhood education for persons who wish to work in nursery schools, day care centers, or child development centers.

While such programs vary, the majority meet a general set of requirements for content. Course work is generally required in human growth and development, in methods and curriculum, and in the history, theory, and philosophy of early childhood education. A general education background is also a normal expectation. Courses in health, nutrition, parent education, or family relations might also be required. Each program has a requirement for direct experience with children, either in student teaching, a practicum, or an internship. Many of these programs have recently undergone changes, often in response to state teacher-certification requirements (Spodek, Davis, & Saracho, 1983).

Many programs in two-year and community colleges look much like early childhood teacher-training programs at the university level, although there are fewer course hours offered in each area of preparation. Other community college programs for early childhood practitioners, however, are considered vocational programs and focus more on the practical and less on the theoretical and foundational levels of teaching. Recently, the National Association for the Education of Young Children (NAEYC) has developed a set of guidelines for four-year and five-year programs of early childhood teacher education (NAEYC, 1982) that are being provisionally implemented by the National Council for the Accreditation of Teacher Education. Plans currently exist to establish similar guidelines for programs at two-year and community colleges.

TEACHING INTERACTIONS

There are many functions in the role of the early childhood teacher. Teacher-child interactions serve many purposes. However, the classroom behavior of teachers is not all there is to teaching. Much of the activity of teaching occurs away from children. This activity includes the determination of what to teach; the selection, procurement, and organization of materials and equipment for teaching; the evaluation of learning; and the recording and reporting of children's progress.

Philip Jackson (1966) has differentiated between two modes of teaching behavior—*preactive* teaching and *interactive* teaching:

> Preactive behavior is more or less deliberate. Teachers, when grading exams, planning a lesson, or deciding what to do about a particularly difficult student, tend to

ponder the matter, to weigh evidence, to hypothesize about the possible outcomes of a certain action. During these moments teachers often resemble, albeit crudely, the stereotype of the problem solver, the decision maker, the hypothesis tester, the inquirer. At such times teaching looks like a highly rational process.

. . . In the interactive setting the teacher's behavior is more or less spontaneous. When students are in front of him, and the fat is in the fire, so to speak, the teacher tends to do what he *feels,* or *knows,* rather than what he *thinks,* is right. (p. 13)

Understanding the intuitive nature of interactive teaching helps to explain why this form of teaching is so resistant to change through the tactics used in most teacher-education programs. The behavior of teachers, however, does have a rational basis. How one behaves is a function of how one feels he ought to behave, and what one feels is right cannot be fully separated from what one thinks is right. Teachers' behaviors go hand in hand with teachers' beliefs.

THE ROLE OF THE TEACHER

The teacher of young children plays many roles. The way in which these are acted out are responses to the school situation and its expectations, the expectation of the profession, and the expectations of the teacher. Teachers may be involved in all the major decisions relating to children and what they learn, or be told what to do. Some schools place great stress upon *caring* for children; others, only upon *instruction.* Whether a range of teaching styles is encouraged varies among schools.

In all situations, to a greater or lesser extent, teachers seem to serve a nurturant role, an instructional role, and a relational role. Each role contains both an action element and a decision-making element. A teacher should be aware of these many role dimensions.

Teaching as Nurturance

Young children are relatively dependent upon adults for their health, care, and safety. Teaching in the early years requires one to be nurturant. Children cannot learn if they are hungry, ill, frightened, or uncomfortable. From its inception, the nursery school provided for the care of children. Day care centers were specifically designed to provide this care. Kindergartens and elementary schools accepted responsibility for caring elements as well, feeding breakfast and lunch to children and providing various screening tests to identify physical problems. The responsibility for this care often falls on the classroom teacher.

Teachers of young children have to go beyond these basic nurturing responsibilities. They need to provide love and comfort. They may, in a limited sense, serve as parent substitutes. They may even be called upon to toilet train a child. All these are important and reasonable educational requirements.

However, problems arise when the nurturing acts become the only interrests of the teacher. It is easy to become aware of the children's needs for nur-

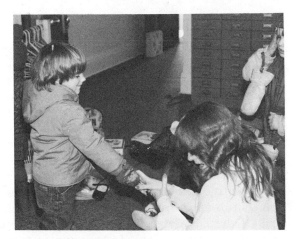

FIGURE 1-1
Teachers provide basic care to young children.

turing; in some circumstances they cry out for response. They should never be ignored. Some of the other educational needs of children are less apparent and thus more easily overlooked. When the teacher's nurturant role becomes the only role dimension that is manifest, the program is apt to be more a child-minding operation than an educational endeavor. This shortchanges children.

Teaching as Instruction

When we think of teaching, we usually think of the instructional role of the teacher. The conventional view of a teacher is of a person who transmits knowledge to others. Telling and demonstrating comprise a direct form of instruction. Other more indirect forms of instruction can also elicit learning. Indirect instruction includes creating learning situations, planning for encounters with instructional resources, and asking questions that cause children to think and test perceptions of reality. These techniques cause the children to act upon their perceived world to create their own knowledge.

Each view of instruction is based upon a set of assumptions about knowledge and schools that often remain unexamined. One assumption is that knowledge consists of a body of facts and information to be assimilated by an individual. The teacher must determine what knowledge is important. Then the teacher "tells" the children what they must know through lectures, storytelling, demonstrations, or the use of computers, films, sound recordings, or television. Over the years that children attend school, they accumulate more facts and information, and thus become more knowledgeable.

Other views of education and the development of knowledge require different forms of instruction. Knowledge is not the result of an accumulation of facts and information but rather the result of an integration of information within some structure that gives it meaning. Facts are the raw data from which knowledge is developed, and they may be easily discarded, once used. To create knowledge, a person must do something to these facts, becoming an active seeker and creator of knowledge. Passively receiving information is not enough.

Within the role of instructor, the teacher serves as a curriculum designer, a diagnostician, and an organizer of instruction. In designing curriculum, the teacher plans an organized set of experiences to promote those learnings judged appropriate for children. The scope of intended learnings, the sequence in which they will be offered, and the balance of different elements within the school life of the child must all be considered.

Some educators suggest that the scope of educational experiences offered to children should be narrow to allow schools to ensure success in the most important elements of education. Those who advocate going "back to basics" feel that when the school curriculum is too broad, energies and resources get spread too thin to allow for the adequate teaching and learning of basic academic skills. Others, however, believe that education must be broad based and related to children's current lives. To limit unnecessarily the area of the school's concern is to limit children's learning in a way that is inadequate for dealing with children's current lives and social needs.

Sequence refers to the way learning experiences are organized over time. Some educators believe that education is most effective when children are provided with a series of hierarchical experiences, with the achievement of simpler goals leading to the achievement of more complex goals. Others feel that learning activities should be sequenced in relation to children's developmental levels. Still others feel that children should be offered choices from which they may select activities based on their interests rather than on some organization that teachers impose.

There have been a range of models developed in the field of early childhood education based on different assumptions relating to the nature of schooling, the nature of knowledge, and the nature of young children. Teachers can select from among those models and modify them to fit their particular circumstances. In selecting and modifying existing programs, the teacher designs a curriculum for a particular group of children after carefully considering issues of scope, sequence, and balance.

Once a teacher has designed a program for a group of children, interest must turn to assessing the learning capabilities of the children. Teachers must come to know each child in order to create an appropriate match between children's learning abilities and styles and the teaching methods and materials to be used. In doing this, teachers must draw upon their knowledge of how children learn and develop as well as their knowledge of early childhood practices and procedures.

As diagnosticians, teachers collect relevant information about each child for use in program planning. Some of this information comes from others, including parents, psychologists, learning specialists, and former teachers. In addition, teachers continually collect their own information about the children in their class through observing children's behaviors, analyzing children's products, and administering both standardized and teacher-made tests. The infor-

FIGURE 1-2
Teachers provide direct
and indirect instruction
to young children.

mation that teachers collect should be recorded systematically. Program plans can take this information into consideration from the beginning of the school year and, as the school year progresses, such information is used to modify the evolving curriculum.

Once these tasks are performed, it becomes the responsibility of teachers to deliver those educational experiences that have been designed. Physical and human resources must be gathered and put to proper use. The activities of the classroom must be orchestrated so that each child's individual needs can be met within the total class milieu. Physical space must be organized, materials must be collected and deployed, a daily schedule must be established, and strategies for learning activities must be decided upon and implemented. Especially in the beginning of the year, children must be made aware of the resources available to them. Both direct and indirect methods of teaching can be used by teachers.

The concept of the teacher as instructor is adequate for an understanding of only one of the teacher's roles. It represents part of the whole picture.

Teaching as Relating

While some educators view the instructional role of the teacher as crucial, others view the relational aspect of teaching as being of primary importance. The teacher continually interacts with children during the school day, and the quality of these interactions may be more important than the specific instructional practices.

Arthur Combs (1965) defines the effective teacher as a unique human being who uses oneself effectively and efficiently to carry out personal and social purposes in the education of others. The use of oneself in carrying out the purposes of education goes beyond professional competency. It requires that the teacher's total self, personal as well as professional, be involved in the educational process. Developing ways of relating to and interacting with people is an important part of becoming a teacher.

FIGURE 1-3
The quality of interaction with children is critical to good teaching.

In addition to providing instruction, the teacher serves as a guide and a helper to the children. Teachers create an atmosphere in the classroom in which children gain a sense of trust. They help children feel secure as learners and persons, guiding them in making decisions, and providing a rich environment for learning.

Each teacher brings a set of values to a classroom. These values help determine what is considered important and how to deal with individual children. They even determine the selection and use of material and classroom arrangement. Ultimately, they will influence the values of the children. The value aspects of the program are often described as "caught rather than taught" because of the personal way in which they are expressed and transmitted.

Above all, teachers provide warmth and support for children. Children are accepted as total human beings with strengths and weaknesses. Through personal relationships with children, teachers help them grow.

The relational aspects of teaching are not based upon any set of teacher actions; what is important is that teachers manifest their personalities in authentic ways. Teacher-training programs must go beyond conventional courses in methods and foundations of education; they must help students explore the meaning that education and teaching have for them and help them understand the nature of their relationships with others.

TEACHING: THINKING AND ACTING

Much of what teachers do, labeled the interactive aspects of teaching (Jackson, 1966), is directly accessible even to the casual observer who enters the classroom. Because this aspect of teaching is so accessible, it has been the focus of attention and research for many years. Indeed, up until recently, most of the research on teaching has focused on teacher behavior (see, for example, Rosenshine, 1976). More recently, however, researchers have focused an increased portion of their attention on teachers' thinking. Teachers' thought processes are less accessible than their behaviors and can often be studied only through teachers' reports of what they think. Such research requires a higher level of inference in its analysis. It is no less real, however, nor is it less important. In fact, much of what teachers do is driven by what they think. Among the areas of teachers' thought that have been studied are teacher planning, teacher judgment, interactive decision making, and teachers' implicit theories (Clark & Yinger, 1979).

The research summarized by Clark and Yinger suggests that teachers begin their planning by considering the content of what is to be taught and the setting in which teaching will take place. Teachers then focus their attention on the need for student involvement. The activity, rather than its goal, is the focal point of planning which becomes a progressive elaboration of a major idea. In thinking about teaching, teachers make judgments about their students, about the materials available to them, and about themselves. Evidence points to the fact that teachers' judgmental policies are responsive to training.

Among the studies of teachers' thinking is a wide range of studies about teachers' implicit theories. Teachers hold a variety of curriculum constructs (Bussis, Chittenden, & Amarel, 1976), or theories-in-use (Argyris & Schön, 1975), that drive their actions. The knowledge that teachers gain in university courses, in in-service training sessions, or in their professional reading is sifted through these belief systems. Teachers accept or reject the information they gather. The theories they hold help teachers create meanings from the information they receive. Such theories allow teachers to behave in a consistent manner as they work under a variety of circumstances with a range of children. Within this consistency, however, teachers must respond flexibly to particular conditions.

In becoming a teacher, each individual constructs his or her own set of theories of education. The theories are built out of the information gained in teacher-training programs—theories of learning and development that are expounded upon in classes along with knowledge of methods and materials gleaned from courses. Practical experience in classrooms with children provides a test for the theoretical knowledge gained in teacher preparation as well as another source of information upon which to build and modify a personal set of theories of education. Finally, what comes to be known professionally must be matched with a set of personal and social values each teacher has which relate to the importance of childhood, the importance of the individual, the importance of the school, and the effectiveness of all that we do with and for children.

The process of becoming a teacher, which is a continual one, may begin in a college course but should not end there. It includes the continued development and modification of theories about education as well as the continued improvement of teaching skills. It is in the integration of thinking and acting that teaching reaches its highest professional stage.

REFERENCES

ALMY, M., and SNYDER, A.   The staff and its preparation. *Early childhood education.* 46th Yearbook of the National Society for the Study of Education, Part II. Chicago: University of Chicago Press, 1947.

ARGYRIS, C., and SCHÖN, D. A.   *Theory in practice: Increasing professional effectiveness.* San Francisco: Jossey-Bass, 1975.

BUSSIS, A. M., CHITTENDON, E. A., and AMAREL, M.   *Beyond surface curriculum.* Boulder, Colo.: Westview Press, 1976.

CLARK, C. M., and YINGER, R. J.   Teachers thinking. In P. L. Peterson, and H. J. Walberg (Eds.), *Research on teaching: Concepts, findings and implications.* Berkeley, Calif.: McCutcheon, 1979.

COLLINS, R. C.   Child care and the states: The comparative licensing study. *Young Children,* 1983, *38*(5), 3–11.

COMBS, A. W.   *The professional education of teachers.* Boston: Allyn & Bacon, 1965.

JACKSON, P. W.   *The way teaching is.* Washington, D.C.: Association for Supervision and Curriculum Development, 1966.

LEEPER, S. L.   *Nursery schools and kindergarten.* Washington, D.C.: National Education Association, 1968.

ROSENSHINE, B.   Recent research on teacher behaviors and student achievement. *Journal of Teacher Education,* 1976, *27,* 61–64.

SPODEK, B., DAVIS, M. D., and SARACHO, O. N.   Early childhood teacher education and certification. *Journal of Teacher Education,* 1983, *34*(5), 50–52.

WARD, E. H., and the Child Development Associate staff.   The child development associate consortium's assessment system. *Young Children,* 1976, *31,* 244–54.

SUGGESTED READING

ALMY, M.   *The early childhood educator at work.* New York: McGraw-Hill, 1975.

GORDON, I. J. (Ed.).   *Early childhood education.* 71st Yearbook of the National Society for the Study of Education. Chicago: University of Chicago Press, 1972.

HYMES, J. L., Jr.   *Early childhood education: An introduction to the profession* (2nd ed.). Washington, D.C.: National Association for the Education of Young Children, 1975.

SPODEK, B., and WALBERG, H. J. (Eds.).   *Early childhood education: Issues and insights.* Berkeley, Calif.: McCutcheon, 1977.

SPODEK, B. (Ed.).   *Handbook of research in early childhood education.* New York: Free Press, 1982.

2

Schools for Young Children

Early childhood education in the United States is practiced in nursery schools, day care centers, Head Start programs, kindergartens, and primary classes. Although there are many common elements among these institutions, differences in institutional setting, age of children served, traditions from which the programs developed, goals set for programs, and psychological theories subscribed to all influence the program. A look at the traditions of early childhood education and contemporary schools should help in understanding the field as it is organized.

Early childhood education programs have been offered in one form or another in the United States since colonial times. The estimates of enrollment in preprimary education for three-year-olds, four-year-olds, and five-year-olds for the year 1980, the most recent figures available at this writing, show a continuation of a trend toward increased enrollments of children at the nursery-kindergarten level.

In October 84.7 percent of the five-year-olds, 46.3 percent of the four-year-olds, and 27.3 percent of the three-year-olds were enrolled in schools (Grant & Eiden, 1982).

THE ROOTS OF EARLY
CHILDHOOD EDUCATION

Some of the differences in schools for young children stem from the distinct traditions and backgrounds that helped develop the separate institutions of the nursery, kindergarten, and primary grades. Each institution was developed and influenced by educators and philosophers with different points of view and from different cultures. As the years have passed, the institutions have been modified, influenced by varied schools of educational thought and assorted cultural contexts.

The Primary School

The primary school was conceived to provide instruction in the basic skills subjects. Reading, writing, and computational skills are the core of learning and teaching at this level. Although other areas of study may be included in the primary grades, these are never afforded the status of the skill areas.

The goals of contemporary primary education descend directly from those of colonial primary education. Especially in the New England colonies, the pressure of religious belief required that persons be able to read the scriptures in the vernacular. This led to the establishment of primary schools under the supervision of the community church. The content of the schools was the teaching of reading, with instruction in spelling, grammar, and arithmetic added later.

The preamble to the Puritan School Law of 1647 gives evidence of the religious roots of colonial primary education:

> It being one chief point of that old deluder, Satan, to keep men from the knowledge of the Scriptures, as in former times, by keeping them in an unknown tongue, so in these latter times, by persuading from the use of tongues, that so at last the true sense and meaning of the original might be clouded by false glosses of saint-seeming deceivers, that learning might not be buried in the grave of our fathers in church and commonwealth, the Lord assisting our endeavors,—It is therefore ordered that every township in this jurisdiction, after the Lord has increased them to the number of fifty householders, shall then forthwith appoint one within their own town to teach all such children as shall resort to him to write and read. (Nohle, 1924)

As the American colonies became a nation, schools lost some of their religious flavor as concern for developing patriotism in children grew. The content of primers used for reading instruction in the late eighteenth century shifted from excerpts from or about the Bible to tales of patriotism and morality. In the nineteenth century the education of children became a public concern, and schools began to receive financial support from the states. At this time the concept of universal education began to take hold, and children of all backgrounds were admitted into the publicly supported schools.

It was not uncommon in this early period to see very young children enrolled in primary schools. Children were viewed then as being capable of high levels of intellectual development. They often learned to read at age three or four while Latin instruction might begin at age five or six.

After statehood, schools in Massachusetts changed from religious to secular institutions. By the beginning of the nineteenth century, most towns in that state offered private and public schooling to the young. School attendance remained high for the very young. In 1826, 5 percent of all children below the age of four, including 20 percent of all three-year-olds, were enrolled in school. A number of reasons are given for the declining enrollment of the young, including (1) an increased emphasis on the role of the mother at home, including her role in educating her young children; (2) a greater concern for the balanced development of young children, including a fear that excessive intellectual activity in young children could cause insanity; and (3) the growing bureaucracy of the public school which, in the 1840s and 1850s sought to exclude, not only the under-fours, but four-year-olds and five-year-olds as well. The reasons given included concern for the well-being of young children as well as the well-being of the school, including better attendance, more disciplined classes, and financial savings (May & Vinovskis, 1977).

While the primary school of the early nineteenth century was basically concerned with teaching the "Three R's," new elements of instruction were slowly added to the curriculum: arts and crafts, nature study (later to be supplanted by science), geography (later to be incorporated into the social studies), music, and physical education.

Teachers in the colonial primary schools were hired with little regard for professional qualifications or credentials. Indentured servants and widowed women often served as teachers. The method of instruction consisted mainly of recitation and rote memorization, with the limited number of textbooks available providing the core of the instructional program.

New educational methodologies developing in Europe during the nineteenth century affected the American primary school. Interpretations of the Pestallozzian system of education, with its emphasis on education through objects, were leading to new developments in German primary education. Reports about these schools influenced American educators to modify their verbal methods of teaching and to enrich their curricula. The establishment of normal schools for the preparation of teachers helped to increase the concern of American educators about teaching methodology.

During the latter half of the nineteenth century, the educational philosophy of the German educator Johann Friedrich Herbart greatly influenced the American primary school. Educational lessons were organized into five steps of the Herbartian system: preparation, presentation, association, generalization, and application. All lessons were to start with preparation of the class and all learnings were to culminate in the child's demonstration of his ability to apply new learning. Remnants of the Herbartian method still remain in the organization of lesson plans, which may begin with "motivating the children" and end in a "culminating activity."

The American Progressive Education movement had a great impact upon the organization of instruction in the primary grades during the first half of the twentieth century. In many cases the Herbartian lessons gave way to the more organic *project* method, which in turn led to the *unit* approach.

The move toward urbanization and the development of large schools and school systems in the nineteenth century also led to a change in the organizational patterns of primary education. The nongraded structure of the one-room country school was supplanted by the multiroom school organized by grade, with instructional objectives determined and all children of like age being grouped together in a single class.

The Infant School, a form of primary education in Britain, was founded in 1816 in New Lanark, Scotland, by Robert Owen, the social reformer. The original principles of infant education were

> that the children were to be out of doors as much as possible and to learn "when their curiosity induced them to ask questions," to dance and sing and not to be "annoyed with books." They were to be educated and trained without punishment or the fear of it, no unnecessary restraint was to be imposed on them and they were to be taught only "what they could understand." The teachers were told to think about such matters as forming good habits and helping the children to treat each other kindly. (Gardner, n.d., p. 6)

Owen's school, designed for the children of workers in his mill, was conceived as a part of a broader program of social reform. Owen's conception of the Infant School foreshadowed the concerns of many contemporary educators.

Owen's idea of using the infant school to serve the needs of poor and working class children spread beyond his mill town. By 1825 there were at least fifty-five infant schools in England, Scotland and Ireland, along with a number of infant school societies. Owen's books were circulated throughout Continental Europe and the United States. By 1827 infant schools were being established in Hartford, Connecticut; New York City; Philadelphia; Boston; and other American cities. Robert Owen himself came to the United States during this period and lectured extensively about his new views of society and about education. He purchased the settlement of New Harmony, Indiana, from the Rappites, a religious group, and set his son up to establish a communitarian society there along with an infant school. Both the school and the community had serious problems and failed. Infant schools did flourish for a while, though, in New England and in middle Atlantic communities for about another decade. By the mid-1830s the infant school movement in America had faded.

The infant schools that evolved were felt to embody the humane innovations and principles of education that could prove valuable to the public primary schools. More important, these infant schools were underwritten by social reformers who saw them as ways of combatting the ills of urban life. Infant schools, it was felt, could permanently eliminate poverty by educating and socializing young children from poor families. They provided a means for both moral and literary instruction for the children of the urban poor while at the same time freeing their mothers for work (May & Vinovskis, 1977). Less than a quarter of a century after the demise of the infant school movement, the Froebelian kindergarten was introduced to the United States.

The Froebelian Kindergarten

The kindergarten was developed in Germany in the first half of the nineteenth century. Based upon a mystical religious philosophy relating to the unity of the individual and nature, God, and other people, Friedrich Froebel designed a series of activities for children aged three to six to symbolize these relationships. The Froebelian kindergarten was composed, in essence, of the use of the *Gifts,* the *Occupations,* and the *Mother's Songs and Plays,* as well as the care of plants and animals.

The *Gifts* were sets of small manipulative materials to be used by children in prescribed ways. The first was a series of six yarn balls, each a different color. The single surface of the ball, a sphere, symbolized the unity and wholeness of the universe. The next set—a wooden sphere, a cylinder, and a cube—represented unity and diversity, as well as the mediation of opposites—the sphere and cube representing opposites, the cylinder representing a mediating shape. Other *Gifts,* including a cube broken up into smaller cubes, followed by square and triangular tablets, were presented to children in a prescribed sequence. At each presentation, children were supposed to build specific forms, each representing some deeper meaning. Throughout the manipulations, little attention was paid to the physical properties of the objects, for sensation and perception of the real world were not considered important.

The *Occupations,* consisting of weaving, paper-folding, cutting, sewing, drawing, painting, and clay modeling, reflected the activities of primitive people. They also provided the children with opportunities for artistic expression. The *Mother's Plays,* specifically designed songs and games, were derived from the play of peasant women with their young children and from the activities of the social and natural world.

In time, the Froebelian kindergarten began to expand as an educational movement. With the extension of kindergarten education came a need for train-

FIGURE 2-1
Froebel's Kindergarten Gifts.

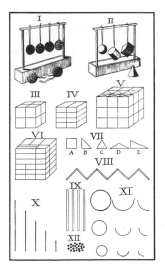

ing kindergarten teachers. Soon kindergarten training institutions began to attract a number of young German women as their students.

With the wave of German migration in the mid-nineteenth century, many women with kindergarten training came to the United States. The desire to apply the principles of the Froebelian kindergarten to their own children led many to establish kindergartens in their homes. Margarethe Schurz, who was trained as a kindergartener in Germany, invited the children of relatives into her home to join her children in what became the first American kindergarten, in Watertown, Wisconsin in 1855. Other kindergartens were established in various communities in the United States in the 1850s and 1860s.

Elizabeth Peabody, who became interested in kindergarten education through her reading and through contact with Margarethe Schurz, who established the first English-speaking kindergarten in Boston in 1860. The philosophy of Froebel was compatible with that of New England Transcendentalism, a philosophic movement that provided intellectual support for the establishment of kindergarten programs in America. Although kindergartens were introduced into the public schools of St. Louis by 1873, the inclusion of kindergarten in public education did not become common for at least two more decades. Kindergartens were being established in many cities during this time, however, by various associations and mothers' clubs and by philanthropic agencies.

The kindergarten was seen as especially useful to the children of the poor in these early days. With the rapid rise of urban centers, the immigration of Europeans to America, and the growth of large city slums, philanthropic kindergartens were established in many areas. Arguments, not unlike those heard today in support of the Head Start program, were used to support kindergarten education for the poor:

> Centering among, and concerning itself with, the children of the poor, and having for its aim the elevation of the home, it was natural that the kindergarten as a philanthropic movement should win great and early favor. The mere fact that the children of the slums were kept off the streets, and that they were made clean and happy by kind and motherly young women; that the child thus being cared for enabled the mother to go about her work in or outside the home—all this appealed to the heart of America, and America gave freely to make these kindergartens possible. Churches established kindergartens, individuals endowed kindergartens, and associations were organized for the spread and support of kindergartens in nearly every large city. (Fisher, 1908, pp. 19–20)

By the beginning of the twentieth century a significant rift had developed in American kindergarten education. Traditional kindergarten educators felt that Froebel had discovered the significant elements of education for young children that were relevant to all children at all times. A more liberal group saw greater meaning in Froebel's educational philosophy than in the specific educational activities and methods derived from it. This liberal group felt that although the original kindergarten program was a step in the right direction, specific activities ought to be discarded when inappropriate. The emergence of the Child Study Movement, which was then establishing an empirical base of knowledge about childhood through the study and observation of children, and the progressive education movement, with its emphasis on freedom and activity in the classroom, lent support to the liberal kindergarteners.

The emerging philosophy of the reform kindergarten movement was probably best stated by Patty Smith Hill in the *Second Report of the Committee of Nineteen of the International Kindergarten Union* (1913). According to her, the content of the kindergarten program should be related to the present life of the child rather than to the life of children of another culture and another generation. The child should be helped to acquire the knowledge of the civilization, which is best done by using the child's personal experiences as a means of achieving insight into knowledge. Hill proposed concrete child-oriented experiences and classroom play that was based more upon the natural activities of childhood, in which the child was free to reconstruct his own reality. The reform movement tried to retain the philosophy of Froebel while doing away with the unnessary formalism of kindergarten method.

Some of the elements of Froebelian philosophy supported by these educators included the following:

1. THE CONCEPT OF DEVELOPMENT IN CHILDHOOD. Froebel suggested that education for young children ought to differ in form and content from that offered to older children. While Froebel's conception of child development is incompatible with present knowledge, the educational implications of the assumption that education ought to be developmentally oriented remains sound.

2. EDUCATION AS SELF-ACTIVITY. Education takes place as the human organism unfolds. The child's movement in educational activity supports this unfolding process. While child development has moved from an acceptance of an "unfolding" process, the concept of education as self-activity is still supported in education.

3. THE EDUCATIONAL VALUE OF PLAY. Froebal saw play as an important activity in helping the child mature and learn. In play, Froebal observed the child's symbolic reproductions of adult activity. He attempted to abstract the significant elements of these and provide them in a meaningful order in his educational program. This idea of the use of play in the education of young children is still supported by educators.

The kindergarten reformers felt that many of the Froebelian *Occupations* were too tedious and required hand movements too small for young children. They also felt that other arts and crafts activities could be profitably included in the kindergarten program. Since the play of the American child was different from that of the German child, different kinds of play activities should be encouraged. In addition, the reformers felt that the child's current life should provide a source of learning. School play became freer and more reflective of the child's life. Large blocks replaced the *Gifts* for constructions, and dolls and miniature housekeeping materials were included in the program.

The reform of kindergarten education continued through the 1920s and 1930s, leading to the creation of the modern American kindergarten we find in many schools today. A number of factors have influenced the development of kindergarten education since the 1920s. The changing economy of the 1930s and 1940s saw a lessening in the number of public school kindergartens as shortages in funds and building space led to the exclusion of this level of education from the public schools. The influence of the mental health movement led to an increase in concern for social-emotional learnings and a deemphasizing of the "habit-training" of the 1920s. In the late 1950s and 1960s kindergarten education began to receive more positive attention. A concern for intellectual development in children led to a reexamination of kindergarten curricula. In addition, psychological theory pointing up the importance of early education gave support to increased public aid for kindergartens and the extension of kindergarten education to large numbers of children in many states.

The Nursery School

The nursery school movement developed from a different cultural context than did the kindergarten. Out of their experience in English health clinics for children of the poor, Rachel and Margaret Macmillan conceived of the nursery school as a preventive for children's illnesses, both mental and physical, that were so prevalent in the slums. The basic philosophy of nursery education was one of *nurturance.*

Nurturance was conceived of as dealing with the whole child, including the social, physical, emotional, and intellectual aspects of the human being. The responsibilities of the original nursery school included bathing the children, dressing them in clean outfits, resting them, and seeing that they got plenty of fresh air—all while being educated. The original nursery schools established in the slums of London were single-story buildings with large doorways or French windows opening into gardens and large play spaces. Children's play flowed freely between indoors and outdoors.

The educational program developed by the Macmillans was social rather than religious in origin, concerned with helping the child learn the observable rather than the symbolic. The Macmillans were influenced more by Edward Seguin than by Froebel. This French educator had developed many activities to improve the sensory education of retarded children. His influence can be seen in current programs for "special" children as well as in the Montessori method.

For three-year-olds and four-year-olds, the program of the nursery school included learning the skills involved in caring for oneself (washing, tying shoelaces, and so forth) and taking responsibilities for plants, keeping animals, or cleaning the school. In addition, specific activities were included to develop the "senses," such as music and rhythmic activities, language activities, and activities that teach form and color. Activities leading to reading and writing as well as number work and science work were recommended by Margaret Macmillan, while Grace Owen, another nursery school pioneer, objected to the introduction of the "Three R's" and object lessons in the curriculum. Free play activities were included in the program, with opportunities for art construction and work with water, sand, and other nonstructured materials.

The work of the Macmillans was so successful that nursery schools were recognized by the Fisher Act of 1918, which allowed for the establishment of nursery schools in local school systems throughout England. Unfortunately, the funds needed to establish these programs were not forthcoming and the expansion of nursery education was a slow process.

In about 1920 a number of teachers who had worked with Margaret Macmillan and Grace Owen came to the United States to demonstrate English nursery education. Nursery schools were started at Teachers College, Columbia University, the Merrill Palmer School of Motherhood and Home Training, and several other agencies in the United States.

During the next decade nursery schools spread slowly throughout the United States. A survey of nursery schools in 1931 listed 203 in existence. About half these schools were related to colleges and universities, a third were private schools, and a fifth were part of child welfare agencies. This diversity of sponsorship, a continuing characteristic of nursery schools, paralleled their diversity of function. All nursery schools were concerned with educating children. Additional purposes varied with the sponsorship of the school:

> A large number of colleges and universities use the nursery school as a laboratory for the preparation of teachers and for research. The schools sponsored by departments of home economics in colleges and universities act as laboratories and demonstration centers for preparental education and instruction on home management. Relief of parents from daytime care of their children is chiefly supported by nursery schools connected with day nurseries and conducted by family welfare or philanthropic organizations. (Davis, 1933, p. 31)

FIGURE 2-2 Early nursery school.

The Great Depression of the 1930s had its impact on the development of nursery education. With incomes low and tax collections down, many school systems curtailed educational services and released teachers whose salaries they could no longer pay. In 1933 the federal government, first under the Federal Emergency Relief Act (FERA) and then under the Works Projects Administration (WPA), provided money to establish nursery schools to hire unemployed teachers. These nursery schools operated through normal public school channels. Emergency teacher training programs were instituted to provide teachers with the necessary skills for working with young children.

Many communities provided WPA nursery schools, which offered relief to unemployed teachers and a valuable educational experience to children. Federally sponsored schools were operated in most states in the United States and ran into the thousands, far outstripping the number of nursery schools that had been in existence in this country up to that time.

The end of the depression and the beginning of World War II brought an end to the WPA nursery school as teachers ceased to be an unemployed group. The burgeoning economy and the manpower needs of the armed services and the defense industry required additions to the labor force. As women were hired for war work, agencies were needed to care for their children. Under the Lanham Act, the federal government established child care centers in most centers of war industry to provide care and education to the children of working mothers. Support for these programs was withdrawn shortly after the end of the war. In many cases, however, since the need for day care remained, they continued to operate under the sponsorship of local governments or philanthropic agencies.

The decade of the 1950s saw the expansion of parent-cooperative nursery schools. The desire for high quality nursery education at a reasonable cost, as well as for increased parent education, supported this development. Parents own parent-cooperative nursery schools and may serve as participants in the children's program as well. Adult classes or parent meetings relating to child development, child rearing practices, or other topics are often included as part of the program.

Nursery school education continued to develop slowly under its varied sponsorship until the mid-1960s, when the federal government again became involved in providing preschool education for disadvantaged children under the Economic Opportunity Act and the Elementary and Secondary Education Act.

While nursery school education went through a series of changes, its development did not elicit the deep theoretical conflict that characterized the development of the kindergarten. The original eclectic approach to nursery education was broad enough to encompass modification and diversity without serious conflict.

Among the important changes that took place in nursery school thought are the following:

1. THE CHANGE FROM NURSERY EDUCATION AS A PROGRAM FOR THE POOR TO ONE FOR THE AFFLUENT. The originators of nursery school conceived of their programs as an antidote for problems of poverty. In the United States, the nursery school became a source of information about children, a place for young women to practice for motherhood and home management, a place to "keep" children, or a place to educate middle-class children. This change was a consequence of the sponsorship of nursery schools in the United States. Without government support, most nursery schools outside of philanthropic agencies were supported by tuition payments, thereby limiting opportunities for nursery education primarily to children of the affluent.

2. A DEEMPHASIS OF THE HEALTH ASPECTS OF NURSERY EDUCATION. Because the children served by American nursery schools had less need for the total care provided by the English nursery schools, programs were shortened to half-days or school hours, and the responsibility for nutrition, health, and hygiene was omitted. Only in day care centers and Head Start programs do we see a manifestation of the original concept of nurturance.

3. A SHIFT FROM THE EMPHASIS ON "TRAINING THE SENSES" TO A MORE BROADLY BASED EDUCATION. The same conditions that led to the reform movement in the kindergarten led to the shift in emphasis in nursery education. There was less concern for cognitive learning and more for emotional and social learning than in the kindergarten. With the current return to a concern for intellectual learning in young children, nursery educators have generally supported broad cognitive skills and strategies rather than the too-specific learning tasks of the original nursery school.

The Montessori School

Paralleling the development of the nursery school in England, a similar institution developed in Italy, the *casa dei bambini*. Dr. Maria Montessori, the originator of this new educational institution, attempted to break from traditional Italian education just as Macmillan had broken from the formalism of the British primary schools. While Montessori education has developed separately from nursery and kindergarten education, interesting parallels exist between the systems as well as an evident intertwining of ideas.

Montessori began her work as a physician dealing primarily with retarded children. Impressed by her knowledge of the work of educators of retarded children, such as Seguin, she began to use and modify some of their methods and materials. She moved from working with retarded children to creating an educational program for normal children in the slums of Rome. The target population and the root methods of the nursery school and Montessori school were basically the same. They both worked with children of the poor, they were both influenced by the work of Seguin, and they both saw sensory education as important. The British nursery school was more broadly conceived, however, and took responsibility for aspects of development and work with parents that was essentially absent in the Montessori system. The freedom from a specific dogma also allowed nursery educators to develop programs more fully and more flexibly, utilizing new knowledge that became available and responding to new so-

FIGURE 2-3   Sensory education in the Montessori School.

cial situations. The Montessori method, however, strongly influenced the content and method of nursery schools.

Montessori philosophy also shows some interesting parallels with Froebelian educational thought. Montessori saw the development of the young child as a process of unfolding, as did Froebel. Montessori perceived education as self-activity, again an idea found in Froebel's work, as were the ideas of self-discipline, independence, and self-direction. A significant difference in philosophy was the Montessori emphasis on sensory education, less important to Froebel than symbolic education and the identification of sensitive periods of instruction in the development of the child.

The Montessori movement expanded, first in Italy and then throughout the world, with Montessori schools being established in several communities in the United States in the 1920s. While Montessori schools remained well-established in Europe, most of them disappeared in the United States during the 1930s and 1940s, either closing down or becoming nursery schools not unlike others around them.

At the beginning of the 1960s, a resurgence of Montessori education occurred in the United States. Montessori schools for children were reestablished as well as training programs for teachers. Some of these schools adhere exactly to the regimen of activity set down by Montessori in her original writings; others modify these activities or include additional activities found in non-Montessori nursery schools, such as block-building and dramatic play activities.

The genius of American early childhood education has been in its eclectic nature. Rather than reject new or foreign methods and theories, American educators and the public to which they are ultimately responsible have been willing to accept them at least in some limited form. Seldom, however, has any "pure" form of early childhood education remained uncontaminated. As a result of the interaction of ideologies and the pragmatic approach of many educators, an American form of early childhood education emerged, consistent yet flexibly developed, taking the best from Froebel, Montessori, Macmillan, and other European theorists and incorporating American theories and techniques. Just as the above-mentioned European educators influenced early childhood education, so did Americans such as John Dewey, Patty Smith Hill, Caroline Pratt, and a host of others.

Today many educators view the kindergarten and the nursery school as a downward extension of the primary school. The goals for the nursery school and kindergarten are exactly those goals set for all schooling. The differences in activities found at these earlier levels stem from developmental differences in the clientele rather than from philosophic differences or differences of purpose. The form and content of early childhood schools must be related to how we define the goals of the school and how we conceive of schooling.

The Child Care Center

Unlike the institutions previously discussed, child care centers—or day care centers or day nurseries, as they have alternatively been called—were originally designed to serve a custodial rather than an educational need. The American day nursery was fashioned after the French *crèche,* which literally translates as "crib." The first *crèche* was established in Paris in 1844 to help working mothers, fight infant mortality, and teach hygiene. The first American day nursery was established in New York City in 1854 by the New York Nursery and Child's Hospital (Forest, 1927).

Child care centers are a product of the Industrial Revolution. Prior to that period, women's work, even for pay, was done in a home—theirs or someone else's—where children could be kept near at hand. With the establishment of the factory system and the subsequent hiring of large numbers of women and children, a need arose to care for young children who were separated from their mothers during the long work day. The day nurseries served the working class during this period, for the middle and upper classes had access to servants to care for their young.

During the latter half of the nineteenth century a number of day nurseries were established in the United States, often by settlement houses or philanthropic groups wishing to help the children of immigrant and poor working women. Sometimes Froebelian activities were provided to the children; often the only responsibility of the caregiver was to keep the children fed, clean, and safe. Matrons cleaned and prepared meals, in addition to caring for the children. A broad range was enrolled, including infants and toddlers along with nursery-age children.

Not until the 1920s, with the introduction of the nursery school into the United States, did day nurseries begin to implement educational programs. During the period that followed, child care centers structured their age groups

FIGURE 2-4   A day nursery in the 1920s.

much as the nursery schools did, limiting the age range to children already toilet-trained. Staff members prepared as nursery school teachers began to work with more informally trained caregivers.

During World War II the number of child care centers in the United States dramatically increased. The Lanham Act of 1941 provided federal funds for child care on a matching basis to war-impacted communities, to help increase the number of women in war work. Many of these Lanham Act centers were high quality, even though created by an emergency program. They provided staff training and adequate support for materials and equipment. Some centers operated as many as twenty-four hours daily to match the three shifts on which mothers worked (Hymes, 1972).

In 1946, shortly after the end of the war, the Lanham Act was terminated and with it federal support for child care services. Where day care continued to be provided, it was much more limited. Often it was considered a child welfare service, a temporary aid to a family in difficulty that could not assume traditional child-rearing responsibilities.

In the past two decades the demand has heightened for child care as a normal service to families. Women from the middle and lower classes were seeking greater equality and finding that the lack of child care interfered with continual employment and promotion to positions of greater responsibility.

The history of child care centers includes several periods of growth and re-conceptualization. Margaret O'Brien Steinfels (1973) has identified three periods in the history of the field. In the first, prior to 1920, child care centers were seen as an essential service to poor working mothers. The availability of such a service often allowed both father and mother to work, thus hastening their social movement upward. From about 1920 to 1940 child care services were curtailed and limited, provided only in cases of special need. A stigma was attached to them through the 1960s. Since the mid 1960s child care services have again been seen as essential to working women, poor or not. The feeling has increased that this service should be available to mothers who want to work as well as those who need to work.

The change in attitude toward child care centers is the result of many diverse factors. Certainly the changing status of women in our society is one, as are the increase in urbanization and the shift to a nuclear family. Just as important is the developing body of knowledge that demonstrates that a good-quality care child care program does not have a negative effect on young children, and that daily separation of mother from child during working hours is not comparable to a total separation such as family break-up or death. Increased concern for the adequacy of child care services and the quality of facilities, program, and staff, needs to be exhibited by those who advocate and provide expanded child care services.

THE CONTEMPORARY SCENE

Viewing the field of early childhood education within an historical context allows one to have a deeper perspective and should lead to a better understanding of contemporary practice. While the field of early childhood education may be overshadowed by other fields that are presently receiving greater public attention, it is a field that has grown and has taken on increasing importance in recent years.

There are a great many more children in early childhood education programs today than ever before, indicating that the field is developing a greater level of acceptance and is serving important social needs. In October, 1966, for example, there were fewer than 30 percent of the three-year-old to five-year-old children enrolled in programs (King, 1974). In October, 1980, that had increased to 52.5 percent, including 27.3 percent of the three-year-olds, 46.3 percent of the four-year-olds, and 84.7 percent of the five-year-olds (Grant & Eiden, 1982). Thus, the statistics show a steady increase in enrollments of children in early childhood programs with kindergarten education approaching universality.

Another indicator of the acceptance of early childhood education is the continuous growth and popularity of the Head Start program. Proposals for 1984 will permit an expansion of Head Start into over 1,200 communities with about 429,000 low income and minority children served (Collins, 1983). This growth takes on added significance with the realization that most federally supported social programs have been diminished during recent years.

Added to these impressive figures is the steady increase in the last decade of early education programs for handicapped children. The impetus of Public Law 94–142, the Education for All Handicapped Children Act, along with increased legislation among the states, has created a network of programs that serve handicapped children prior to the normal school entrance age.

The increased acceptance of day care services for children must also be noted. Not only are many more day care programs available today than in decades past, but the sponsorship of these programs has changed as well. Formerly, the majority of day care programs catered to needy families and were sponsored by community and philanthropic agencies, with a minority of centers privately owned, often by the persons who operated them. Today, most centers operate for profit, often as one of a chain of corporately owned centers or as a franchise. Children from all social strata are served in these centers.

Early childhood programs have been nurtured by social necessity. Day care is provided to serve mothers who are increasingly entering the work force and seeking careers. Other programs for young children serve the need to ensure the successful school achievement of all children. The increased knowledge of positive outcomes in early childhood education has also led to its increased acceptance. Evidence is growing that good early-childhood education programs do not harm children and, indeed, there can be long-lasting positive effects.

For many years early-childhood educators have been driven by a belief that what they do with young children makes a difference in their current and future lives. Too often this belief lacked substantial support. Over the last two decades there has been increasing evidence to support that belief.

One of the more interesting studies focused on the effects of first-grade teachers on students' subsequent adult status. Longitudinal data and independent measures and estimates of characteristics and achievement were collected on a group of sixty children from a disadvantaged urban neighborhood. The study supports the hypothesis that "a good first grade teacher can provide children with such a head start that the effects, in terms of academic self-concept and achievement, will continue to be felt later in life" (Pederson, Faucher, & Eaton, 1978).

Positive, long-lasting results have also been shown for preschool programs. A number of university-sponsored early-education programs were developed for poor and minority children during the early 1960s. Many of these demonstrated immediate gains on academic and intelligence tests for their students. More recently, the Consortium for Longitudinal Studies has followed up the children in these programs. According to Irving Lazar and Richard Darlington (1982), who reported on the work of the Consortium in relation to six of these programs, there are four areas in which early education has had lasting effects: school competence, developed abilities, children's attitudes, and family outcomes. There were fewer retentions in grade and fewer assignments to special education for children in these programs. These children also performed better on tests of achievement and intelligence, although the heightened scores on IQ tests were not sustained. The children who graduated from these programs showed more positive attitudes toward school and gave more achievement-oriented responses in interviews. In addition, their mothers were more satisfied with their school performance and seemed to exert more pressure on them to achieve.

These reported effects relate to special programs implemented in controlled settings. Similar results have been found in relation to Head Start programs. Raymond C. Collins (1983) reports the following results of the Head Start Evaluation, Synthesis, and Utilization Project:

> The data show clearly that Head Start programs have grown more effective over the years. Effect sizes calculated for children who attended Head Start since 1970 are nearly twice the size of cognitive gains reported for children who attended Head Start in the start up years 1965–69. Other specific findings pertaining to cognitive development are:
>
> - Children make immediate gains in basic cognitive competence, school readiness and achievement.
> - Head Starters generally outperform other low income children into elementary school (but continue to score below norms on middle class tests).
> - Head Start children usually perform better than non-Head Starters on real work indicators of school success (less likely to be retained in grade; avoiding inappropriate placement in special education; reduced drop out rates).
> - Head Start children sometimes maintain superiority on achievement test scores into later school years.
> - Head Start improves language development, especially for bilingual and handicapped children.
> - The children who appear to benefit the most from Head Start are the most needy (children from families whose mothers had a 10th grade education or less; children of single-parent families; and children with low initial I.Q. at the beginning of Head Start.)
> - Children in classes of mixed minority enrollment (26%–89% minority) averaged gains nearly twice as high as those in classes where minority enrollment ranges 90–100%.
>
> Results of the Head Start Synthesis Project to date validate to a considerable extent in a Head Start context similar findings to those revealed in other contemporary child care research. Further analysis is necessary, particularly of the longitudinal studies, to confirm these preliminary results.*

Much of the early research on day care was designed to determine if there were negative effects on children of placement in these programs in relation to having children cared for at home. Later studies attempted to identify elements in day care programs that are associated with positive effects. A review of this research by Bettye M. Caldwell and Marjorie Freyer (1982) demonstrates the positive effects of good day care in both large-scale and small-scale studies. As a result of their review, these educators suggest that day care programs should be small, that attachment to parents is not impaired by early day care, that staff turnover in centers may be less debilitating than was feared, that the health of infants can be maintained in day care programs, that the effects of prohibitions and controls in day care programs need to be considered, that research offers

---

*Raymond C. Collins, "Headstart: An Update on Program Effects." *Newsletter of the Society for Research in Child Development,* Summer, 1983, p. 2. Reprinted with permission.

little curriculum guidance for day care programs, and that parental involvement takes many forms and remains elusive and difficult to attain in many day care programs.

The increased acceptance of early childhood education cannot be taken for granted by educators. While positive effects have been shown for programs of high quality, the availability of such high-quality programs still remains a problem. Good education for young children is expensive. Competent teachers require high salaries to be retained. Programs should remain small and child-staff ratios low. Physical facilities, furniture, equipment, and supplies are also expensive. As long as preschool programs must depend on tuition payments alone, or on low fees for purchase of service, quality will remain elusive.

All states have licensing standards that define minimum acceptable levels for day care; nursery schools are often included in these standards. Similar state standards often apply to public schools. Standards of quality remain low in early childhood education, partly due to the nature of the states' regulatory powers, and partly due to pressures to maintain low standards or to exclude blocks of centers from compliance. In addition, requirements for early-childhood staff outside the public schools remains low.

The National Association for the Education of Young Children has developed guidelines for accrediting four-year and five-year programs to prepare early-childhood personnel. Similar guidelines are being explored for two-year programs as well. The Association at present is also in the process of developing guidelines for accrediting programs for young children that will go beyond minimum licensing standards. Such efforts can affect the field and increase the quality of personnel and programs for young children. Financial support for maintaining high-quality programs, however, continues to be elusive. Only when services for young children are adequately funded and teachers of young children are given higher status, higher salaries, and better working conditions will the problems of high-quality programs be properly addressed.

REFERENCES

CALDWELL, B. M., and FREYER, M.   Day care and early education. In B. Spodek (Ed.), *Handbook of research in early childhood education*. New York: Free Press, 1982.

COLLINS, R. C.   Headstart: An update on program effects. *Newsletter of the Society for Research in Child Development*. Summer, 1983.

DAVIS, M. D.   *Nursery schools: Their development and current practices in the United States*. Washington, D.C.: U.S. Government Printing Office, 1933.

FISHER, L.   Report of the Commissioner of Education, as quoted in N. Vanderwalker. *The kindergarten in American education*. New York: Macmillan, 1908.

FOREST, I.   *Preschool education: A historical and critical study*. New York: Macmillan, 1927.

GARDNER, D. E. M.   *Education under eight*. London: Longmans, Green and Co., n.d.

GRANT, W. V., and EIDEN, L. J. *Digest of educational statistics.* Washington, D.C.: National Center for Educational Statistics, 1982.

HILL, P. S. Second Report in Committee of Nineteen, *The Kindergarten.* International Kindergarten Union, 1913.

HYMES, J. L., Jr. The Kaiser answer: Child services centers. In S. J. Braun and E. P. Edwards (Eds.), *History and theory of early childhood education.* Worthington, Ohio: Charles A. Jones, 1972.

KING, I. A. *Preprimary enrollment, October, 1974.* Washington, D.C.: U.S. Government Printing Office, 1975.

LAZAR, I., and DARLINGTON, R. Lasting effects of early education: A report from the Consortium for Longitudinal Studies. *Monographs of the Society for Research in Child Development,* Serial No. 195, 1982, *47,* Nos. 2–3.

MAY, D., and VINOVSKIS, M. A. A ray of millenial light: Early education and social reform in the infant school movement in Massachusetts, 1826–1840. In T. Harevan (Ed.), *Family and kin in urban communities, 1700–1930.* New York: New Viewpoints, 1977.

NOHLE, E. *Report on the United States Commissioner of Education* (1897–98), I, 24–25. As reported in C. S. Parker and A. Temple, *Unified kindergarten and first-grade teaching.* Chicago: Department of Education, University of Chicago, 1924.

PEDERSON, E., FAUCHER, T. A., and EATON, W. W. A new perspective on the effects of first-grade teachers on children's subsequent adult status. *Harvard Educational Review,* 1978, *48,* 1–31.

STEINFELS, M. O. *Who's minding the children? The history and politics of day care in America.* New York: Simon & Schuster, 1973.

SUGGESTED READING

BRADBURN, E. *Margaret Macmillan.* Nuffield, England: Denholm House, 1976.

BRAUN, S. J., and EDWARDS, E. P. *History and theory of early childhood education.* Worthington, Ohio: Charles A. Jones, 1972.

DOWNS, R. B. *Friederich Froebel.* Boston: Twayne, 1978.

HARRISON, J. F. C. *Utopianism and education: Robert Owen and the Owenites.* New York: Teacher College Press, 1968.

KRAMER, R. *Maria Montessori.* New York: Putnam, 1976.

LILLEY, I. M. *Friedrich Froebel: A selection from his writings.* Cambridge, England: Cambridge University Press, 1967.

MACMILLAN, M. *The nursery school.* New York: Dutton, 1919.

MONTESSORI, M. *The Montessori method.* New York: Schocken Books, 1964 (Originally published 1912).

ROSS, E. D. *The kindergarten crusade.* Athens, Ohio: Ohio University Press, 1976.

SNYDER, A. *Dauntless women in childhood education.* Washington, D.C.: Association for Childhood Education International, 1972.

STEINFELS, M. O. *Who's minding the children? The history and politics of day care in America.* New York: Simon & Schuster, 1973.

WEBER, E. *The kindergarten: Its encounter with educational thought in America.* New York: Teacher College Press, 1969.

WHITBREAD, N. *The evolution of the nursery-infant school.* Boston: Routledge & Kegan Paul, 1972.

3

Early Childhood Curriculum

Schools for young children are expressly designed to achieve certain goals. School personnel fill the day with activities designed to achieve these goals—to develop a school curriculum. How does one derive a curriculum? The curriculum may be defined as the organized experiences designed to provide opportunities for learning to children in a school setting. It can be both formal and informal. In this chapter the sources of an early childhood curriculum and its appropriate goals are discussed.

THE SOURCES OF EARLY CHILDHOOD CURRICULA

During the past two decades, many innovative programs have been proposed for the education of young children. Although some programs described as "new" are essentially modifications of existing practice, differences between innovative programs and traditional nursery school and kindergarten practice exist. The difference in the sources of these curricula is even greater.

Children as a Source of Curricula

According to some theorists, early childhood curricula should originate from children themselves. Both Friedrich Froebel and Maria Montessori, pioneers of early childhood education, used their observations of children as the main source of their curricula.

The kindergarten of Friedrich Froebel consisted of the ordered use of manipulative activities, or *Occupations,* and the use of songs and finger plays, his *Mother's Plays and Songs.* Froebel viewed these activities as they were revealed to him by the children themselves (Lilley, 1967). Similarly, Montessori observed the uses children made of didactic materials provided them, abstracting the essential elements for learning and ordering them into her famous *Montessori Method.* These observations became the basis of Montessori's scientific pedagogy (Montessori, 1964). Froebel's analysis of child behavior was more mystical than scientific.

The use of "natural" childhood activities as the source of curricula is a romantic ideal that can be traced as far back as Jean-Jacques Rousseau. The ideal of the unsocialized savage whose best instincts are destroyed by the surrounding culture is echoed by contemporary critics. Educators who use such arguments feel they are not violating the child in any way but are "doing what comes naturally."

Unfortunately these arguments do not hold up well. There is nothing natural about any school, even a preschool and its activities cannot be directly derived from the natural activity of children. Play activities provided to children in these settings are modified by teachers who allow certain activities to take place, disallow other activities, and intervene directly and indirectly to make these activities educational. Selecting a room's furniture, materials, and equipment is one form of intervention. The very nature of effective education requires that the child be modified as a result of his experiences within it. All schools are cultural contrivances to *do* things *to* children—to change them.

Looking at the curricula derived from observations of children, one becomes aware of the selectivity of both the observations and their uses. When one observes an object, one defines certain attributes as critical, providing a focus for observing and describing. Other attributes are overlooked because they are considered uncritical. The purpose for which one is observing determines what one will see.

In analyzing the arguments about the natural activity of childhood as a source of the curriculum, one becomes aware that the purposes of the observer determines what is seen. One educator may see a set of potentials while another sees only deficits; one may see only the intellectual behavior of the child, another only the emotional or social behavior. One educator may view a particular child as a problem solver, while another may see him as a respondent to external rewards. The natural child becomes a product of the theoretical scheme that helps to determine which observations should be attended to and which discarded in a complex organism.

Few contemporary educators can fail to see the contrived nature of both the Froebelian kindergarten and the Montessori school. If one is to understand the curricula determined by Montessori, Froebel, or any other educational developer, one must go beyond simple natural observation and identify the basis for selecting the observations and the conceptual framework used to give meaning to these observations in developing educational experiences for children.

Developmental Theory as a Source
of Curricula

A second source of curricula used by early childhood educators has been child development theory. One such theory, derived from Arnold Gesell's research, considers child development as primarily maturational. The developmental norms produced by Gesell and his colleagues are based on many observations of children of various ages. As a result, children have been grouped by age and provided with experiences that are considered appropriate for their age level.

Arguments derived from Gesellian theory have been used to exclude activities thought to be inappropriate and to insure inclusion of appropriate experiences in the school life of children. However, age norms do not adequately describe the range of heights, weights, skills, abilities, or other attributes of children at any age. Nor would these attributes remain constant at all times for all persons in all cultures. Average heights and weights of children have risen in the last fifty years and vary from one geographic area to another, not necessarily as the result of natural differences but rather of environmental differences. Other attributes of childhood vary as a result of the environment—cultural as well as physical. What a child is at any level of development is to some extent a result of what a culture says he ought to be.

Psychoanalytic theory, concerned primarily with the personality, has also been used to formulate curricula for young children. Interpretations of the work of Sigmund Freud, Carl Jung, and Erik Erikson have led to emphasis on expressive activities, dramatic play, and group interactions. When carried to excess, educational practices based upon this theory resembled child therapy sessions as much as educational activities. With the increased emphasis on ego development, however, psychoanalytic thinkers became concerned less with catharsis and more with building an integrated self requiring personal competencies, and many of the excesses eventually disappeared.

Recently, George E. Forman and Catherine T. Fosnot (1982) defined four propositions as underlying Piaget's constructivist theory: (1) knowledge as a construction of our own inference making, (2) a belief in the individual's internal self-regulating mechanism, (3) a view of knowledge as resulting from an individual's actions that include both activity and reflection, and (4) a view that knowledge results from conflict resolution. These authors then analyzed six Piagetian early childhood programs in relation to these propositions. Each program focused on the propositions differently and interpreted them in terms of varied activity prescriptions. Thus, there was both a selection from among elements of the theory and a freedom of interpretation evident in the uses made of the theory.

Such an analysis raises the question as to whether there can be a purely developmental theory–based early childhood program. In translating theory to practice, elements of the theory get discarded and other elements are added.

Thus, even when programs are rooted in the same developmental framework they can differ from one another in essential and significant ways.

Is child development theory, Piagetian or otherwise, a legitimate source of educational curricula for young children? The "child development point of view" has been popular in early childhood education for many years. However, one may seriously question its appropriateness as the prime source of curricula.

Child development is a descriptive science; it can tell us what *is*. Education deals with what *ought* to be. Choices and preferences are involved in creating educational experiences that cannot be rationalized by recourse to child development theory.

In their discussion of developmental theories and early education, Greta Fein and Pamela Schwartz (1982) suggest that developmental theory provides a rich source of information about the intricacies of human growth. While this is necessary, it is not sufficient for generating practice. What may be needed, however, is a theory of practice (Bronfenbrenner, 1979). Such a theory would include statements about how controllable resources would be obtained and allocated, and allow for the creation of conceptions of educational environments.

Learning Theory as a Source of Curricula

Just as child development theory has been identified by program developers as a source of curricula, so have learning theories of intelligence. Developmental theory deals with change in the human being over long periods of time. Learning theory attempts to account for short-term change. The recourse to learning theory as a source of curricula has been manifest in several different ways.

The "conduct curriculum," developed in the early childhood program at Teachers College under the leadership of Patty Smith Hill (1923), gives evidence of the influence of Edward L. Thorndike's school of behaviorism. Kindergarten was seen as a place for habit training to take place. Lists of appropriate "habits" and recommended stimulus situations for five-year-olds were developed for kindergarten teachers at this time.

Today the theories of behaviorist B. F. Skinner are having similar influence. Skinner's learning theory contains six major concepts:

1. *Operant conditioning.* Reinforcing operations or responses that occur normally.
2. *Reinforcement.* A stimulus that increases the rate at which an operation occurs is called a *reinforcer,* such as: food, toys, money, tokens, or praise.
3. *Immediate reinforcement.* There should be a minimum delay in time between the operant behavior and its reinforcement.
4. *Discriminated stimuli.* Behaviors that should be emitted under specific circumstances are reinforced only under those circumstances.
5. *Extinction.* A response can be decreased by its failure to be reinforced.

6. *Shaping*. Complex behaviors can be analyzed into simple components which can be built up to the complex behavior (Bugelski, 1971).

"Third force" or phenomenological psychologists, view behaviorism as too mechanistic and simplistic to provide an adequate framework for understanding complex human processes. They suggest an alternate approach in dealing with human learning.

Donald Snygg and Arthur Combs (1949), for example, view the process of education and of learning, as a process of change in the phenomenological field. How a person behaves, they suggest, is a function of his understanding of a situation. The meanings of behavior and of situations become the focal point of learning. Meanings are personal and therefore vary from individual to individual and cannot always be fully verbalized. The goals of learning are also individual. What a person learns depends upon his goals and needs, which are not always externally manipulatable.

Within phenomenological psychology, the *self* plays an important role. How a person views himself affects his behavior and what he learns. A child who views himself as competent will be more ready to learn and will learn more than one who thinks of himself as incompetent. The school, it is suggested, needs to concern itself with developing adequate selves in its pupils.

Phenomenological psychology leads to a different set of instructional strategies in classrooms than does behavioral psychology. Complex learning situations are used intact, with children being helped to develop their own meanings; their behavior is not "shaped," nor are specific behavioral goals predetermined. Instead, the teacher is concerned with moving children in the direction of appropriate behavior—a wide range of behavior is acceptable. Such an approach allows a greater degree of freedom for children, enabling them to select alternatives and develop personal responsibility for their learning and their growth.

Psychological theory focusing on behavior and behavior modification has determined the structure of a number of curricula in early childhood education. While short-term change is easily observed and evaluated, there are seldom any attempts to study long-term effects of these curricula. In the final analysis, such programs may be based as much on ultimate faith as are any of the more traditional programs. The description of a program in psychological terminology and the great emphasis on the evaluation of effectiveness without analyzing ultimate goals may, in the long run, obscure the ultimate consequences of these programs.

Nor can phenomenological psychology help us to determine what should be taught to children. At best, learning theory can help us in developing new instructional methodologies and in analyzing and assessing established methodologies. This, in itself, is no small role.

One other facet of psychology that is often used for formulating curricula is psychological testing and evaluation. Many of the programs in early childhood education, for example, have been justified as ways of increasing intelligence, and one way of judging the intelligence of children is through the administration and scoring of intelligence tests. Such tests consist of items that purport to sample a broad range of intellectual behaviors in children. Each item achieves its validity from the fact that it represents many other kinds of behaviors that might have been elicited from the total number of intelligent behaviors.

Since the effectiveness of educational programs can be demonstrated by students' achievement of higher scores on intelligence tests, it is easy to allow tasks taken from or related to intelligence tests to become the content of the program. Justification for this approach to curriculum development often suggests that since these items are samples of intelligent behavior, having children practice these behaviors allows them to practice behaving in an intelligent manner.

Such distortions of psychological testing and curriculum development are not limited to the area of intelligence testing. They take place in language development, in academic achievement, or in any other area where samples of behavior are mistaken for the total population of behaviors they represent. The small number of items that determine the difference in age or grade placement on a test make this form of justification all too attractive for short-term intervention techniques for young children.

Organized Knowledge as a Source of Curricula

More than two decades ago, Jerome Bruner (1960), suggested that the organized fields of knowledge should become the basis of educational curriculum for children at all levels. The "structure of the disciplines," it was argued, could provide a vehicle to insure that school learning would be intellectually significant. Key ideas in each area of knowledge would be revisited in more sophisticated ways as children moved through their academic careers. These key ideas could be taught in an intellectually honest way at every level of development. *New Directions in the Kindergarten* (Robison & Spodek, 1965) provides examples of how this proposal could be translated into early childhood programs in the fields of science, social science, and mathematics.

The proposal to develop school curricula based on the structure of knowledge was attractive and a number of curriculum development projects were organized along these lines.

As the work in these projects continued, a number of problems became evident. Scholars identified many different structures and some disciplines, such as social science, did not seem unified. Another problem was that identifying intellectual structures did not help to determine what school experiences would help children attain significant understandings in a field. The strategies for understanding the sciences did not seem to help in understanding the arts and the humanities. In addition, fewer projects dealing with these areas and with the expressive elements of school learning were mounted.

The relationship between the conceptual structures of mature disciplines and children's less mature understandings is more complicated than was originally thought. Issues dealing with relevance to children, individual learning rates and style, personal interests, and so forth complicated what had once seemed a simple task. Although the content of the disciplines—the areas of knowledge—could help to determine the significance of school content, by itself it was inadequate for determining school curricula at any level, especially at the early childhood level.

School Content as a Source of Curricula

Another source for developing early childhood programs has been the content of later schooling. "Reading readiness," for example, is considered important because it prepares children for reading instruction. Readiness skills have no importance in themselves, but they and certain other kinds of learnings prepare children for later school expectations. Thus the pressures of later life and schooling are heaped upon the child in anticipation of what is to come.

Such a justification is to be found in the Bereiter-Engelmann Program (1966). Its content (reading, language, and mathematics) is required of children in primary grades. The program also prepares children for behaving appropriately for their school life ahead; whether such preparation will benefit students later is debatable.

One of the few long-range studies of the effects of education, the *Eight-Year Study* (Aiken, 1942) of progressive high schools, demonstrated that children in open school situations did better than those from more restrictive school environments when they went to college. This study certainly raises some questions about the desirability of providing children with rigid early schooling as preparation for rigid later schooling. In addition later school learning is not a goal in and of itself, but a means to a goal. Using such a justification only delays decisions about curriculum content. As it is, too little concern is given to the proper source of curriculum.

THE PROPER SOURCE OF CURRICULA

The sources of curriculum theory used through the years have been reviewed and analyzed. Neither test items nor school content can be viewed as proper sources of any curriculum. Using either represents circular thinking that supports existing practice because it exists. School content is devised to achieve societal aims. To support school content as an end in itself is to deny the purposes of schooling and to legitimize activity solely on the basis of tradition.

Test items are designed to help judge educational experience; to use them to determine curriculum content is to distort both the educational process and the evaluation process. Rather, test items should be determined by educational practices.

Using children themselves to determine educational programs might also be questioned. Since what we see in children is determined by prior conceptions, it might be more fruitful to make them explicit by defining the developmental theories and learning theories to which we adhere when we observe children's behavior. Learning theory, developmental theory, and conceptions of organized knowledge and ways of knowing are all sources of curriculum. But only within the context of human values can these sources function properly.

Schools at all levels help children learn those behaviors required to function in society. They also help children lead personally satisfying lives. To the extent that schools help to define the "good life" and the "good society," they are moral enterprises. The values growing out of this enterprise determine how we use our knowledge of human development, human learning, or knowledge in determining educational experiences for young children.

In addition to child development or learning theory, school programs are derived from statements about social purpose and forms of knowledge. All schools, including those for young children, are designed to serve social purposes. These purposes can be identified by studying the cultural values, levels of technology, cultural organizational forms, and cultural symbol systems of the school's community.

Cultural values tell us what is important for an individual to know, and thus help us judge the worth of educational content. Our society is based upon such values as liberty, justice, equality, and the dignity of the individual. Our valuing of the individual's dignity causes us to consider the way we treat children in school and the nature of the materials we use. Individuals or groups should not be demeaned. Our concern for equality leads us, under one interpretation, to treat all children alike and demand the same language learning for each; under another interpretation, we support diverse programs for different children, such as bilingual-bicultural education. Our valuing of cooperation, competition, or independence can also directly influence the kinds of materials we provide young children and the forms of behavior we reward or restrict.

A society's level of technology determines to a great extent what forms and levels of knowledge an individual must acquire to cope with community life and to be productive. The change from teaching "nature study" to teaching "natural science" during the twentieth century is an example of how changing school content responds to changing levels of technology.

Forms of social organization also have their impact on school programs. In the primary grades, for example, we study families, communities, and community workers, making children aware of roles and structures in their communities.

Cultural symbols allow us to share ideas and feelings. Consequently, language instruction is a basic part of all school programs. Other symbols are taught as well—music, art, and movement provide nondiscursive symbolic forms. Our flag is another type of symbol; even the clothes we wear can take on symbolic meanings.

These are but a few examples of how our culture sets requirements for what is taught in school. These cultural imperatives become so much a part of our thinking that we seldom identify them explicitly. Cultural options, sometimes referred to as "stylistic differences," also exist.

FORMS OF KNOWLEDGE

Human development theory can tell us what children can learn. The cultural context of schools can tell us what children ought to learn. The content of schools must be abstracted from existing forms of human knowledge. A number of attempts have been made over the years to identify the varying forms of knowledge that can be used as the basis for school curricula.

During the colonial period, the primary schools which young children attended were mainly concerned with teaching literacy. Literacy was the foundation of education, since the ability to read gave the individual direct access to the Bible. Schools at all levels were taught or supervised by ministers. When Thomas Jefferson attended the College of William and Mary, all but one of the faculty members were ordained ministers.

Since the Middle Ages, the Bible was seen as the source of knowledge in Western society. When a theory or a set of observations was not consistent with the teaching of the Bible, the theory or observations were considered in error. Thus, when Galileo began charting the skies and determined that the sun rather than the earth was the center of the universe, he was considered in error because his theory ran counter to the view of the universe presented in the Bible.

As the period of the Enlightenment developed, it became more generally accepted that there were other views of the world besides those presented in the Bible, and there were other ways of validating knowledge besides recourse to the Scriptures. During this Age of Reason, rationalism and empiricism evolved as significant conceptions of knowledge and with these developments came changes in early childhood curricula.

Rationalism provided the epistemological basis for the Froebelian kindergarten. Rationalism held that truths were composed of self-evident premises that were not derived from experience but were held to be logically and undeniably true. Froebel's view of the world suggested that the key idea was the unity of humanity, God, and nature. This and related ideas were presented to children through a set of materials and activities that symbolized them: the *Gifts,* the *Occupations,* and the *Mother's Songs and Plays.* The kindergarten curriculum was designed to present these ideas to children through continued contact with symbolic representations. The ideas themselves were never tested in the program, nor was there a concern with helping children understand objective reality except how that reality expressed those ideas.

Empiricism gave the central role in knowledge to sense perceptions. One comes to know the world as a result of one's experiences. The information generated by those experiences is internalized through one's senses. To become more knowledgeable, one must have a greater number or range of experiences and a greater sensitivity to the external world.

The development of the Montessori method reflected the belief that human knowledge results from experiences. Montessori education is sensory education. Children are trained through apparatus that isolate particular attributes of experiences, helping children become aware of resulting sensory experiences, and learning to order them. Children discriminate between and order objects by their color, size, weight, or shape.

Sensory elements, however, do not account for generating meanings from information—that is, the creation of knowledge. While the colors or shapes of an object are inherent within the object itself, the ways in which we classify objects and put them into a sequence are independent of the objects themselves and of our sensory experiences with them. It is the structure that we apply to our experiences that gives them meaning.

In recent years, early childhood programs have been developing based upon the research and theory of Jean Piaget. Piaget viewed knowledge as resulting from something more than a person's experience. The child or adult constructs knowledge through the application of mental processes. The mental structures created by the individual interact with sensory information in the creation of knowledge. Knowledge is neither simply the accumulation of sensory experiences nor the accumulation of innate ideas; rather, it is a human creation that uses sensory data—information resulting from experiences—to create ideas that can be tested against additional experience, to be discarded, elaborated, modified, or affirmed.

Constance Kamii (1973) has used a Piagetian framework to identify objectives of early childhood education that include five forms of cognitive knowledge. These are:

1. *Physical knowledge*—the observable properties and physical actions of things
2. *Logico-mathematical knowledge*—the relation between and among objects, such as classifications, seriation, and number
3. *The structuring of time and space*—although these are observable in external reality, reasoning is required in the creation of these structures
4. *Social knowledge*—the social conventions that are structured from people's feedback
5. *Representation*—the development of symbols and signs that can stand for objects

Kamii and Rheta DeVries (1978, 1982) have used this scheme to design activities to teach logico-mathematical knowledge and physical knowledge to children.

Using the framework above, one may know many things about a table, for example. A child may determine if the table has a hard or soft, smooth or rough surface, if it is high or low, and if its top is round or rectangular. These are elements of physical knowledge directly accessible through the child's senses. The child can then place the table he or she has observed into a previously constructed category of objects called "table," containing similar objects that may actually look different in many ways. The child can also distinguish this table from objects that are not tables; The child can count the tables in the room, and order them by size, by height, or by some other attribute. These are forms of logico-mathematical knowledge. The child can identify where the table stands in relation to other objects in the room and recall whether the table was covered with a cloth last night, thus placing the table in a structure of time and space.

The child learns that it is permissible to place things on, write on, and eat from the table, but not to sit on it or jab a sharp knife into it. These learnings are not directly accessible through sensory experience, nor are they the result of logical processes. They are matters of social knowledge, common as they may seem, and must be communicated to the child, directly or indirectly. Finally, the child may represent the table by drawing a picture of it, creating a model of it, or writing the word *table*.

These various forms of knowledge deal with the same object, but each is derived and verified in a particular way. This Piagetian framework is limited to cognitive knowledge; however, early childhood curriculum that deals only with the intellectual realm is too narrow a focus for early childhood programs. A conception of knowledge must go beyond cognitive knowledge.

Other conceptions of knowledge, developed by philosophers of education, should prove useful to early childhood educators (for example, Phenix, 1964; Hirst & Peters, 1970). Some of these have been elaborated elsewhere (Spodek, 1977).

Our views of the school's role, the relationship between individuals and their development, society's demands, and the sources of knowledge can be used to identify goals for education. R. F. Dearden (1968), for example, has suggested that the goal of education is "personal autonomy based upon reason," which seems quite appropriate as *one* of the goals of early childhood education. He describes this autonomy as follows:

> There are two aspects to such an autonomy, the first of which is negative. This is independence of authorities, both of those who would dictate or prescribe what I am to believe and of those who would arbitrarily direct me in what I am to do. The complementary positive aspect is, first, that of testing the truth of things for myself, whether by experience or by a critical estimate of the testimony of others, and secondly, that of deliberating, forming intentions and choosing what I shall do according to a scale of values which I can myself appreciate. Both

understanding and choice, or thought and action, are therefore to be independent of authority and based instead on reason. This is the ideal. (p. 46)

This concept of autonomy is not alien to the education of young children. Erikson's framework (1950) for human development includes the stage of autonomy just after the development of trust. As the child's intelligence continues to develop, the basis for personal autonomy becomes more rational.

If we accept the goal of "personal autonomy based upon reason" for early childhood education, then psychological theory can help us determine ways of testing the effectiveness of a program in achieving this ideal. In addition, knowledge of developmental processes can help us order activities which can serve an educational purpose to a child at a particular level of development. We can determine whether children can adequately cope with the degree of autonomy we provide. Developmental theory becomes a tool for the analysis of curriculum. The forms of knowledge also can help to determine whether the methods of teaching are consistent with what is being taught, and whether children can become not only independent learners, but independent verifiers of what they have come to know. The content of school programs must be recognized as a product of educators' imaginations, to be tested by psychological means rather than as natural consequences of children's behavior, adults' thinking, or institutional organization.

ESTABLISHING GOALS FOR EARLY CHILDHOOD EDUCATION

One of the prime goals of early childhood education, as of all education, is the development of knowledge in children. Knowledge, however, must be broadly defined, and continually redefined as the socio-cultural context changes. We should provide children access to not only formal scholarly disciplines, but also self-knowledge, that is, knowledge of what one can do, feel, and communicate to others. Values, aesthetic appreciations, attitudes, and predispositions are communally shared forms of knowledge that children must also learn. These cannot be isolated by subject area. Knowledge of the culture's symbol system, both linguistic and otherwise, must be developed by children.

The attainment of knowledge is a lifelong task. Although this can begin in the early years, the goals of education can never be fully attained in these years. Therefore, teachers must identify *instrumental* goals as well as *terminal* goals. Instrumental goals are those that must necessarily be attained if our terminal goals are to be achieved. For example, children might be taught to discriminate among and to name different colors and shapes in kindergarten. The names of colors and shapes are not significant in their own right. However, the processes of discrimination, categorization, and labeling are important cognitive processes. Once learned, these processes can be applied to many similar activities. Since they can be achieved through studying colors and shapes, the activity of sorting and naming has educational merit.

Sometimes we teach things to young children that they will have to unlearn later. This occurs when these early learnings are a necessary step to mature knowledge, even though they are inadequate for the mature scholar. Beginning reading instruction is a case in point. A mature reader does not sound out words or use a large memorized sight vocabulary to gain meaning from the printed page. Such an approach to reading hinders the mature reader's progress in gaining meaning efficiently. But we can see no way for the young child to become a mature reader without learning a sight vocabulary and a set of letter-sound associations. These constitute a transitional stage, and the child must be helped to discard them later. Our instrumental goals, although they might not look like our terminal goals, must be directly related to them in a psychological if not a logical way.

MODELS OF EARLY CHILDHOOD CURRICULA

Within the last two decades a range of program alternatives have been developed for the education of young children. Many of these programs can be found in the Planned Variations program of Head Start and Follow Through. It is beyond the scope of this chapter to present the content of each program. The various curriculum models can be found elsewhere in detailed description and comparison (see, for example, Evans, 1975; Day & Parker, 1977; Spodek, 1973). Rather, the discussion that follows will concern itself with ways of analyzing and comparing models.

Early childhood programs have been traditionally identified with various theories of child development. The Educational Products Information Exchange (EPIE) report on early childhood education (1972) seems to take this point of view. This report helps the reader determine educational program preferences. In the process they first ask of the reader, "Where do you stand on human development?" identifying three views on human development: a behavior-environmental view, a maturational-nativist view, and a comprehensive-interactionist view. In the behavior-environmental view, development is seen as an accumulation of learning or sets of responses related to cues that elicit them and reinforcers that sustain them. In the maturational-nativist view, the emphasis is on the role of the individual's genetic make-up that allows development to unfold. The comprehensive-interactionist view sees developmental tasks, consultation with other people, and interactions among all of these. The reader having determined a personal point of view on development, can use the rest of the report to identify parallel program preferences for early childhood education.

Lawrence Kohlberg and Rochelle Mayer (1972) suggest that programs of education differ on the basis of ideologies—prescriptions of practice based upon value assumptions about what is ethically good or worthwhile and theoretical assumptions about how children learn or develop. They identify three ideological thrusts of education, similar to the EPIE views of development: a romantic thrust, a cultural transmission thrust, and a progressive thrust. Underlying the romantic thrust is a conception of development as a process of unfolding, with education as essentially a support for development. The cultural transmission thrust is concerned with transmitting elements of the culture from the older generation to the younger generation with little concern for maturation. Within the progressive thrust, development is seen as occurring through an interaction of the individual with his environment, with the individual essentially creating his own development.

Conceiving of educational programs as based in ideologies suggests that programs can be generated with many different goals, yet rooted in the same developmental or learning theory. The Behavior Analysis Program of Project Follow Through, sponsored by the University of Kansas, is geared toward a set of rather narrow goals. It focuses essentially on social and classroom skills and the core subjects of reading, mathematics, and handwriting (Bushell, 1973). Sidney Bijou (1976), operating from a behavior analysis framework suggests goals for the development of abilities and knowledge such as body management and control, physical health and safety, self-care, recreation and play, social behavior, aesthetic knowledge and abilities, everyday mechanical know-how, knowledge of how things work in the community, academic and preacademic subjects, and the methods and content of science. The extension of motivation involves the preservation and extension of ecological reinforcers, the development of attitudes and interests in people, and a positive attitude toward school. In the area of self-management skills, Bijou includes personal self-management techniques, and problem-solving and decision-making skills.

Thus, in assessing early childhood education program models, one needs to know more than just the developmental theory associated with the model. The basic assumptions underlying the model are necessary, including assumptions about the client, the educative process, the school, and the teacher. One needs to identify the long-range and short-range goals of the program, the curriculum and teaching methodology, the style of teaching prescribed, and how the model handles the organization of time, space, physical resources, and human resources. If one is concerned with implementing a model, one should know whether this has been done and how effective the implementations have been. Practical issues regarding costs of implementation, requirements of staff and materials, and the availability of supportive services can also affect a decision regarding the worth of a program (Spodek, 1973).

It is not surprising that different programs of early childhood education lead to different learning outcomes when their goals are as diverse as those described above. When assessments are made of these programs in terms of academic achievement alone, some programs seem more effective than others. However, broader assessment techniques show that differences among programs are not just a matter of one program teaching *more* than another, but of programs geared toward different goals.

Different programs have different impacts on children. One must select a program not only because it works, but because what it achieves is considered worthy. Early childhood programs represent ethical principles. Our selection of goals and means to achieve them should come from an awareness of the options available and a judgment of the goals we consider appropriate for young children. The match between goals and curriculum method can then be made.

Selections of educational activities are among the choices teachers can often make. The chapters that follow look at the various subject matter areas, presenting a summary of the knowledge available about each area and a sample of strategies for teaching children that grows out of the basic summary. Organization by subject matter areas is used because it is a convenient way of talking about program content that has been used traditionally in education. While the framework is handy, the reader should continually be on the lookout for ways of crossing these subject lines, of integrating content through activities, and of seeking relationships in terms of children's interests and experiences.

REFERENCES

AIKEN, W. M.   *The story of the eight year study.* New York: McGraw-Hill, 1942.
BEREITER, C., and ENGELMANN, S.   *Teaching disadvantaged children in the preschool.* Englewood Cliffs, N.J.: Prentice-Hall, 1966.
BIJOU, S. W.   *Child development: The basic stage of early childhood.* Englewood Cliffs, N.J.: Prentice-Hall, 1976.
BRONFENBRENNER, U.   *The ecology of human development.* Cambridge, Mass.: Harvard University Press, 1979.
BRUNER, J. S.   *The Process of education.* Cambridge, Mass.: Harvard University Press, 1960.
BUGELSKI, B. R.   *Psychology of learning applied to teaching* (2nd ed.). Indianapolis: Bobbs-Merrill, 1971.
BUSHELL, D., Jr.   The behavior analysis classroom. In B. Spodek (Ed.), *Early childhood education.* Englewood Cliffs, N.J.: Prentice-Hall, 1973.
DAY, M. C., and PARKER, R. K. (Eds.).   *The preschool in action: Exploring early childhood programs* (2nd ed.). Boston: Allyn & Bacon, 1977.
DEARDEN, R. F.   *The philosophy of primary education.* Boston: Routledge & Kegan Paul, 1968.
EDUCATIONAL PRODUCTS INFORMATION EXCHANGE.   *Early childhood education: How to select and evaluate materials.* New York: EPIE Institute, 1972.
ERIKSON, E. H.   *Childhood and society.* New York: W. W. Norton & Co., Inc., 1950.
EVANS, E. D.   *Contemporary influences in early childhood education* (2nd ed.). New York: Holt, Rinehart & Winston, 1975.

FEIN, G., and SCHWARTZ, P. M.   Developmental theories in early education. In B. Spodek (Ed.), *Handbook of research in early childhood education.* New York: Free Press, 1982.

FORMAN, G. E., and FOSNOT, C. T.   The use of Piaget's constructivism in early childhood education programs. In B. Spodek (Ed.), *Handbook of research in early childhood education.* New York: Free Press, 1982.

HIRST, P. H., and PETERS, R. S.   *The logic of education.* Boston: Routledge & Kegan Paul, 1970.

KAMII, C.   A sketch of a Piaget-derived preschool curriculum developed by the Ypsilanti early education program. In B. Spodek (Ed.), *Early childhood education.* Englewood Cliffs, N.J.: Prentice-Hall, 1973.

KAMII, C.   *Numbers in preschool and kindergarten.* Washington, D.C.: National Association for the Education of Young Children, 1982.

KAMII, C., and DEVRIES, R.   *Physical knowledge in preschool education.* Englewood Cliffs, N.J.: Prentice-Hall, 1978.

KOHLBERG, L., and MAYER, R.   Development as the aim of education. *Harvard Educational Review,* 1972, *42,* 449–496.

HILL, P. S., et al.   *Conduct curriculum for kindergarten and first grade.* New York: Scribners, 1923.

LILLEY, I. M.   *Friedrich Froebel: A selection from his writings.* Cambridge, England: Cambridge University Press, 1967.

MONTESSORI, M.   *The Montessori method.* Cambridge, Mass.: Robert Bentley, 1964.

PHENIX, P.   *Realms of meaning.* New York: McGraw-Hill, 1964.

ROBISON, H. F., and SPODEK, B.   *New directions in the kindergarten.* New York: Teachers College Press, 1965.

SNYGG, D., and COMBS, A.   *Individual behavior.* New York: Harper & Row, Pub., 1949.

SPODEK, B. (Ed.)   *Early childhood education.* Englewood Cliffs, N.J.: Prentice-Hall, 1973.

SPODEK, B. (Ed.)   *Teaching practices: Re-examining assumptions.* Washington, D.C.: National Association for the Education of Young Children, 1977.

SUGGESTED READINGS

DAY, M. C. and PARKER, R. K. (Eds.).   *The preschool in action: Exploring early childhood programs.* (2nd ed.) Boston: Allyn & Bacon, 1977.

DEARDEN, R. F.   *The philosophy of primary education.* London: Routledge & Kegan Paul, 1968.

EVANS, E.   *Contemporary influences in early childhood education* (2nd ed.). New York: Holt, Rinehart & Winston, 1975.

FORMAN, G. E. and KUSCHNER, D. S.   *The child's construction of knowledge.* Washington, D.C.: National Association for the Education of Young Children, 1983.

NIR-JANIV, N., SPODEK, B. and STEG, D. (Eds.)   *Early childhood education: An international perspective.* New York: Plenum, 1982.

SPODEK, B.   *Early childhood education.* Englewood Cliffs, N.J.: Prentice-Hall, 1973.

4

Language Learning in Early Childhood Education

Perhaps the most important area of learning in the education of young children is that of language. Although reading is obviously crucial to all later school learning, other aspects of language learning—such as speaking and listening—are equally important. As a matter of fact, learning to read is predicated upon a great deal of prior language learning.

Language is a code that allows ideas about the world to be represented through a system of arbitrary signals, primarily vocal. As a system, it has a set of rules that determines which sounds can be combined into words and which words into sentences. Members of a community arbitrarily agree on the use of rules, sounds, and words so that utterances can be communicated and understood as representing knowledge, thus allowing the encoding and decoding of messages (Bloom & Lahey, 1978).

Children entering the classroom receive verbal messages from many sources, giving specific directions for actions, providing information about the world, and offering opportunities for enjoyment, aesthetic appreciation, and comfort. They must act on the messages received, understanding and responding to them if appropriate. Children also send messages to others. They respond to teachers and attempt to influence the behavior of their peers; making their needs and wishes known to others; expressing the ideas and feelings they have developed. The continual verbal give-and-take of the active school day presents endless opportunities for speaking, listening, reading, and writing. These then become the basis for social interactions as well as for the development of cognitive processes.

EARLY LANGUAGE DEVELOPMENT

School does not provide children their first language learning situation. The most important part of this learning has taken place before school. The role of the school is to extend and enrich language learning and to provide remediation if necessary.

This extension and enrichment role is important. In entering school, children find themselves an environment that often requires them to be understood in ways not required at home. The communication demands made upon children by both the teacher and other children require an adjustment to an environment less responsive than those previously experienced.

Children produce verbal utterances from birth. They cry, coo, and babble in their first year, soon eliminating those sounds not found in their native language. Single word utterances develop at about the end of the first year and phrases by the end of the child's second year.

Most young children have learned to use the basic sentence forms of the language of their culture appropriately by the time they enter school. The basic acquisition of grammatical speech is complete by age three and one-half, often before the child enters nursery school. By the time first grade is reached, they are competent performers in language. They have probably mastered a listening and speaking vocabulary of about twenty-five hundred words and the basic rules for combining these words into complex sentences and phrases. Although it would not be possible for young children to parse a sentence or recite the rules of grammar, by this time they have developed an intuitive sense of the structure of the language.

Through interaction with others, children have somehow learned, for example, that adding "-ed" to a verb places it in the past tense. The conversational mistakes that teachers so often report grow out of the children's applying rules logically to words that happen to be exceptions to those rules. Rules are seldom misapplied by young children, however. You may hear a child say, "He dided it," but you will seldom hear him add the "ed" to the end of a noun.

Individual children vary greatly in their language development. There are early talkers and late talkers, talkative children and quiet children. Some differences are a function of the way children react to a specific environment, others are developmental. Psychologists report that sex, class, position in family, and ethnic group membership are all related to the child's rate of language development. Differences reported by psychologists are usually differences in *group trends;* individuals may differ markedly from the norm of their group.

HOW DOES LANGUAGE DEVELOP?

The study of language development in children has a long tradition that spans over a century. The earliest of these studies consisted of parents' diaries, often focused upon the beginning of a new form of vocalization in their child. Events of the past three decades have been extremely generative of studies of child language development. The field has been spurred by the theories of Noam Chomsky and others, and by the social issues related to dialect differences and bilingualism. Much of the research on language acquisition is not directly relevant to classroom situations at the early childhood or later levels, since it deals with even younger children; also, few studies relate to the effects of environmental manipulations on language acquisition. An understanding of the evolving theories, however, can help in understanding the conflicting prescriptions for educational practice that are available.

Chomsky (1957) has proposed a transformational grammar as a way of understanding language. Children's mastery of language depends on their intuitive knowledge of this grammar.

According to his view, two levels of structure exist in language—a surface structure and a deep structure. The surface structure represents the pattern of words that are used; the deep structure represents the pattern of meanings underlying the words. Chomsky also differentiates between language competence and language performance. Competence is a person's knowledge of language; performance represents the use of that knowledge. Children's performance at any language task is only a partial indicator of their language competence.

Chomsky uses transformational grammar to develop his model of language acquisition, which cannot be explained by modeling or repetition alone. Each utterance of an individual, including that of a very young child, is a unique sentence that may never have been articulated before in that particular way. Thus, children do not repeat phrases and sentences that they hear. Rather, they use a set of rules to transform components of language that is heard to create their own peculiar message. They continually test the rules they have created about language. The responses received allow them to refine and elaborate their language competence and performance. Given a finite set of rules for grammar, any individual can construct an infinite number of sentences.

This view of language acquisition gives an active role to children as the constructor of their own language within a cultural framework. The ideas and arguments that developed from the articulation of this theory have provided a basis for a range of current language research, much of it focusing on how children develop syntactical structures. Ursula Bellugi and Roger Brown's (1964) work, for example, focused on the process by which children develop syntax in language as a process of interaction between parent and child.

Just how educators can best use the research in language development is not completely clear. Early researchers were concerned with normative studies, attempting to find the regularities in the development of language in children or attempting to discover the language acquisitions of children at different age levels. Later researchers focused more on the theoretical aspects of language development, studying the process of language acquisition or the factors that affect the development of language in children.

Eric Lenneberg (1967) has developed a theory of the biological foundations of language that is compatible with the work of Chomsky. He analyzes knowledge of language development in human beings alongside biological knowledge about human and nonhuman animals, synthesizing them into a theory. He suggests that latent language structures are biologically determined and that they need to be actualized within a sound setting through exposure to adult language behavior. The schedule for language development seems to follow a biologically programmed schedule. For example, the period of language readiness for such actualization, it is suggested, is from two years to the early teens. In this period, children recreate the language mechanisms of the culture.

While Lenneberg's theories provide great opportunities for speculation, they give little guidance in how best to "actualize" language structures—the key role of language education. Education and child development specialists have developed research related to engineering the social setting to enhance language development.

B. F. Skinner (1957) has also developed a theory of language acquisition based upon behavioral principles. He believes the infant's original vocalizations and babblings reinforce themselves. After a while, adults around the infant selectively reinforce sounds that are a part of the native language, thus strengthening them while allowing the others to fade. Language forms are taught through imitation. Children learn grammar and proper word orders as they distinguish sentences from nonsentences during listening. Thus speech is learned first, followed by grammar. Although Skinner's theory could explain repetition of language, it does not explain grammar-generating rules that have been observed by linguistic scientists. However, this behaviorist approach has been the basis for language learning programs in schools.

Another view that is being tested to explain language acquisition in children sees language as an adjunct to cognitive processes. A number of developmental psychologists, including Jean Piaget and Lev Semenovich Vygotsky, have discussed the relationship between language and cognitive development. Marilyn Edmonds's (1976) research seems to indicate a direct relationship between stages of intellectual development and stages of language development in children. There is general agreement that a relationship exists between language and cognition, but the nature of that relationship remains open to further study.

Language and Dialect Differences

Children learn the language they most often hear spoken by the significant adults around them. Most American children learn English; children in Japan learn Japanese just as easily. But the various forms of the English language spoken in American subcultures may differ markedly from one another. These differences are called *dialects.*

Speech patterns may differ in many ways. There can be differences in the pronunciation of words or in speech inflections. Differences may exist in the labels ascribed to familiar things; what is called a "sack" in one area may be called a "bag" elsewhere. There may also be syntactical differences among dialects, making understanding difficult because the structure of statements carries much of their meaning.

The dialect prevalent in the schools and generally heard over radio and television has been called *Standard American English*. However, many children have been raised in an environment in which different dialects prevail.

Bilingualism refers to speakers who have achieved competence and performance in two languages (Gingras, 1983). Most bilingual speakers tend to be stronger in one language than in the other. The language first mastered in childhood is often referred to as the child's *native language* or *first language*.

Most studies of language acquisition focus on children's learning of their first language. Children seem to acquire their second language in much the same way and appear to be able to keep the two languages apart. A bilingual child, however, may go through a silent period in the second language until competence is built up. The pace of second-language acquisition varies among children. However, there does seem to be a consensus about the desirability of beginning second-language learning early, although just how early is not clear.

The fact that many children enter school with a langauge background not shared by their teacher and significantly different from the language upon which most school learning is based has many implications for programs and for teaching.

Dealing with Language Differences in the Classroom

Some educators suggest that differences in the language backgrounds of children are irrelevant in determining instructional goals. Since the school uses Standard English, one should teach Standard English, even if it means suppressing the child's language. Others suggest that the child's language is important and should be reflected in the school; one ought not to teach a single system of language, but teach the use of language appropriate to the situation in which it is used. Using the Spanish language in school would be justifiable if there were a number of Spanish-speaking children in the class. The black dialect of the urban ghetto could also be recognized as a valid and useful form of verbal communication.

Language serves many purposes. These purposes become the basis for establishing the goals of a language arts program in school. Speaking a dialect or using a particular style of language establishes an individual as a member of a specific group. To attempt to change this language system might have significant implications beyond learning the use of proper syntax.

Preschool teachers who have in their classroom children for whom English is not their native language might speak English as a *caretaker language.* This would require that English be spoken simply and slowly, using frequently repeated syntactic patterns to help children deal with the here-and-now. Whether formal instruction in English should begin before or about the age of six is questionable (Gingras, 1983). When it is begun, Standard English might be taught in a number of ways.

Use of naturalistic methods. One way to teach Standard English is to model the natural processes of language acquisition. This could be done by surrounding the child with people, both adults and children, who speak the majority dialect. Their natural interactions would help the child acquire this dialect.

Courtney Cazden (1968) reports using a process known as *expatiation* in improving language of children. This process requires the adult to react to the child's utterances by expanding them ideationally rather than linguistically. The child's remark, "Dog bark," may be responded to by, "Yes, he's mad at the kitty." Marion Blank and Francis Solomon (1969) also used a naturalistic strategy in elaborating children's language. They suggest a one-to-one relationship basing instruction on the child's utterance but reflecting open-ended questions that move beyond his or her original statements. This strategy allows the tutor to make judgments about the child's level of language development by listening to specific utterances. This information is used in framing the next question, to move the child along a developmental continuum. The program was not designed to teach language per se but to develop within the child the linguistic base for thinking.

In the Tucson Early Education Model, developed for Mexican-American children, the child is given opportunities to speak, and the language he or she brings to school is valued. The teacher responds in Standard English, acting as a model for the child. Through the interactions of adult and child, the child's language is expected to be transformed.

Arline Hobson (1973), working within this model, systematically utilizes those elements found within the natural adult-child interaction patterns that support language acquisition. These elements, according to Hobson, are

1. *Corrective feedback*—providing omissions, proper labels, proper word order, and appropriate vocabulary
2. *Summary feedback*—gathering together ideas that have been expressed by the children, thus expanding the relationships among ideas
3. *Elaboration and extension*—extending language and ideas beyond the immediate
4. *Extending knowledge*—providing information beyond what is immediately available
5. *Reinforcing*—providing generous and specific reinforcement for appropriate language generation

Use of synthetic techniques. Shari Nedler (1970) and Robert Reeback (1970) use synthetic approaches to teach English to non-English-speaking children. The teacher, using their patterned drill approaches, states a sentence or asks a question and the children must give the desired response.

Nedler (1975) has described the process of developing and testing approaches to teaching English to non-English-speaking children. After the experience with two synthetic approaches of teaching language, which did not have transferable outcomes that children could assimilate into their day-to-day verbal interactions, Nedler's group moved to a more naturalistic approach aimed at teaching English vocabulary and elements of syntactical structure.

The naturalistic and synthetic approaches to language instruction parallel the theories of language acquisition supported by the transformationalists and the behaviorists. The transformationalists—who view the child as an active participant, generating rules to be tested and modified to create internal language structures—believe the school should provide opportunities for these language acts to occur, and feedback to allow children to test the rules they create. The behaviorists see the school as providing an opportunity for a more efficient, more systematic scheme of language instruction than can be provided in the home. By using explicit instructional strategies and manipulating rewards in the environment, the teacher can help the child move quickly through successive approximations toward mature language behavior. To do this, educators must clearly define goals of language instruction as behaviors and determine the conditions for achieving these behaviors.

GOALS OF LANGUAGE LEARNING

Language arts programs in the early years have multiple goals. In general, the goals are as follows:

1. THE DEVELOPMENT OF VERBAL COMMUNICATION SKILLS. Young children are constantly interacting with those around them, transmitting and receiving messages. Their ability to function in the world is determined to a great extent by their ability to communicate their wants, needs, ideas, and feelings, and to receive and interpret similar communications from other persons. These two skills are in large part the goals of language arts programs. As children mature, the communications sent and received are put into written as well as spoken forms—reading and writing become important skills. This requires extended knowledge of vocabulary and structural forms as well as skill in forming letters, words, sentences and paragraphs.
2. DEVELOPMENT OF RICH LANGUAGE REPERTOIRE. Language is an extension of the person. To function effectively in the community, young children must have a sense of the shared meanings of words and of the structure of the language that allows them to be linguistically effective. They need to learn about the variety of styles and uses of language that are available. Chomsky's "deep structure" becomes important here.
    A language repertoire also serves as an aid to thinking. Since mature thought

processes are so closely related to language both in structure and in content, growth in language will also support growth in thought.

3. DEVELOPMENT OF AN ABILITY TO USE LANGUAGE TO INFLUENCE AND BE INFLUENCED. Until the time children reach nursery school age, they are manipulated and manipulate others physically. As they enter school, the manipulation is more by the use of words. The teacher gives instructions in words; language, in this sense, is a tool. Children satisfy social needs more by talking to other children. The give-and-take of human relationships becomes a function of language. Even in the dramatic play of children, verbal statements soon take the place of actual physical movements. All this suggests that the appropriate use of language is one of the most important social skills young children can learn.

4. DEVELOPING PERSONAL SATISFACTIONS AND AESTHETIC APPRECIATIONS OF LANGUAGE. Although much of the language arts program in the early school years is primarily utilitarian in nature, aesthetics should not be excluded. The use of literature, poetry, creative dramatics, and other forms of expression can provide great personal satisfactions, aesthetic and emotional, for children.

EXPRESSIVE ORAL LANGUAGE LEARNING

There are many opportunities for oral language learning in the early years of school. Specific times are set aside for group discussion, story reading, and sharing, or "show and tell." Although such large group activities may be suitable for teaching some receptive language skills, they are not efficient for teaching expressive skills, since each child spends too much time waiting for a turn in a large group. Alternate approaches need to be developed. Some of these approaches require a teacher's sensitivity to the time when language learning can occur naturally in a small group setting or in individual interaction. These small settings are usually more appropriate for language learning than are total class instructional settings.

The Activity Period

Most nursery-kindergarten programs set aside a good portion of the day for an activity or work period. When primary grades are organized into activity centers which children use throughout a long period, these opportunities are also available. Some of the activities of the work period provide greater opportunities than others to support language learning.

Dramatic Play

Dramatic play is an important area for language learning. This involves the children in role playing with no predetermined script or plot. It might include family play in a housekeeping area or playing other roles reflecting a range of social situations such as in supermarket play, or garage play. In dramatic play children can put into action their personal constructions of the adult world. The cognitive and affective meanings developed become intertwined in this play.

Although dramatic play is supported most often in nursery-kindergarten activities, similar play interactions can be developed by primary-grade children. These may be more narrowly focused and closely guided and related to specific learning situations. Often social studies activities include dramatic play incidents to explore social roles. Dramatic play is symbolic play. It requires the interaction of children in interlocking roles: they must communicate with one another to carry on the play. Language often substitutes for the actions of the playing. Sarah Smilansky (1968) found that a teacher may use specific techniques that work to enrich children's dramatic play.

Educational play requires active guidance, although the teacher should allow the children to structure their own play activities within the established theme and the setting. Through observation, the teacher becomes aware of possibilities in the play that are not evident to the children. Moving into the play, momentarily assuming a role, and directing it through verbal interactions one can actively guide it. Asking key questions of the play participants that will suggest new alternatives or providing additional props will also move the play forward.

The key to supporting language learning in dramatic play is not in simply setting up the children's play activities and leaving them alone in their corner. Helen Robison and Bernard Spodek (1965) used the term *directive teaching* in describing how a teacher might guide the play of children. The teacher functions not only as an observer but also as a guide and a source of information and play materials. In functioning in this manner, the teacher must be careful not to impose too heavily on the play of children.

Other Areas

Although few activity areas are as productive for language learning as dramatic play, there are other opportunities for language learning. More mature block-building often involves verbal and social interaction.

As the children move beyond the manipulative stage of blockbuilding, a strong dramatic element takes over. This may be used in much the same way as dramatic play to support language learning. Teachers can add to available opportunities, however, by holding intimate conversations with the children.

Children who are shy and reticent in a large group situation will often speak more freely when alone with the teacher. Conversations can relate to the children's activities or to the materials they are using, allowing the child to focus on something outside himself, and to refer to things immediately available. Teachers can use open-ended questions like, ''Tell me what you have there,'' or ''Are there other ways you could make something like it?'' to elicit language expressions. These questions can be followed up to continue the conversation.

Marion Blank (1973) designed a tutorial approach that emphasized both language and cognitive goals. The tutorial was essentially a dialogue between the preschool child and the teacher. By asking questions about common occurrences and materials, the teacher could extend the child's language and thinking skills. Children's difficulties were attended to and children were helped to deal with ideas on a more abstract level. Tutorial sessions are short but frequent in the Blank approach.

A teacher can set aside some time within the daily schedule to meet briefly with those children who are having language difficulties. Brief dialogues could be planned relating to occurrences in the classroom and children could be helped to think through and articulate their thoughts about those events. This form of interaction could help extend language and thinking skills.

Having the teacher immediately available as a respondent to the child makes these small verbal interactions very useful. If a teacher aide or volunteer is in the classroom, a great amount of teacher-child interaction can take place in an activity period, since two persons can be deployed to support verbal behavior.

Discussion Sessions

Discussion sessions involving the entire class, as in sharing and "show and tell" periods, have many advantages.

The sharing period generally requires that each child, in turn, speak to the entire class. An object brought from home may be shown and discussed, or a child may discuss something that has happened. If the child is reticent, the teacher can ask questions about the object. Other children can be encouraged to ask questions, comment, and make observations.

Teachers using this sharing period should avoid its inherent pitfalls. Rejecting objects or incidents from home may teach the child that it is safer not to expose oneself in school, and thereby limit language learning possibilities.

There is also the danger that limiting the length of each contribution, or having the children take turns or wait for their turn longer than they can bear, may have negative influences on language learning. The children should be learning to be listeners and speakers—this is not easily learned in a situation that supports the negative responses of "turning off" and "tuning out."

Several alternatives to the traditional sharing period can increase the benefits of this type of activity. One method is to limit the number of children who will speak at each session. Going through the class alphabetically and assigning five children per session, for example, can keep the sharing period to a reasonable limit. Asking that children bring items to class associated with a specific theme might also limit the range of items discussed and relate the discussion time to other learning situations in the classroom. Children can be asked to bring in something made of wood, something that is attracted by a magnet, something very old, or pictures of objects. The need to focus on some special

FIGURE 4-1   Discussion sessions provide opportunities for oral expression.

area or class of object turns the home search for an object into a problem-solving activity for the child as well as the family.

Another alternative is to make the sharing session a small-group activity. This would allow a degree of voluntarism to the child's involvement, a greater degree of participation among all the children, and far more interaction among children in the discussion situation. The children themselves might take turns asking about objects and events.

Finally, the discussion session might be changed from a situation in which children talk about things outside the school to one in which they talk about what happened in school. If a sharing time is held at the end of the activity period, for example, the children can talk about what they made or did during that time.

The children can be called together in a suitable place. Each child can be asked to talk about what was done or made that day. If a product is involved, the child can show it. The teachers or any of the other children may ask questions about it, or the child can be asked to describe some activity.

As the activities vary, the discussions also vary. Children and teacher share the same reference; if there is distortion, misrepresentation, or confusion, the teacher is able to deal with it. *Sharing* in this situation takes on new meaning, for not only does the child have an opportunity to relate things that are personally important, but the interaction and reporting of activity in the school setting can help establish a feeling of community in the classroom.

Many other opportunities for discussions also can be found. Informal discussions between the teacher and a child or group can take place on any occasion and should be regularly encouraged by the teacher. The greater the amount of the child's verbal expression, and the greater the number of adult-child interactions that take place, the greater the opportunities for language learning in the classroom.

Creative Dramatics

Children can interpret the stories, poems, and songs they hear in a variety of ways. Creative drama allows for such interpretations by focusing on a particular plot, such as a familiar story with a relatively simple, straightforward plot line. The children can be assigned characters and make up their own dialogue, keeping the story line intact. The creative aspect of the dramatic presentation lies in the interpretations of the children, the dialogue they develop, and the actions they assign to particular characters. Children can also base dramatic presentation on their own original stories, which provide them with a greater latitude of plot and character.

Creative dramatic presentations need no audience. They can be organized as a part of the activity period, started spontaneously by the children or encouraged by the teacher. Only a few props generally are needed. A pair of chairs can be made to represent an automobile, a table can become a bridge, or a piece of carpeting an ocean. Odd pieces of drapery material, skirts, and floppy hats can be used for costumes.

The teacher should be careful not to have the children memorize pieces of dialogue or action, but instead to allow the content of the play to be their product. The teacher provides a story that can become familiar to the children through repeated telling, suggests actions and sequences, and refers to the original story as a source of dialogue and action. Often a suggestion such as "What happens next?" or "What did he say in response?" is the only guidance that is needed.

Simple dramatic presentations can be repeated. Children can be encouraged to try new roles, playing them in their own way. If a particular dramatic presentation seems good, there is no reason not to invite another class, the principal, or the children's parents to view it. This can offer the children a great sense of accomplishment.

As children mature, dramatic presentations can become more elaborate, using more extensive stories and characterizations, and more elaborate props and settings. The same story can often be dramatized in a variety of ways in a class. After interpreting a story in creative dramatics, the children can try it with puppets or flannelgraph illustrations. They could also try acting out the story in pantomime—attempting to communicate with actions alone.

Puppetry

Playing with puppets is a good way to get a shy child to vocalize, for the puppet becomes the center of attention rather than the child. A variety of excellent commercial handpuppets is available in supply houses, and simple puppets can be constructed by the teacher or the children.

Stick puppets can be made by pasting faces the children have drawn on paper to a flat stick. The children then hold and manipulate them in a play situation. Puppets can also be made out of paper bags on which a face has been drawn. If the mouth is drawn on both sides of the point at which the square bottom of the bag is folded, it will open and close when held between fingers and thumb. Such puppet manipulations are not really necessary for young children, however.

Teachers and parents can also make interesting puppets out of socks: buttons can be eyes and a piece of felt the mouth. Puppets can be improvised in many other ways. For very young children, a puppet stage is unnecessary, for even if the puppeteer is visible, as in Japanese puppet shows, the audience will focus on the puppets themselves.

Children can be easily bored if they must sit for periods of time watching the unrehearsed and often uncommunicative manipulations of puppets by each member of the class. Puppet shows are best developed in small groups. In fact, an audience is not always necessary.

With older children, puppet making can become a more extensive craft activity with children using papier-mâché or wood for shaping the puppets' heads. Marionettes—puppets that move by the manipulation of strings—can also be used by children in the upper primary grades. As with creative dramatics, there is no age ceiling on the use of puppets, if their use is varied with maturity.

Children's Storytelling

Young children should be encouraged to tell stories in class. These can be their original stories or stories they have heard. The teacher can ask leading questions, or read part of a story and ask the children to complete it or to fill in portions.

Children can also be encouraged to report on important events. They may return from a vacation or a trip and share their experiences with others. These reports may be given to a small group rather than to the entire class. On occasion they should be written down by the teacher to be read back at a later time.

Teachers should take other dictation from children as well. The children's observations of the process of dictating, recording, and reading back stories gives them an understanding of what reading and writing are, and the reasons for our concern for learning these skills. The phrase "writing is talk written down" comes to life in this process. Meaningful associations between their verbal utterances and the books around them are created in this process.

RECEPTIVE ORAL LANGUAGE LEARNING

As children mature, they spend less time speaking and acting and more time listening and watching in school. Opportunities must be provided for children to learn to listen.

FIGURE 4-2   Teachers have many opportunities to take dictation from children.

Children listen at different times for different purposes and with varying degrees of depth. Levels of listening have been classified as marginal, appreciative, attentive, and analytic (National Council of Teachers of English, 1954). Listening to sounds in the background can be characterized as marginal; listening to music or to a story is appreciative listening; attentive listening is listening for directions; analytic listening requires a more active role of the individual, who dissects and evaluates what is heard.

Teaching children to listen is a worthwhile goal for early childhood education, but it is sometimes difficult to determine whether it has been achieved. Children who are watching will usually provide visual cues of their attention: their eyes are focused and their faces turned toward the object being viewed. The child's ears do not give the same clues of attention. A child may be listening while looking away from the speaker, even engaged in other activities. The only way we can actually tell whether a child is listening attentively is to ask him a question that requires him to reflect some element of what he heard, or to do something with what he heard. Young children can be involved in the processes of appreciative, attentive, and analytic listening in schools. Storytelling and discussions about stories will help.

Telling Stories to Children

A large body of children's literature providing a wealth of resources for storytelling has developed in the last few decades in our country. But reading books to children should never completely eliminate telling stories. Teachers can familiarize themselves with stories from children's books, which they can retell in their own words.

The story might be a fanciful, contemporary tale or a traditional story culled from the folk literature. Stories may also be the outgrowth of the children's experiences. Retelling the happenings on a trip or another experience the children have had, or even an occurrence from the childhood experience of the teacher, provide excellent resources for stories.

Teachers often find that props or pictures help them dramatize a story. Simple figures for use on a flannel board, simple objects, or pictures are commercially available.

Reading to Children

Any nursery or kindergarten class should have a good stock of well-written and well-illustrated books for children. Collections of stories, or anthologies, even when not illustrated, are also useful. Teachers can get help in selecting books from other teachers and supervisors, librarians, and local colleges and universities. In addition, several printed resources are available to help teachers select books. These include

> *Bibliography of Books for Children.* Washington, D.C.: Association for Childhood Education International, 1980.
>
> Gillespie, John T., and Gilbert, Christie B. *Best Books for Children.* New York: R. R. Bowker, 1981.
>
> Larrick, Nancy. *A Parent's Guide to Children's Reading* (4th ed). Garden City, N.Y.: Doubleday, 1975.
>
> Peterson, Linda K., and Solt, Marilyn L. *Newberry and Caldecott Medal and Honor Books.* Boston: G. K. Hall, 1982.
>
> Tway, Eileen. *Reading Ladders for Human Relations* (6th ed). Washington, D.C.: American Council on Education, 1980.
>
> White, Mary Lou. *Adventuring with Books.* Urbana, Ill.: National Council of Teachers of English, 1981.

In addition, each spring *Young Children* publishes a series of annotated bibliographies of outstanding new books for young children.

Books should be selected carefully; they should be of interest to the children. Information books should be accurate and authoritative—accuracy of information may take precedence over literary style. The teacher might select stories to prepare children for a future study, or a book because the theme concerns her. Books are also read simply for good fun.

Leland Jacobs (1972) has suggested that a collection of books in a classroom be balanced. The balance should be between contemporary works and classics, between realistic and fanciful literature, between fictional and informational material, between popular and precious reading matter, between expensive and inexpensive books, between periodicals and books, and between prose and poetry. No one type of children's literature should be selected to the exclusion of others.

Good children's literature has themes that are the central focus of young children's concerns. Books provide a way of learning about things outside the immediate in time and space, thus expanding the child's horizons. Persons different in manner and dress can be introduced to children through books. And certainly the world of whimsy and fantasy should be a part of the child's literary experience.

Books can often help the young child deal with the resolution of his own problems and conflicts; they may have a mentally healthful effect by showing the child that the problems encountered are not his or hers alone. Some educators have suggested that teachers systematically use books and discussions to help children cope with the problems they encounter. Such an approach, called *bibliotherapy,* is seen as having preventative powers as well as therapeutic values in maintaining a child's mental health.

In addition, books that depict children from minority groups in realistic ways are becoming increasingly available. Athough such books are no substitute for an integrated classroom, they help the majority culture member realize that people who may seem different are really not that different. Providing such books in school also shows the minority-group child that members of his group are worthy of being depicted in the national literature. Teachers need to review the materials in their classroom to see if they are free of racial and sexual stereotypes. *Guidelines for Selecting Bias-Free Textbooks and Storybooks* (1980) by the Council on Interracial Books for Children should prove helpful.[1]

It is important that teachers be familiar with the books read to children. New teachers often find it helpful to take books home and practice reading them aloud. The stage should then be set for a pleasurable reading experience. An informal arrangement helps; seating the group informally on a rug so that each child has an undisturbed line of vision to the teacher is helpful. Chairs can also be informally arranged for reading—especially if a picture-story book is being read.

It is disturbing to have to interrupt a story constantly to admonish a child who is misbehaving or inattentive. Teachers sometimes place obstreperous children near them to forestall the need to interrupt. Making story listening a voluntary activity, with choices of other non-noise-producing activities available, is also useful. Often a child will begin to pay attention simply because it is not required.

Teachers generally read stories to children themselves, but it is beneficial to have an aide or a volunteer parent come to school and read. If more than one person is available, a story-reading time need not involve the entire class. Making the story-reading period more intimate is helpful in developing language

---

[1]For information about books dealing with minority children, see the list of books suggested earlier in this chapter, as well as Bernard Spodek et al., *A Black Studies Curriculum for Early Childhood Education* Rev. (Urbana, Ill.: ERIC Clearinghouse for Early Childhood Education, 1976); and *Interracial Books for Children Bulletin* (Council on Interracial Books for Children, 1841 Broadway, New York, N.Y. 10023).

learning. Children in the upper grades may be invited to read to the class, as may the better primary readers.

Reading a story will often stimulate discussion. Teachers sometimes also like to ask questions to see if the children have understood the story. Although this is a good technique for ferreting out misconceptions, it can be overdone. Care must be taken to see that story-reading remains pleasant and does not become burdensome to children.

Browsing through Books

Children need opportunities to look at books themselves, to get the feel of books even before they learn to read them. A good library area has books attractively displayed and available for children. Books may be laid on a shelf or placed in a rack so that the child can easily see covers in order to select books that seem interesting. There ought to be a place where children can comfortably look through the books, examining the pictures, reading, and discussing them with other children. A rocking chair, a table and chairs, a group of pillows on the floor, or even a small rug all make inviting settings for browsing through books. Of course, lighting must be adequate and there should be a degree of isolation to the area. Children should also learn to care for books. When books are changed at frequent intervals, some new and exciting reading material is always available.

It is useful to allow children to take books home if possible. Particularly when a child has few books at home, the teacher should try to arrange to lend books. Inexpensive reprints of good children's books are available that make the cost of this activity reasonable. Parents should be encouraged to read to their children. Sometimes a simple instruction sheet sent home to the parent is enough; at other times, the teacher might wish to devote a parent meeting to working on the specific skills of reading to children.

Poetry for Young Children

Children enjoy listening to poetry, for it combines the rhythmic flow of words with a concern for their sounds. A range of poems for young children from Mother Goose rhymes and A. A. Milne to the works of many contemporary poets can be introduced. The repetitive quality of much of children's poetry will sometimes help the children learn the poems themselves.

Often, reading poetry in a class will lead children to an interest in the sounds of words. Rhyming and alliteration may fascinate some children who simply enjoy the sounds of the words and the way they feel on their tongues. Play with words should be encouraged, but teachers should be forewarned that young children can be terrible punsters. Poems should be read aloud so that the rhyme and rhythm become more readily apparent.

Teachers of young children often use poems along with finger plays. These activities may lack literary value, but they are useful as time-fillers and are enjoyed by children. Finger play has a venerable tradition in early childhood education, originating in Froebel's kindergarten.

Using Audio-Visual Aids

In most classrooms the teacher is limited in the variety of listening activities that can be provided for the children. If a story is read to the children, then nothing else can be done and story times become total class activity times. Many teachers have found that using audio-visual aids can extend their ability to provide receptive language activities under a variety of conditions and with smaller groups of children.

Commercial long-playing and cassette tape recordings of many children's stories are available. In addition, teachers have found it helpful to make their own recordings of stories. Most children at the nursery level can learn to handle a cassette tape recorder on their own. Providing children with a tape recording of a book along with the book itself allows them to listen to the story and look at the pictures at the same time. Recording an auditory signal for turning the page is helpful.

Many classes are equipped with *listening centers,* consisting of headphone attachments to a phonograph or tape recorder with multiple jacks so more than one child may listen at a time. Although some listening centers are designed with carrels to separate the children, such separations are unnecessary unless there is a severe attention problem. Listening to a story can and ought to be an experience a child can share with others. The headsets are used primarily so that the sounds of the record do not interfere with other activities that may be occurring in the classroom.

Motion pictures and sound filmstrips can also be used to extend children's receptive language experiences. A number of excellent children's stories are now available in these media and rooms can be arranged and equipped to allow viewing by a single child or a large group.

FIGURE 4-3
Headphones can create a listening center almost anywhere.

Using the Normal Occurrences of the Day

Teachers can find many opportunities to support language learning throughout the school day. Continual language instruction, however, requires a sensitivity to the potentials of learning in each situation.

A cooking activity might start with a planning discussion: "What needs to be done?" "How will we go about it?' "Who will do each task?" "What materials and equipment are necessary?" Questions can elicit responses in a planning discussion from all the children. Recipes need to be read several times, during both the planning and the cooking. The teacher can review the entire cooking sequence at its termination and write a chart describing the experience.

In dramatic play situations, signs can often be made by the teacher and used by the children. In music, the teacher might have the children listen carefully to the words of a song, then talk about the sounds of the words as well as their meaning. Singing a repetitive verse can teach new words, or children can be asked to create their own verses. The need for finding rhymes will help the children to learn to listen to the word endings and to compare the sounds of words. Each activity needs to be explored for the language learning that can be found therein.

Other Language-Related Activities

In addition to the areas discussed, other opportunities exist for language learning in the classroom. In most classrooms, a number of manipulative materials are provided in support of language learning. The use of these materials can extend an understanding of specific language attributes.

Lotto games are a good example. In playing Lotto, children have to identify a picture, label it, and match it with another picture on a card; thus Lotto games can be used to teach names of categories of objects, names of objects, or names of actions, in addition to teaching visual matching skills. Sequence puzzles, in which the scenes from familiar stories must be placed in proper order, help children learn the sequence of events in a story. Then they may be asked to relate the story after the pictures are ordered. There are also many reading-readiness materials that can be used. Three-dimensional letters allow children to make up words and learn the letters without coping with the problem of forming the letters themselves. They also provide a tactile experience in perceiving the shape and form of letters. A number of reading-readiness games and materials can also be included here.

Many of the games in the manipulative material area can be used by children individually or in small groups. Once children have mastered the skills and rules needed for their use, they can often work independently, with the teacher periodically checking on the accuracy of the activity. This independence allows the manipulative materials to be used during many different times of the day.

Continued involvement in oral language activities, discussions, creative dramatic productions, and listening to stories and poems has a direct connection with involvement in written language activities. There is less separation of the language arts in life than in school programs, which are too often segmented and compartmentalized. Reading and writing must go hand in hand with listening and speaking in the classroom.

WRITTEN LANGUAGE LEARNING

Primary teachers in particular are concerned with the mechanics as well as the expressive content of reading and writing. Much activity in the area of written language learning can be approached informally. However, teaching the skills of reading and writing requires some systematic approach to learning.

Writing

Most schools today teach young children to write in manuscript, a simple form of calligraphy using unconnected letters. The switch to cursive writing, in which all the letters in a word are connected, usually comes about the middle or end of second grade. Children often begin writing in kindergarten by learning to write their names. Sometimes they have learned this skill at home. It is helpful if kindergarten children learn to use manuscript rather than block printing to avoid an additional transition.

The beginnings of letter writing actually start even earlier. Children in nursery school and kindergarten have already used crayons and paint brushes. If the children learn to hold and use these implements properly, the transition from drawing to writing is simplified. Children can be provided with pencils in the kindergarten for both drawing and beginning writing. By this time children are usually aware of what letters look like and can distinguish between letters and letter-like forms and other markings. They can be helped to make the strokes necessary for manuscript writing: the circle and the horizontal, vertical, and slant strokes.

A variety of techniques can be used to teach the formation of letters, including the use of templates, and wooden or sandpaper letters. This lets the child feel the shape and form of letters. Letters can be formed in the sand or on a blackboard before using paper and pencil. Children can then copy letters the teacher writes or those printed in work sheets or exercise books, or write over letters formed by the teacher. Teachers may also give a child models printed on paper placed under acetate sheets so that the first writing is directly on the model. When such activities are provided, they should be provided only to those children who are interested and who can benefit from them rather than as a whole class assignment.

One intriguing sequence in teaching children to write was observed in an English infant school. Children from the day of admission (about age five) were given a book of their own, several sheets of paper stapled together along the left edge. Each day every child was to "write" in his book. The "writings" at first were pictures drawn by the children. The teacher would write a short narrative about the picture as dictated by the child. Later, the children were asked to write with a pencil over the teacher's writing. Still later the children copied the teacher's narrative directly below her words on the paper. Finally, the children were expected to write their own short narratives with the help of the teacher or another child.

In many cases, children will be able to *use* writing long before they have perfected the ability to write each letter clearly, legibly, and without error. They should be encouraged to do so, since unnecessary attention to the mechanics of writing without any concern for its use may lead them to lose interest. It is useful to have the children write words, sentences, and stories as early as possible.

Many kindergarten and primary classrooms have primer typewriters available. Their large type and simplified form of the letters make them an extremely useful addition to the classroom. Children can begin early to type their own stories on these machines, and they can be read by other children with ease. The typewriter frees the young child from his concern with coordinating the muscles of his hand to form the letters. Words come out with ease. In its introduction, the typewriter often stimulates children to play with the forms of letters and punctuation marks. Soon children will move from this exploratory stage to a more goal-oriented stage, using the typewriter as a writing implement. More than one child might wish to be at the machine at the same time—for dialogue as well as discourse can be typed by children.

With the introduction of computers into early childhood classes, especially at the upper primary level, children have a new writing tool. Once the keyboard is mastered, word processing programs, like the *Bank Street Writer,* allow children to focus on the content of what they write rather than the mechanics. Errors can be corrected and the content can be revised without requiring a complete rewrite—and the final product is always presentable.

Teachers who have been taking the dictation of children, can move slowly to the children's writing. The teacher might begin by having the children dictate a short story, using only a few words that they can copy. The children might also be given the opportunity to illustrate the story on large sheets of paper. The copying of short stories can be extended as stories become more elaborated. Stories can be written by groups of children, but they should be encouraged to write their own stories as soon as possible.

The stories children write should be read, either to the teacher or to other children. They may also be sent home. It is helpful to collect the writings of children stapled together into a book with covers and illustrations done by the children, to show progress in school and to read for pleasure. The volume can be displayed or put into the reading area for others to read as well.

Providing children with thin writing tablets at the beginning of the year gives them a sense of writing a book. Care should be taken that there are not too many pages in these tablets; otherwise, completing them will seem an overwhelming task. A home-made book, used in the infant school as described above, is often sufficient.

Children should be encouraged to write as much as possible. They can write about experiences out of school as well: starting with reporting incidents may help the children become writers. As time goes on, they can become more creative in the writing, composing fanciful tales and poetry.

Spelling is not too important in the beginning and should not be stressed. Children need to feel comfortable in writing; premature criticism can stifle the child's early attempts. The work can be corrected later by the teacher or by other children. Eventually children will develop the habit of proofreading their written work. It is helpful to provide them with primary dictionaries so that they can begin to look up the spelling of words. A file box and a set of cards or a notebook with each page devoted to a single letter of the alphabet can help them develop their own dictionaries or word lists. Children can put into their dictionary new words that they have learned to spell and define. They will soon begin to use one another as well as the teacher as resources for proper spelling.

There is not complete agreement in the field as to when a systematic program of spelling construction ought to begin for children, nor is there agreement as to the nature of such a program. In the past, many spelling programs consisted of providing children with lists or books of words used in their particular age-groups. Since it was felt that English spelling was highly irregular, most programs had the children memorize the spelling of lists of words in some fashion. Sometimes pretests were given weekly and children wrote the words they could not spell periodically until they were retested at the end of the week. Often the length of the word was the criterion for determining its suitability for children, with young children asked to learn shorter words. They were often helped to focus on the visual aspects of the word to enhance retention.

Studies by Paul and Jean Hanna and others (1967) have shown a high degree of regularity in the spelling of English words. This would suggest that spelling patterns can be abstracted and words taught to children in a more rational manner. It also suggests that the errors of children who spell words as they sound could also be used to greater advantage by teachers, for even when mistakes are made, some errors may be more logical than others.

Grammar

Recent changes in linguistic theory have had a profound effect on the teaching of grammar at the secondary school and college level. It is only possible to speculate about the extent to which these changes call for modification of early childhood programs. Current theory conceives of grammar as a process by which an infinite variety of sentences can be derived by transformation from a limited number of basic sentence forms. The theory of transformational grammar as postulated by Noam Chomsky (1957) and others would suggest that grammar ought to be taught not as a series of rules that lead to "proper" language usage, but as a series of rules from which new structure can be generated.

In the early years we are concerned with having children become good users of language rather than scholars of the structure of the language. From this point of view, the teacher's concern needs to be about how the newer grammar could provide insights that would help to extend children's language.

One possible approach is to provide children with opportunities to "play" with the structures of language just as they play with the sounds of words. Children can be given simple sentences and asked to transform them in a variety of ways. Given a declarative sentence, children could be asked to state it as a question or as a command. They could add modifiers to noun or verb phrases, thus becoming more specific in their language use. They could also be asked to place words in different sequences to try to change the meaning of sentences or to become sensitive to grammatical and ungrammatical structures.

Teachers need to be aware of the beauty of language that can be found in the ways children express themselves. Often the idiosyncratic phrases of children in the nursery years are subdued because they do not seem proper. Subcultural groups have expressions that have enriched our language, yet we often exclude these from our schools. Teachers should support and cherish these rather than try to eliminate them. The beauty of the language is enhanced when communication is a personal statement rather than a stereotyped series of phrases.

English primary schools can be characterized by the amount of writing in which the child engages. American schools can be characterized by their emphasis on reading. Carol Chomsky (1971) suggests that the natural order of progression is from writing to reading. Starting written language instruction through writing makes the child aware that the written work is an extension of his consciousness. Beginning reading can grow out of the child's writing. Begin-

FIGURE 4-4
Opportunities for children to write can be built into many learning activities.

ning spelling can be invented by the children following the sounds of words, thus making them aware of letter-sound associations. More formal spelling instruction can take place later.

Instruction in reading and writing needs to go hand in hand. Having the children write early is consistent with a number of methods of teaching reading reviewed in the next chapter. It can also help the classroom teacher develop an integrated approach to the language arts in her classroom.

Reading

As we wish to develop writers through our primary programs, we also wish to develop readers. Reading has to become a meaningful and personally satisfying experience. This can happen only when the child reads because he wants to rather than because he has to. If a child is to become "hooked on books," the book has to be introduced early in his reading experience.

Children need to be provided with opportunities for free browsing and reading. They should be able to determine what they will read, when they will read, and for how long. Even nursery-school children need opportunities to look at books and get their feel before being required to learn to read them. Once children develop reading skills, they should have many opportunities for independent study.

The books available in a class should range broadly in topics and reading levels. If a book is interesting, children will be able to read beyond their level as well as beneath it. A child needs a place to sit or stretch out and read undisturbed. Conversation should not be limited in a reading area, for a child who is truly interested in a book will want to share its contents with others. If the school has a library, it is important to schedule times for children to read or select books in it. However, a school library is a supplement, not a substitute, for a classroom library. Children need continual access to books. If they are reading independently, a record-keeping system will enable teacher and children to keep track of books read.

Children learn much by observing the behavior of teachers. Teachers who wish to teach them to enjoy reading must be readers themselves, able to communicate their enjoyment of reading. Reading stories to the class is one way of showing this enjoyment. There are other ways as well. A teacher can bring special books into class on occasion and tell the children about them, or feature them in a display. A teacher can have conferences with the children, asking them to describe the books, telling if they enjoyed them and why. A teacher can allow the children to write about the books they read, and can schedule time for them to read books of their choice during the school day.

More than anything else, the climate of the classroom and the values the teacher's behavior reflects will determine the nature of the language program. The same room with the same materials can be a dull setting or it can be an exciting place with children eagerly learning, listening, reading, talking, and writing. It is what the teacher does with the materials at hand that makes the difference.

REFERENCES

BELLUGI, U., and BROWN, R.   The acquisition of language. *Monograph of the Society for Research in Child Development,* 1964, *29* (2).

BLANK, M.   *Teaching learning in the preschool.* Columbus, Ohio: Chas. E. Merrill, 1973.

BLANK, M., and SOLOMON, F.   How shall disadvantaged children be taught? *Child Development,* 1969, *40,* 47–63.

BLOOM, L., and LAHEY, M.   *Language development and language disorders.* New York: John Wiley, 1978.

CAZDEN, C.   Some implications of research in language development. In R. Hess, and R. Bear (Eds.), *Early Education.* Chicago: Aldine, 1968.

CHOMSKY, C.   Write now, read later. *Childhood Education,* 1971, *47,* 296–299.

CHOMSKY, N.   *Syntactic Structure.* The Hague: Mouton and Co., 1957.

COUNCIL ON INTERRACIAL BOOKS FOR CHILDREN.   *Guidelines for selecting bias-free textbooks and storybooks.* New York: The Council, 1980.

EDMONDS, M. H.   New directions in theories of language acquisition. *Harvard Educational Review,* 1976, *46,* 195–198.

GINGRAS, R. C.   Early childhood bilingualism. In O. N. Saracho, and B. Spodek (Eds.). *Understanding the multicultural experience in early childhood education.* Washington, D.C.: National Association for the Education of Young Children, 1983.

HANNA, P. R., HANNA, J. S., HODGES, R. E., and RUDORF, E. H.   A summary: Linguistic cues for spelling improvement. *Elementary English,* 1967, *44,* 862–865.

HOBSON, A. B.   *The natural method of language learning: Systematized.* Tucson: Arizona Center for Educational Research and Development, 1973.

JACOBS, L. B.   Providing balanced contacts with literature for children. In L. B. Jacobs (Ed.) *Literature for children.* Washington, D.C.: Association for Childhood Education International, 1972.

LENNENBERG, E. H.   *Biological foundations of language.* New York: John Wiley, 1967.

NATIONAL COUNCIL OF TEACHERS OF ENGLISH.   *Language arts for today's children.* New York: Appleton-Century-Crofts, 1954.

NEDLER, S. E.   Explorations in teaching English as a second language. *Young Children,* 1975, *30,* 480–485.

NEDLER, S. E.   Early education for Spanish-Speaking Mexican-American Children. Paper presented at the annual meeting of the American Educational Research Association, March, 1970.

REEBACK, R. T.   Teacher's manual to accompany the oral language program (3rd. ed.). Albuquerque, N.M.: Southwest Cooperative Educational Laboratory, 1970.

ROBISON, H., and SPODEK, B.   *New directions in the kindergarten.* New York: Teachers College Press, 1965.

SKINNER, B. F.   *Verbal behavior.* Englewood Cliffs, N.J.: Prentice-Hall, 1957.

SMILANSKY, S.   *The effects of sociodramatic play on disadvantaged preschool children.* New York: John Wiley, 1968.

SUGGESTED READINGS

ANDERSON, P. S. *Language skills in elementary education* (3rd. ed.). New York: Macmillan, 1979.

BLOOM, L., and LAHEY, M. *Language development and language disorders.* New York: John Wiley, 1978.

BURNS, P. C., and LOWE, A. L. *The language arts in childhood education* (4th ed.). Skokie, Ill.: Rand McNally, 1979.

CAZDEN, C. B. (Ed.). *Child language and education.* New York: Holt, Rinehart & Winston, 1972.

—— (Ed.). *Language in early childhood education* (Rev. ed.). Washington, D.C.: National Association for the Education of Young Children, 1980.

CHUKOVSKY, K. *From two to five.* Berkeley: University of California Press, 1963.

DEVILLIERS, J., and DEVILLIERS, P. *Language acquisition: Structure and function.* Cambridge, Mass.: Harvard University Press, 1978.

GLAZER, J. I. *Literature for young children.* Columbus, Ohio: Chas. E. Merrill, 1981.

HUCK, C. S., and YOUNG, D. A. *Children's literature in the elementary school* (4th ed.). New York: Holt, Rinehart & Winston, 1979.

LEE, D. M., and RUBIN, J. B. *Children and language.* Belmont, Calif.: Wadsworth, 1979.

TIEDT, I. M. *The language arts handbook.* Englewood Cliffs, N.J.: Prentice-Hall, 1973.

TOUGH, J. *Talking, thinking, growing: Language with young children.* New York: Schocken Books, 1974.

5

Teaching
Beginning Reading

Reading is often considered the most important subject in the school curriculum. Success in school achievement in general is heavily dependent upon the ability to read, not only in the elementary school, but at levels beyond as well. While universal literacy has been the goal of public education in America for generations, this goal has never been totally achieved. The fact that some children complete schooling without having basic reading skills, and that others have difficulty in learning to read, has led to a wide range of recommendations and proposals concerning when to begin reading instruction, what instructional program to use, and how reading should relate to the entire early childhood education program.

Deciding how reading should fit into an early childhood program reflects each teacher's fundamental assumptions and convictions about language, development, learning, and the role of the school. In presenting a discussion about reading in the early years, various definitions of reading and conceptions of the reading process are offered. These are related to different reading programs that are available. Reading instruction is also discussed in the context of other language arts activities. Finally, a conception of an early childhood reading program is offered.

In proposing an early childhood reading program, we must distinguish between reading as a mature process and learning to read. Just as a good bicycle rider does not attend to or do all the things a beginner feels are important, so the mature reader attends to different things and reads differently from the novice reader. An analysis of reading will help in understanding the goals of the reading program. The ways in which these goals are achieved cannot be directly derived from this description.

DEFINING READING

Some of the controversy about reading instruction arises from the way in which the reading process is defined. Some educators contend that it is basically a decoding process—learning the relationship between written symbols and spoken sounds. Once these associations are learned, the child is a reader. Since the young child already has a body of knowledge available to him in relation to meanings and processes in oral language, beginning reading teachers need not worry about these. What the child does with the information gleaned from the written page is not considered the domain of reading. Further, the goal of reading instruction, according to this point of view, is to provide children with the key letter-sound associations that will unlock the written code.

Although few will disagree with the need for the successful beginning reader to learn letter-sound associations, many suggest that the reading process is more than "code cracking." Different experts extend their interpretations of the reading process and include much more. Some claim that reading is "gaining meaning from the printed page." They take reading one step beyond the first approach, suggesting that *interpreting* the sounds associated with the letters is also a part of the reading process and needs to be included in any program of instruction. Educators supporting this theory even suggest that the derivation of meaning for the printed word, rather than "code cracking," be emphasized in any reading instructional program.

Still others suggest that the reading process is really an extension of intellectual processes, for the interpretation of meaning is a significant part of reading also. Critical reading, problem solving, and other complex processes need also to be included in any reading program.

Frank Smith (1971) sees reading as gaining meaning from the printed word. He identifies two ways of achieving comprehension in reading. The first, *immediate comprehension,* is accomplished by going directly from the visual features of writing to their meaning. The second, *mediated comprehension,* requires a prior identification of words. The fluent reader reads primarily by way of immediate comprehension, using alternative sources of redundant information to speed the process along. This information comes from word forms, syntactical structures, and the context of words. Only when difficulties arise does the fluent reader use mediated comprehension.

Smith believes the problems of the beginning reader are compounded by a lack of experience with the reading process and suggests that traditional programs allow him to achieve the experience he needs to create rules of reading for himself. The fact that the redundancy of information is used by mature readers may explain why different programs stressing different reading skills may be equally successful in teaching beginning reading.

The arguments have been presented as "either/or" alternatives. In reality, most reading programs differ in emphasizing the teaching of reading subskills, or the gaining of meaning from the context of the passage read and the reader's language background; few totally exclude either approach. In fact, a number of reading specialists suggest synthesizing these alternatives as the basis for teaching reading.

John Carroll (1978) for example, defines reading as a process of gaining meaning, and sometimes sound, from print by converting print into inner representations analogous to speech. The written language, he suggests, is understood much like speech. Readers use their knowledge of the letter representations of sounds, of their vocabulary, of the way words are arranged in the language and their knowledge of the meaning of speech utterances within situations to gain meaning from print. Graphemic cues are used to reduce the uncertainty of intended meanings of words. According to Carroll, an awareness of the way language is segmented into phonemes, syllables, and words and an ability to use these language units are critical to learning to read, just as practice is critical to achieving reading competence.

Relationship of Reading to Language

When discussing language, one needs to include the four modes of communication: speaking, listening, reading, and writing. The linguists study written language as a way of expressing oral language in visual symbols. The writer takes oral language and encodes it into a series of characters that can be decoded in order to ascertain their meaning.

There are many ways of encoding language. Early people used pictures to illustrate the things they wished to communicate. Some people eventually developed abstractions of these pictures, replacing them with a set of symbols, each symbol reflecting a single idea. The advantage of this ideographic approach was that the symbols could be combined to create representations of abstract ideas and actions. The traditional Chinese written language is composed of such ideographs. While the written symbols relate to the spoken language ideationally, they have no relationship to the sounds of the language. The advantage of such a written system is that it allows one to communicate across languages and dialects without sharing a common spoken language. The disadvantage lies in the large number of symbols that need to be learned to establish basic literacy, let alone the vast number needed for a person of scholarship.

In our system one can read any material, no matter how complex, by mastering a set of twenty-six symbols and their multiple sound relationships. The symbols reflect sounds in the spoken language rather than ideas or objects. The need to crack the code of letter-sound association, therefore, becomes obvious, for the written symbols carry no meaning outside their oral counterpart. Some reading specialists suggest that one of the major problems in reading stems from the fact that a sound can be represented by more than one letter, and letters or combinations of letters can represent a multitude of sounds. Still, there is a high degree of regularity between the sound symbols and the visual symbols of our language.

Reading requires decoding written symbols. The written word in our language is derived from the spoken word, but this does not mean that the reader must translate each word read into a word heard. Rather, once reading skill is achieved, the individual has two parallel forms of receptive language available. In the early years of schooling, children may have to move from the novel (for them) written symbol to the more familiar spoken symbol before meaning is achieved. At this point, the meanings gained from the written word are usually those the children already learned in relation to their knowledge of the spoken word. Only as they approach maturity does the reading vocabulary outstrip the listening vocabulary. Few books developed for reading instruction under any system contain a vocabulary that is beyond the listening vocabulary of the children for whom the book is designed.

Defining the process of reading does not solve the issues inherent in reading instruction, though it is a necessary first step. The crucial issues relate to *how* children can best learn the reading process. Is meaningful or meaningless material best for teaching the code-cracking system? This is one question that even the proponents of "phonics only" or linguistic approaches to reading raise. Another relates to the appropriateness of using cues other than letter-sound associations in gaining meaning from the printed page. Yet other issues relate to the form, organization, and materials of instruction in reading. Some of these issues might be clarified if we fully describe the process of reading.

The Reading Process

Even in its simplest form, the reading process seems to involve a broad range of perceptual, associative, and cognitive elements. While these processes may be analyzed and described separately, they are intertwined so that the individual does not practice each one separately as he reads. Nor is reading simply a matter of making a series of letter-sound associations. The scene of the preschool child roaming the aisles of a supermarket and identifying and reciting labels of packages made familiar through television commercials is not unusual. Although this might not be labeled *reading,* much early reading seems to mirror this process for in attempting to gain meaning from the written page, the young child uses a variety of approaches and clues.

Young children can learn a reasonable number of words without using any analytic techniques. The associative learning technique used in the "look-say" method has proved successful and is probably responsible for the very young child being able to read product labels. The continually repeated association between the picture of the product and its name on television helps the child learn the words and recall them when the symbol is seen. Other techniques can be used for associating visual cues with the sounds of words.

The shapes of beginning and ending letters provide clues to the word. Using these visual cues, the child can be helped to make the association between the written symbol and the spoken word. Children also learn to use a word's context as a clue to reading it. The structure of the language and the meaning of phrases have a degree of regularity that creates a fairly high chance of success in the use of context clues.

As children begin reading instruction they learn other techniques of word recognition. Structural analysis—the breaking of large words into their parts—is an important one. Phonetic analysis, one way the child can identify letter-sound associations, is another important technique. Phonetic analysis is not the *only* method, however, that young children can use in learning to read, nor is it necessarily the first. It would be unfortunate if we did not provide children with as many different ways of unlocking the mystery of the written word as they can use, for it is the synthesis of many skills that helps make a competent reader.

It is important to note that word identification, although important, is just one part of beginning reading. Meanings must become evident to children. They must associate the written words with the spoken words and move quickly from reading *symbols* to reading *ideas*.

John Carroll (1970) has identified the necessary elements of a reading instructional program. He suggests that the disagreements about how reading should be taught are actually disagreements about the order in which these skills should be taught. The skills identified are

1. The child must know the language that he is going to learn to read.
2. The child must learn to dissect spoken words into component sounds.
3. The child must learn to recognize and discriminate the letters of the alphabet in their various forms.
4. The child must learn the left-to-right principle by which words are spelled and put in order in continuous text.
5. The child must learn that there are patterns of highly probable correspondence between letters and sounds.
6. The child must learn to recognize printed words from whatever cues he can use.
7. The child must learn that printed words are signals for spoken words and that they have meanings analogous to those spoken words.
8. The child must learn to reason and think about what he reads (pp. 31-33).

APPROACHES TO READING INSTRUCTION

There are many different reading programs available today, some quite similar to one another in approach. There are differences that can be found among these programs, however, in the stress placed upon the teaching of letter-sound relationships, on how reading instruction is related to the entire language arts program, and on the way that the instructional program is organized. Differences can also be found in the conceptions of the reading process upon which the program is based.

M.J. Adams, Richard Anderson, and Dolores Durkin (1978) suggest that reading programs are based on one of three conceptions of the reading process. Some programs are *data driven,* some are *conceptually driven,* and others are *interactive.* In the data-driven programs, the reader attends to the printed letters and develops expectations from the words spelled out by them. These expectations are built upon as the reader deals with larger units going from words to phrases to sentences. These programs are seen as using a *bottom-up* process.

Philip Gough (1972), for example, proposed a linear model of the reading process that can be considered data driven. Reading proceeds from identifying letters to forming words from these letters, representing these words in sounds. Syntactic and semantic rules are then applied to these representations to derive meanings. The process is a linear one, and no stage can be bypassed.

In the conceptually driven programs, readers use their knowledge of the language to approach reading by testing hypotheses against what is printed. The context of a passage and the reader's knowledge of syntax provide important cues for developing hypotheses. This psycholinguistic approach to reading has been characterized as *top-down* processing.

Kenneth Goodman (1968) has proposed a conceptually driven model of reading in which the child goes through three stages or proficiency levels. Although the first two levels require rather complex processing, from graphic input to meaning at the highest level, the focus is on gaining meaning almost directly through input from large graphic sequences. The process of decoding graphemes for meanings in this model seems to be similar to those used in oral language.

The third conception of the reading process sees both top-down and bottom-up processing occurring simultaneously. This process is *interactive.* Within this conception readers are as much dependent upon what they already know as what the author has put in the text for gaining meaning from the printed page. Both conceptually driven and interactive conceptions of reading view the process as consisting of something more than decoding, while the data-driven conception sees reading as a process of changing written language into its oral counterpart, with meaning embedded in oral language.

David Rumelhart (1976) has developed an interactive model which conceives of reading as utilizing both top-down and bottom-up processes. There is little emphasis on abstract letter or word recognition. Rather, the perceptions of letters and words are dependent upon the surrounding letters and words. Thus, knowledge of syntactical and semantic rules helps the reader judge what letter or word should be perceived and thus drive word and letter identification. Interpretation of the written symbols is determined by the context in which those symbols are embedded, hence the comprehension process becomes critical.

Programs that Focus
on Letter-Sound Associations

Phonics-oriented programs and programs that use a transitional orthography or alphabet to provide a greater degree of regularity to the relationship of letters to sounds can be considered essentially data-driven programs. They are less concerned with reading comprehension in the early years, since they view comprehension as embedded in oral language, which is a different part of the school curriculum.

Teaching reading through phonics may require the children to sound out the letters in a word and then blend the sounds to create the word, or to analyze speech sounds in words and then relate them to letter representations. Although some programs depend upon phonics entirely, it is usually taught in combination with other reading skills. One often finds a phonics workbook added to a basal reading program. Phonics lessons are also outlined in teachers' manuals and in most basal series reading textbooks.

In recent years a number of programs labeled "linguistic" or "modified linguistic" approaches to reading instruction have reached the market. These programs attempt to teach the child the rules of letter-sound associations in the language. They often start with those letters that have a regular relationship to specific sounds in the English language, progressing slowly to letters with less regular relationships, and from there to those with the most irregular relationships. Instruction in this approach may place little reliance on understanding meaning as a way of learning to read, so reading might be taught through the use of nonsense words as well as meaningful words.

Approaches that use artificial orthographies cannot truly be classified as programs that teach letter-sound associations, since an orthography can be used in many ways. Because these orthographies tend to produce a greater degree of regularity between written symbols and the sounds they represent, and because this aspect has been highlighted by most developers, they are discussed here. The most widely known of all the artificial orthographies is the Initial Teaching Alphabet (*ita*). First introduced into British schools, this approach to reading has had a good deal of exposure in American schools. It consists of a forty-four-symbol alphabet that, while not completely regular, is more regular in its letter-sound associations than our traditional twenty-six-letter alphabet. The child is introduced to both reading and writing instruction with materials using this alphabet. After he has achieved a degree of competency with it, he is helped to make the transition to the traditional form of reading and writing. One can find both simple trade books and reading textbooks available in *ita*.

Relating Reading to Children's Language.

The Language Experience Approach to reading may be considered a top-down or interactive model. This approach conceives of reading as integral with writing, speaking, and listening as a unified whole of language experience in the life of the child. Of all the possible approaches to reading, this one places the least emphasis upon learning the code-cracking skills in some systematic fashion. Some proponents of the Language Experience Approach would caution teachers that premature focus on reading skills will thwart rather than help the child's acquisition of them. Since focusing on a single word or part of a word would slow down the child's rate of reading and is counter to the natural way mature readers function, teachers are cautioned not to start the child with improper reading habits. Word attack skills are often taught to individuals and small groups as the need arises.

The Language Experience Approach would allow reading to be learned in a natural manner. The desire to learn to read would grow from the children's need to communicate in writing as well as in speech. Reading and writing would go hand-in-hand in the classroom, with children often beginning by reading what they have written themselves. This approach would also make the greatest use of children's understanding of the oral language as well as of their awareness of print.

It is important for teachers using this approach to find out what children already know about reading and to build upon the children's existing knowledge and competence. Teachers must also create an environment that is rich in written materials and in the functional uses of the written language. Play activities can provide the basis for developing literacy, and reading would be related to all school subjects as well as to the other language arts. The reading experiences provided would reflect a range of language functions (Goodman & Goodman, 1979).

The Language Experience Approach works most effectively in a classroom that is filled with stimulating learning opportunities. As children involve themselves in classroom activities, they feel the need to communicate what they are doing. Early communication takes the form of speaking and listening, then a natural transition to reading and writing takes place. Children first dictate stories about their experiences to the teacher, who writes them on experience charts; the children learn to read from these charts.

Children are also encouraged to write early. Soon they are writing their own stories rather than having the teacher do the writing. These stories become the content of the child's reading. Since the children have written the material themselves, there is seldom difficulty with vocabulary, for even difficult words are remembered.

The next transition is from reading one's own writing to reading someone else's writing, and each child is encouraged to read other children's work as well as many books available in the classroom. Stories and experience charts can also be written as a group endeavor.

The Language Experience Approach to reading does not deny the need to crack the code of letter-sound associations. Rather than being learned from lessons designed specifically to this end, however, they are learned through the organic activities provided. The process of learning to read more closely parallels learning a native language than a second language.

Organizational Patterns of Teaching Reading

In most primary classes, reading instruction is provided to groups of children, most often using a *basal* reading series. In other classes one can find an *individualized* approach to the teaching of reading. These represent the two most popular ways of organizing for reading instruction.

The basal approach consists of teaching reading through a series of ordered reading textbooks. Along with the textbooks, and often available from the same publisher, come workbooks and other instructional aids, such as flash cards, pictures, films, filmstrips, and records. The children in most classrooms are divided into groups for instructional purposes based upon reading ability: one group of high ability, another of low ability, and a third, usually the largest group, in the middle. This limits the range of ability within each instructional unit, a range that would be great in most classrooms.

Most basal reading programs are carefully designed, eclectic ones containing some balance of reading skill and comprehension activities. Teachers are provided with a detailed manual of instructions describing the content of the program and the activities to be used. The use of textbooks and related activities may be carefully prescribed for the teacher. In addition, the books are carefully graded so that teachers need only to take their class through the books and related exercises provided to successfully carry on the program. Generally, all groups will go through the same reading program, but the pace of instruction will vary.

Basal reading programs are modified from edition to edition to mirror the changes that take place in reading instruction theory. Changes in the content of basal readers also reflect the changing social scene. Many have begun to change their illustrations to reflect the multiracial nature of our society. The characters now reflect greater sexual and cultural equity. Series (such as the *Bank Street Readers,* and the *Skyline Readers*) have been developed in which the story lines relate to an urban context. Additional changes include newer format designs for basal reader series, especially the use of smaller books and integrated audiovisual aids.

Most basal reading series begin by providing pupils with a limited sight vocabulary of words and names of characters in the stories. The vocabulary is carefully restricted and constantly repeated. As the program's sight vocabulary increases, a variety of word recognition skills, including phonics and structural analysis are introduced.

Although basal reading programs have been discussed as a group here, there is considerable variation in methodological emphasis and textbook content among basal reader series.

Individualized reading programs have been conceived of to deal with the inherent problem of the inappropriate fit of instructional programs to the diverse needs of children in any group. Within a single group of children there are differences in learning skills, styles, interests, and reading abilities. While grouping might limit the range of differences in one dimension, differences in children continue to exist in other dimensions.

Individualizing reading instruction provides neither a single medium nor a single organizational framework for instruction. Instead, a great variety of books are provided for the children—both trade books and basal readers. Trade books vary in topics and level of difficulty, and so are selected by the child as he sets his or her own learning pace.

Central to the organization of the individualized reading program is the pupil-teacher conference. Several times each week the teacher meets with each child in conference. The conference is used to review the child's progress in reading and to plan new work for the future. The teacher often asks children to read aloud, and asks questions about what the child has read to check on his degree of comprehension.

An individualized program requires an extensive amount of record-keeping and planning. The teacher keeps records on the books the child has read as well as on the content of their conference. These records might include notes about the child's progress in reading and the problems encountered that need to be dealt with. Planning consists of selecting and providing books, then suggesting specific books for particular children.

If more than one child manifests the need for instruction in a particular set of reading skills, the teacher may organize a group for instructional purposes. The group is convened for a particular task and may include children of different levels of reading ability but with the same instructional needs. When the instructional task is completed, the group may be disbanded. Practice in reading skills may also be provided through worksheets and other materials. Some teachers may begin a program of instruction with individual lessons, but more often such a program is designed to extend from some form of group instruction. As the children show competence in reading skills, they are allowed greater degrees of freedom in reading.

Computer-assisted instruction.   Recent years have seen an increase in the availability of microcomputers in schools and in early childhood classrooms. This has led to the development of a number of projects in the utilization of computers in early childhood education.

Computer-assisted instruction (CAI) teaches through an interaction of computer with student, thus enabling instruction to be individualized. Three forms of interactions have been noted in CAI reading programs: drill and practice, tutorial, and dialogic. In drill and practice programs, exercises are presented on the screen to students who type a response on the computer keyboard. The material offered to children in this approach is essentially similar to that in a workbook. With the computer, however, students are given immediate feedback on the correctness of their response, and a record of errors can be stored for review by the teacher.

The tutorial mode of CAI allows the computer to present a concept or skill to the student, offering tutorial assistance to help students understand the concepts and correct their responses. The dialogic mode allows students and computers to explore a curriculum together. A vast array of information and potential responses needs to be programmed into a computer for it to function in a dialogic mode (Saracho, 1982).

Most CAI reading programs fit within the drill and practice mode, with material similar to that found in workbooks provided to children through computers. Given the high cost of computers, the fact that only one child can use a computer at a time in such a program, and the need for adult intervention when young children work with computers, one can question their practicality for basic classroom instruction.

Elizabeth H. Brady and Shirley Hill (1984), in reviewing research on young children and computers, raise serious questions about what constitutes appropriate computer experiences for young children. They fear that the overenthusiasm educators often have for new technologies will create a bandwagon approach to the use of computers in early childhood education without a critical look at the consequences and outcomes related to their use. They cite the limitations of existing research and voice a concern for the unequal access of all economic groups to computers in schools.

There are, however, some children who will work effectively with a computer but who might not persevere with a workbook. Computers can be a viable alternative to having these children work continually with an adult. Computers with word processing programs that young children can use can also serve as an effective tool in a Language Experience Approach to reading.

Evaluating Approaches to Reading Instruction

Considering the number of possible approaches to beginning reading instruction and programs available within each approach, it becomes difficult for classroom teachers to decide which program to institute in their classroom. In many school systems the teacher has little choice, for the decision has already been made by the administration or by a curriculum committee, usually selecting one reading program to be instituted in all classrooms.

Teachers are usually involved in program selection procedures. They can also supplement any adopted program in their own classroom. Selection should be made among program alternatives, considering evidence of program effectiveness, practicality, content, and the willingness of teachers to use the program.

A READING PROGRAM FOR THE EARLY YEARS

The First Grade Reading Studies (Bond, 1966) suggest that the best results could probably accrue from a program that uses a combination of approaches for teaching beginning reading. Many primary teachers feel comfortable in planning a reading program around a basal reading series. A supplementary program of phonic materials could be added if not a part of the series' program. To round out the program, elements of a Language Experience Approach could be included, such as having the children write stories and using experience charts and group stories for instructional purposes. Finally, ways of individualizing the program could also be devised. Such a program could be implemented by the majority of teachers who are most comfortable using published instructional materials.

The combined approach suggested should not be merely a basal reading program with a few chart stories used at the beginning and a few trade books available for children to read as time fillers. In the program proposed, the range of classroom activity available at any time would be great. The combination program would not be a basal program, but would use basal reading materials.

BEGINNING A READING PROGRAM

A reading program begins long before the child attempts to make sense out of the first preprimer. Reading is an extension of the language process. As such, reading instruction begins in the infant's babbling stage. For most children, the first reading teacher is usually their mother, who helps them develop language skills, who provides an environment in which reading and writing occur, and who provides the motivation for learning to read.

Most schools, however, wait until the child is old enough to be enrolled in an institutional group program before beginning any kind of formal instruction. The age at which a formal reading program might be provided for the child is open to controversy, and it is doubtful if any single age limit would be appropriate for all children.

Beginning Reading Instruction

When should reading instruction begin for the child? In the United States, the traditional age for beginning reading instruction is some time during the child's sixth year. Some countries postpone reading instruction until age seven, while still others begin at age five. Generally, the age at which children begin to learn reading is related to the age at which most children in the community enter the primary school, although there has been some concern with offering reading instruction in kindergarten.

Many books on early childhood education and beginning reading instruction, have stated that children cannot benefit from beginning reading instruction until they have achieved a mental age of six years and six months. This grew out of a study done in a Chicago suburb many years ago which found that children in the Winnetka schools with a mean age of six years and six months benefited from reading instruction (Morpell & Washburne, 1931). A study conducted a short time later by Arthur Gates (1937), however, suggests that the necessary mental age for beginning reading instruction is not rigid, but is related to the size of the group and the flexibility of the program.

When to begin reading instruction depends, to begin with, on the child's maturity, his level of intelligence, and his language background and capability. The decision depends on the particular program of reading instruction and the way in which it is organized. Not all classroom situations or teachers can provide the individual attention or flexibility needed to support an early reading program.

The question of when a child might begin formal reading instruction is best answered on an individual basis. If children can receive individually or in small groups beginning reading instruction at the time they seem most receptive to it, this is probably the best method of matching a program to the children's capability.

Teachers can assess the readiness of the child to benefit from such instruction in a variety of ways. One way is to use reading-readiness tests. Although they correlate well with successful results on reading achievement tests in first grade for *groups* of children, these are not accurate enough to predict the success of any single child. Teachers may also make their own personal assessment of a child's readiness to read. Spache and Spache (1977) suggest that teachers observe their children for good vision, good speech, listening ability, social and emotional behavior, and interest in learning to read as indicators of readiness. Research reviewed by Schickedanz (1982) would suggest that teachers might also wish to assess their children's knowledge of the features of print, of reading processes and functions, of the characteristics of words in print, and of phonemes to provide some indication of their ability to profit from reading instruction. Checklists and rating scales, such as those described in chapter 15, might be selected or developed by teachers to help in the process.

Reading Readiness

The term "reading readiness" might most simply be defined as the predisposition to benefit from reading instruction. To some, it has been seen as a maturational state in a child. If readiness is a function of maturation alone, the teacher who identifies a child as not yet ready to read has no recourse but simply to wait until the child ripens. Little in the school curriculum has any effect on the rate of maturation of the human organism.

Educators have, however, become aware of the inadequacy of the maturation approach to readiness. Success in reading achievement is correlated not just with maturity, but with specific learned skills such as auditory and visual discrimination, familiarity with language and print, and knowledge of letter names. These must be learned before the child is introduced to formal reading instruction. A purely maturational approach to reading readiness is wholly inadequate today.

Formal reading instruction should be considered not the beginning of a reading program but an extension of a program of literacy education that takes place in the school and home that provides children with knowledge and skills that are used in formal reading instruction. Some children arrive at school already knowing what is necessary, having been taught by siblings, peers, or parents or having picked up this knowledge on their own. It is the responsibility of the school to create a program of instruction to foster this readiness for those who lack it.

Designing a Reading Readiness Program

Much of the content of a reading readiness program has already been described in the previous chapter on language learning. Reading is an extension of the language process. Children's knowledge of language and their ability to produce and receive oral language is important in learning to read. The focus on oral language helps the child develop an extensive speaking and listening vocabulary that can be a resource in developing a reading vocabulary. Children can also develop a familiarity with print and printed material. Stories will be read to them and they can have the opportunity to handle books and to see how one can get information from the printed page. The child can also develop simple skills such as how to hold a book, open it, turn its pages, and care for it.

The suggestions provided here are consistent with Dolores Durkin's (1982) proposal for a language arts approach to beginning reading. The nursery school and kindergarten day are full of opportunities to expand language activities. Many of the activities suggested in the previous chapter can be used to provide a beginning to reading and help children see the relationship between the written language that is new to them and the oral language competencies they already have.

Most important, children should develop a sense of what reading is and that the written word has the same power to express meaning as does the spoken word. They should have many opportunities to dictate stories to a teacher who will read them back at a later time. These informal and formal language activities will help children as they move into actual reading.

In addition to these, teachers can provide learning activities that help develop the specific skills upon which the reading process is built. Many of these will be in the area of visual and auditory discrimination.

Visual discrimination.   Many nursery and kindergarten classrooms include materials that help a child develop visual discrimination skills. In using parquetry puzzles, children relate the shape of each piece to the shape of the space in which it is to be inserted, and to the rest of the picture. Pegsets, beads, strings, and similar materials can also be used. Teachers can develop design cards for children to model. A simple pattern of one red and one blue peg alternating along the length of a line of holes in the pegboard is one that children can model, with more complex patterns following. Similar patterns can be made with beads on a string. A series of cards beginning with simple patterns and including complex designs, and design cards used with parquetry blocks of different shapes and colors, are other models. These can be used at the children's own pace, with more complex tasks being offered after the simpler tasks.

Children can also be asked to copy specific patterns from models using crayons or pencils. Etch-a-Sketch boards help children copy models provided by the teacher. Form discrimination tasks can be given to children, starting with simple geometric forms on form boards and continuing to writing letters with letter templates. As children learn to discriminate letters, they can also learn the names of letters.

Auditory discrimination. Music affords many opportunities for this, since the child must distinguish and reproduce pitch in music as well as learn to listen to the words of songs. Instruments allow the children to recreate patterns of sound that differ in pitch and rhythm according to models provided by the teacher.

A number of other techniques for auditory discrimination exist. Books such as the *Muffin* series can be read to make children more aware of sounds. There are many records and sound filmstrips that can similarly be used—for example *Sounds Around Us* (Guidance Associates). Teachers can also create games for teaching listening skills such as sound recognition and discrimination. They may make their own auditory discrimination materials using tape recorders.

Most importantly, teachers need to make children aware of the sounds they hear in the language around them. Word sounds can be the basis for much fun, because children enjoy alliteration and rhyming. While many opportunities for learning may be found in the classroom, teachers should be aware of the need to exploit situations as they arise as well as to create situations for particular purposes.

Creating a language-rich environment. Teachers can support children's literacy learning by helping them build connections between the written word and the spoken word. Many opportunities for this occur in dramatic play, where signs can be used to label places and things, and written messages introduced into the play. Class experiences can be recorded on a chart, with the teacher taking dictation from small groups of children. The charts can then be mounted on a wall or bulletin board and later informally referred to by teacher or children. Each child can develop a collection of written words he or she can recognize. These can be written on individual cards or pieces of paper and kept in a folder or large envelope. Every learning activity in the classroom can be analyzed for potential opportunities to expand language learning and especially learning related to print.

Reading stories to children. Teachers should engage children in the reading process early by reading to them. Successful readers consistently report that they have been read to by parents. Unfortunately, many of the elements that help children understand the reading process when read to one-on-one are eliminated when the reader is distanced from the listener in group reading. Teachers should try to approximate the home reading situation as much as possible.

Schickedanz (1978) suggests having the children sit so they can see the print in the book and even help turn the pages. The same book should be read repeatedly so that the story line can be memorized by the children. The adult should periodically point to words as they are said or ask a child to say the word which will be remembered from previous readings of the story. There should also be free access to books in the class, with tape recordings of stories made available along with books.

A similar but more formal strategy called "assisted reading" has been suggested by Hoskisson (1977) for children ages four and up. In assisted reading the adult reads phrases and the children repeat them. Books and stories are reread many times and the adult moves a finger along the lines as words are read so that children can visually connect the way a word looks with the way it sounds. At some point the children are encouraged to read those words they recognize before the adult reads them. Finally, children are encouraged to read independently with the adult supplying words that children might not know.

In both these strategies, the process of moving from "being read to" to "reading" occurs as a result of hypotheses children develop in relation to the written language they have seen and heard repeatedly. Reading becomes a cognitive-linguistic act with subskills developing gradually and intuitively as the children use a range of strategies to bring order to an already familiar relationship between the printed language and the written language.

FORMAL READING INSTRUCTION

The move from a reading readiness program to a formal reading program should be gradual, almost imperceptible. If the children have been writing stories and charts, it is an easy move for the teacher to begin to use simple short charts for reading. This can be done with individual children or with small groups as the teacher determines their ability to profit from reading instruction. Such a beginning will build upon the language knowledge each child already possesses and will keep reading from seeming like an exotic skill. The charts can become longer and more elaborate as each child progresses. Teachers should have pupils write their own stories on smaller sheets of paper, rather than have all experiences transcribed onto large charts. They can also start children reading books at this time.

Developing Word-Recognition Skills

Many word-recognition skills can be introduced in conjunction with reading experience charts. Because the content of the chart is so close to the children's experience, teaching them to use context clues seems natural. Their intuitive knowledge of sentence structure and the fact that they have shared in the experience recorded on the chart make this an effective technique.

Phonics instruction can also be provided in the program. The child should be made aware of the sounds of words. Initial consonants can be identified and

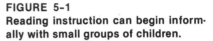

FIGURE 5-1
Reading instruction can begin inform-
ally with small groups of children.

related to sounds. Experience charts have the advantage of extending beyond a limited word vocabulary. Children's experiences and interests are so broad that they cannot be described with only a small number of words. Children's writings and reading will contain a sprinkling of fairly sophisticated, complicated words. The teacher using these methods should realize that some words will not be fully learned by the children. Independent of experience charts, teachers can provide more systematic instruction in reading subskills, including phonics and structural analysis.

Using a Basal Reading Series

Most teachers in the primary grades establish a reading program based upon the basal readers. These are a resource to be used in the teacher's program rather than as a program by themselves. Slavish adherence to teachers' manuals and to the traditional grouping practices should be avoided.

Teachers need to take into consideration their pupils' abilities in planning the reading program. Bright children seem to do better in more individualized programs, while slow readers seem to profit more from a basal reading approach. Brighter children will develop the basic techniques of reading rapidly and should be allowed the freedom to select books to read under the guidance of the teacher. Those children who need the help provided by basal readers, with their controlled vocabularies, should be given the opportunities to use them. But even then, a great degree of flexibility and alternative resources must be employed.

When teachers use the basal readers, they do not need to operate in the traditional "three-reading-groups-everybody-reads-aloud-today" fashion. Opportunities can be provided for silent reading, and conferences can often supplant the group experience. Teachers can use the pupil-teacher conference even when the reading program is not fully individualized and task grouping can supersede ability grouping.

Nor does the teacher need to follow a workbook step by step. In the discussion of reading readiness, no mention was made of using readiness workbooks. Readiness skills can best be taught in an experience context where children learn to use their language skills through interacting with the human environment. Children differ in their educational needs and patterns of learning. Skill learning and practice ought to be a part of a beginning reading program, but all the children need not systematically go through a set of prescribed exercises.

Spache and Spache (1977) suggest that instead of using a single workbook, the teacher should order a few copies of a number of different workbooks and skillsheets. These can be organized into sets of related exercises for each skill area, and placed in heavy acetate folders on which the children can mark their answers.

Using a Classroom Library

The availability of a classroom library has been continually emphasized in this book. If children are to learn to read, they must learn not only the basic skills, but also the uses of reading. The more children practice reading, the more they will master the rules for gaining meaning from the written page. Most reading is an intimate personal experience based upon a person's interest and need for knowledge. Classroom reading should reflect this. As soon as children have mastered a rudimentary vocabulary, they should be introduced to a range of books. Fortunately, books are available that even the first-grade child can read independently. Children who do not know how to read all the words in a book can practice their developing word recognition skills. Books should be carefully selected, with a relatively small number in the room at any one time, and with the selection constantly changing during the year.

Use of Reading in Other Subject Areas

While the appreciation of literature is an important aspect of a reading program, there are other uses of reading. Reading in specific subject areas for particular purposes helps increase the children's comprehension and helps them learn to use reading skills flexibly, reading differently for different purposes. Many information books are available in the various subject areas, written at a primary grade level.

In addition, primary children can begin to use reference books. Encyclopedias, dictionaries, atlases, and other reference books are available in simplified children's forms. This will require that children learn techniques for seeking information. Alphabetization becomes important, since topics are often listed in alphabetical order. Children also need to learn to use the book's table of contents and index.

Teachers can help children to use information books by phrasing questions to guide their reading. At first these questions may be related to the specific content of the book. As the children develop skills in informational reading, more critical elements need to be included in the questions so that they

FIGURE 5-2
Once they have mastered the rudiments, children can read their favorite books to others in the class.

learn to read carefully and make judgments about what they have read. Often, asking children to read and compare material from two different sources on the same topic is helpful.

Teaching reading is not a simple, seldom problematic activity. Many children do learn to read very easily and some even learn to read without a teacher's aid. But a large number of children have difficulty learning to read.

Teaching a child to read requires more than presenting learning activities in some sequential order. Teachers need to make use of children's current language competence and be aware of any disabilities that might inhibit his learning. Most important, they have to sense the forces that would create a desire to read in a child. Children for whom the reading material is irrelevant, dull, or even insulting may not progress readily through the stages of reading instruction. Yet we often present suburban, middle-class-oriented materials to urban, working-class children and female-oriented material to boys. We sometimes make demands on children, for the sake of the reading method rather than the reading process, that are unnecessary and create discomfort or confusion. We sometimes ask children to read in a dialect or language that is foreign to them. This can compound the problems of learning to read, for a new language as well as a new coding system must be assimilated; the cues to unlock language that have worked for children before may no longer have any power at all.

The reading teacher must know not only methods of instruction but also her children—their competencies and their backgrounds. Special procedures must be used with children who have special needs.

REFERENCES

ADAMS, M. J., ANDERSON, R. C., and DURKIN, D.   Beginning reading: Theory and practice. *Language Arts,* 1978, *55*(1), 19-25.

BOND, G. First grade reading studies: An overview. *Elementary English,* 1966, *43,* 464-470.

BRADY, E. H., and HILL, S. Research in review. Young children and microcomputers: Research and directions. *Young Children,* 1984, *39*(3), 49-61.

CARROLL, J. B. The nature of the reading process. In D. V. Gunderson (Ed.), *Language and reading.* Washington, D.C.: Center for Applied Linguistics, 1970.

CARROLL, J. B. Psycholinguistics and the study of reading. In S. Pflaum-Connor (Ed.), *Aspects of reading education.* Berkeley, Calif.: McCutcheon, 1978.

DURKIN, D. *Getting reading started.* Boston: Allyn & Bacon, 1982.

GATES, A. The necessary mental age for beginning reading. *Elementary School Journal,* 1937, *37,* 497-508.

GOODMAN, K. S. *The psycholinguistic nature of the reading process.* Detroit: Wayne State University Press, 1968.

GOODMAN, K. S., and GOODMAN, Y. M. Learning to read is natural. In L. B. Resnick, and P. A. Weaver (Eds.), *Theory and practice of early reading.* Vol. 1. Hillsdale, N.J.: Lawrence Erlbaum Associates, 1979.

GOUGH, P. B. One second of reading. In J. F. Kavanaugh, and I. G. Mattingly (Eds.), *Language by ear and eye.* Cambridge: M.I.T. Press, 1972.

HOSKISSON, K. Reading readiness: Three viewpoints. *Elementary School Journal,* 1977, *78,*(1), 44-52.

MORPELL, M. V., and WASHBURNE, C. When should children begin to read? *Elementary School Journal,* 1931, *31,* 496-503.

RUMELHART, D. E. *Toward an interactive model of reading.* San Diego: Center for Human Information Processing, University of California at San Diego, 1976.

SARACHO, O. N. The effects of computer-assisted instruction program on basic skills achievement and attitudes toward instruction of Spanish-speaking migrant children. *American Educational Research Journal,* 1982, *19,* 201-219.

SCHICKEDANZ, J. A. "Please read that story again!" *Young Children,* 1978, *33*(5), 48-55.

SCHICKEDANZ, J. A. The acquisition of written language in young children. In B. Spodek (Ed.), *Handbook of research in early childhood education.* New York: Free Press, 1982.

SMITH, F. *Understanding reading,* New York: Holt, Rinehart, & Winston, 1971.

SPACHE, G. D., and SPACHE, E. B. *Reading in the elementary school* (4th ed.). Boston: Allyn & Bacon, 1977.

SUGGESTED READING

CLAY, M. M. *Observing young readers.* Exeter, N.J.: Heinemann Educational Books, 1982.

DURKIN, D. *Getting reading started.* Boston: Allyn & Bacon, 1982.

HALL, M. A. *Teaching reading as language experience* (2nd ed.). Columbus, Ohio: Chas. E. Merrill, 1976.

PFLAUM-CONNOR, S. (Ed.) *Aspects of reading education.* Berkeley, Calif.: McCutcheon, 1978.

SMITH, F. *Understanding reading* (3rd ed.). New York: Holt, Rinehart & Winston, 1982.

SPACHE, G. D., and SPACHE, E. B. *Reading in the elementary school* (4th ed.). Boston: Allyn & Bacon, 1977.

6

Science
in the Early Years

Almost from the moment of birth young children reach out to their surroundings in an attempt to gain information about the world through their senses. At first their understanding of the physical world is limited by their perceptual field. Things not perceived do not exist; things perceived often seem to have no explanation.

As children mature and their experiences with the world increase, they become aware of the existence of order in the world. Some cause-and-effect relationships soon become evident. Items previously dealt with as discrete phenomena are now classed with other, similar items and treated accordingly. Children will even try to create order where order does not exist. They develop concepts, both physical and social, about the world that allow knowledge to accumulate from experience and new powers of understanding to develop.

It is easy to see how early observers in the field of child development conceived of children's intellectual development as following the pattern of the development of cultural knowledge; the parallels are striking. Early humans also viewed occurrences as discrete, attributing changes to magical powers beyond human understanding. Human society moved through a series of progressions whereby a person could explain, understand, and to some extent deal with the world of people and things through the development of concepts. The concepts allowed whole classes of objects to be treated as equivalent. Generalizations could then be developed about regularities of relationships among concepts. Systems of knowledge could be created by relating concepts and generalizations to one another.

Knowledge that was created could be accumulated and transmitted from generation to generation. In time, knowledge systems became complex, and divisions were established leading to specialization of inquiry and to more efficient system of knowledge storage and retrieval. This specialization has evolved into the *scholarly disciplines* as we know them today, with separations based upon the subject studied, the basic sets of assumptions, and agreed-upon ways of accumulating and verifying knowledge in each area.

One of the basic purposes of school is the transmission of significant portions of knowledge to the young. This allows each generation to grasp what we know at present about the world, so that they can deal effectively with it, building upon what is already known and, in time, accumulating greater knowledge about it.

School subjects—sciences, social studies, mathematics, and others—closely parallel the scholarly disciplines. Science, mathematics, and the social sciences are the results of intellectual processes by which the physical and social world has been explored. Science is an important method for exploring the world. It deals with the physical properties of the world. It orders these properties, identifies relationships among them, and establishes theories that can be empirically tested to explain the relationships identified. These theories allow us to predict events and the consequences of acts, and thus to develop a technology to harness natural phenomena. Philosophy, literature, and religion are a few of the other tools we have for knowing about the world. Unlike science, knowledge in these areas is personal, often not generalizable, and cannot be validated by recourse to public, empirical testing. Paul Hurd and James Gallagher (1968) have identified the ability to comprehend science as:

(1) the ability to grasp the central theme of a set of observations;
(2) the ability to look at data from a variety of vantage points;
(3) the ability to recognize the effect of changing one variable at a time;
(4) the ability to discount irrelevancies and focus on the useful aspects of information;
(5) the ability to formulate useful hypotheses and test them;
(6) the ability to search for new evidence; and
(7) The ability to reason logically from a model. A good imagination is also helpful. (pp. 5–6)

These skills represent a high order of intellectual development. These higher mental processes are derived from a long train of maturational stages and prior experiences. Thus, the ability to think scientifically requires nurturing from the early years on. The theories of Jean Piaget have provided one framework within which science concepts could be generated in children; learning theory provided another. Models of curriculum development paralleled beliefs about what and how children could learn, models now evident in the newer science programs. Basic to this development in science education is the belief that schools should teach science as an intellectual activity.

THE NATURE OF SCIENCE EDUCATION
IN THE PAST

Science was one of the later subjects to be included in the curriculum of early childhood education. In many of the pioneering approaches we do find nature study—the observation of natural phenomena primarily for the sake of appreciation rather than comprehension. Teachers provided a garden to be cultivated by the children. Small animals were cared for by children. Rocks and leaves were brought into the classroom and arranged on a table for the children to observe. Nature stories were read and pictures exhibited to further children's learning.

The prime purpose of this activity was development of children's reverence for the outdoors and their appreciation of the wonders of nature. In urban schools nature study was especially needed because city children had less opportunity for encounters with nature.

After the first quarter of the twentieth century, the study of science began to replace nature study in elementary and early childhood education. Science education became concerned less with appreciation and more with understanding scientific concepts and the scientific method, even at a rudimentary level. Elements of nature study are still found in early childhood classes today, with teachers displaying materials and reading anthropomorphic nature stories.

Although teaching an appreciation of nature and providing opportunities to observe natural phenomena are worthwhile activities, they are not adequate as a total science program. Teachers need to develop activities that improve children's observational skills, for example. They should also teach children that an appreciation of nature also requires an understanding of how to preserve nature and the consequences of technological activities on nature.

Knowing what science is allows us to use everyday occurrences in a classroom to build a science program. The careful inquiry that takes place in a classroom, and the use of scientific approaches to generate and test ideas, make a science program. Careful observation, description and measurement, development and testing of hypotheses, acceptance of multiple explanations of happenings, adequately explained—this is the stuff of which science programs are made.

SOME MODERN CONCEPTIONS OF SCIENCE
EDUCATION FOR THE EARLY YEARS

What and how one teaches science depends to a great extent upon how science is conceived. Science education is considered part of general education. All persons in our society ought to have some knowledge of science to use in their daily activities. They should have an understanding of the nature of scientific inquiry and the role of science in modern society. Scientific literacy is an educational goal for all children.

SCIENCE AS SYSTEM OF KNOWLEDGE

Science is sometimes considered as a body of knowledge about the physical world. From that point of view, the curriculum should contain those scientific facts most useful to children and adults. These would be accumulated throughout a child's school career.

The problem with this approach is that so many scientific facts continue to be accumulated that it is difficult to select the most significant ones. The number of facts an individual would have to be taught and later have to remember would make science education a formidable task. Teaching a body of scientific fact to children becomes a cumbersome, never-ending task of questionable ultimate value.

This approach to science teaching has generally been discarded in favor of a view of science as a set of organized concepts and generalizations. Scientific information can be organized into systematic sets of concepts that help to order them. The concepts give meaning to the facts by allowing a person to relate pieces of information to a conception of knowledge about the world.

Science is also conceived as a method of generating and verifying knowledge. The methods used by the scientist in observing phenomena, in testing hypotheses, in controlling variables, and in careful reporting and replicating of experiments are all part of what may be considered the *structure* of science. Teaching this structure is the goal of the newer science programs.

The organizing of the content of science into a conceptual structure is not a completely new idea. Gerald Craig's (1927) research in science education in the 1920s was aimed at developing a unified science program for children based upon generalizations that cut across the boundaries of separate disciplines. This work led to the development of a conceptual scheme for education that is still in use today:

1. The universe is very large—*Space*
2. The earth is very old—*Time*
3. The universe is constantly changing—*Change*
4. Life is adapted to its environment—*Adaptation*
5. There are great variations in the universe—*Variety*
6. The interdependence of living things—*Interrelationships*
7. The interaction of forces—*Equilibrium and Balance* (Craig, 1958; pp. 93–101)

Paul Brandwein and his associates (1966) developed a similar conceptual scheme for science teaching:

1. When energy changes from one form to another, the total amount of energy remains unchanged.
2. When matter changes from one form to another, the total amount of matter remains unchanged.
3. Living things are interdependent with one another and with their environment.
4. A living thing is the product of its heredity and its environment.
5. Living things are in constant change.
6. The universe is in constant change (pp. 8–9)

Within this framework, Brandwein and his colleagues have designed an integrated science program for the kindergarten through the sixth grade.

Such conceptual schemes are useful in integrating information into meaningful concepts and generalizations. In addition, almost all scientific knowledge and information fits into a category, programs at different levels can be articulated with one another, and the entire content of science education for the school can be integrated by fitting each science experience into a concept and then determining the level at which it could best be taught. What is taught in the kindergarten can be related to what is taught in the third grade, with little danger of too much overlap in the content of instruction from grade to grade.

This approach is based upon a conception of science primarily as a body of knowledge and information. Scientific concepts are taught through elements of knowledge that reflect these concepts. The concepts, however, order this knowledge and allow for its greatest transferability. This does not allow us to test the concepts' truth or their usefulness.

Other programs of science education have focused on the phenomena of science, the concepts of science, or the strategies of scientific inquiry rather than on scientific knowledge. Robert Karplus and Herbert Thier (1967) have characterized the differences in three science curriculum projects as follows:

> . . . the units produced by the SCIS and the parts written by the AAAS form a complete and integrated curriculum, while the ESS is creating self-contained units that may be fashioned into a curriculum by local teaching groups. He will also find that there are significant differences in emphasis on the three elements—concepts, phenomena, processes—which make up the science course. Thus, the ESS stresses the child's involvement in the phenomena and is confident that he will thereby gain practice with processes and achieve understanding of valuable concepts even though these are not made explicit. The SCIS stresses the concepts and phenomena, with process learning an implicit by-product of the children's experimentation, discussion and analysis. The AAAS stresses the child's practice with the processes and uses the phenomena only as vehicles and the concepts as tools. An added difference is that the AAAS program attempts to appraise the children's progress more systematically and in greater detail than do the others. (p. 8)

Differences in programs reflect not only differences in content emphasis but in ideas about how children learn and develop, and in how people conceive of the nature and purpose of school.

There are also a number of common attributes found in these programs. They are all based upon modern conceptions of science, they conceive of the child as an active learner, and they require active participation in science experiences.

A brief sketch of the three science programs discussed by Karplus and Thier should help to illustrate the likenesses and differences among newer programs. The American Association for the Advancement of Science has developed the program *Science—A Process Approach* (S—APA). The *Science Curriculum Improvement Study* (SCIS) was developed at the University of California under the direction of Dr. Robert Karplus. The *Elementary Science Study* (ESS) is a product of the Educational Development Center.[1]

These are but three of many science programs available today. Barbara Waters (1973) presents six different early childhood science programs for teachers to analyze in choosing a program. In addition to those programs generated as part of the curriculum reform movement, a number of science programs are available for kindergarten and primary grades that have been developed by textbook publishers, often including teachers' manuals and kits of materials. The three presented here have been chosen because each is well conceived, well developed, and represents a distinct point of view about what science is and how children can best learn it.

SCIENCE—A PROCESS APPROACH

The American Association for the Advancement of Science (1967), in its primary science curriculum, conceived of the processes of scientific inquiry as the essential elements of science that one wishes to communicate to children:

> The basic processes of science appropriate for children in the primary grades are identified by the following terms:
>
> 1. observing
> 2. using space-time relationships
> 3. using numbers
> 4. measuring
> 5. classifying

---

[1] More complete descriptions of the content of the various science programs and the materials developed are available from their educational publishers. For information, contact the Webster Division, McGraw-Hill, Manchester, Mo., for *Elementary Science Study;* Rand McNally, Skokie Ill., for *Science Curriculum Improvement Study;* and Ginn, Lexington, Mass., for *Science—A Process Approach.*

6.   communicating
7.   predicting
8.   inferring

A principal aim of the program is to develop skill in the careful and systematic use of these processes in the primary grades as a necessary preliminary to undertaking more complex science learning in the later grades. (p. 3)

The more complex science learning of the intermediate grades includes the skills of formulating hypotheses, defining operationally, controlling variables, experimenting, formulating models, and interpreting data.

Activities in the S—APA primary program are carefully designed to teach children the above processes. Young children observe objects and identify color, shape, and texture within them. They observe weather phenomena, and the various parts of a plant, then describe their observations. In the area of space/time relationships, children learn to identify two- and three-dimensional shapes and angles and deal with concepts of speed. Number work includes identifying and comparing sets, finding the sum of two numbers, and dealing with number relationships. Measures of length, weight, area, and volume are explored by the children in making comparisons and using standard units of measurement.

Specific experiences are provided to help children classify objects by visible attributes, moving from single stage to multistage classifications. Communication requires identifying and naming objects, using graphs, and describing experiments to others. Children are required to draw inferences from information and demonstrate how they may be tested. They also learn to make and test predictions.

The program is hierarchically structured, with simpler activities followed by more complicated ones. Prerequisites for later activities are encased in earlier activities. In the area of observation, for example, early activities include identifying and naming attributes of an object—is it rough or smooth, large or small, or of primary or secondary colors? Later activities require the identification and naming of two or more characteristics of an object, such as roughness and smallness. Similarly, early identification of two- and three-dimensional shapes leads to the identification of two-dimensional shapes that are the components of three-dimensional ones.

This approach conceives of science education as helping children learn the process of scientific inquiry that was identified through a task analysis of the scientist's role. While the facts of science and the level of technology used continually change, the basic processes of scientific inquiry remain relatively constant.

The method of teaching scientific processes in the program leans heavily on learning theory. Readiness is identified as the achievement of prerequisite learnings. Upon successful attainment of one level of skill development, the child moves up to the next. What a child can learn is a function of what he already knows. If he is unable to master a scientific process then he needs to master the prerequisite skills.

Behavioral Objectives

The S—APA program has been organized to achieve specific observable behavioral goals. Identified within each lesson are the goals the child is expected to achieve, specified in behavioral terms. Since these are directly observable by the teacher, immediate evaluation becomes possible.

Critics of this approach are concerned that while it does teach some of the basic processes in science, it omits other important ones, including thinking creatively about phenomena, inventing concepts, and developing divergent notions about aspects of the world. The lack of concern for children's stages of intellectual development has also been criticized.

SCIENCE CURRICULUM IMPROVEMENT STUDY

The Science Curriculum Improvement Study (SCIS) of the University of California sees science education as a way to help children form "a conceptual framework that permits them to perceive phenomena in a more meaningful way. This framework will also help them to integrate their inferences into generalizations of greater values than they would form if left to their own devices" (Karplus & Thier, 1967, pp. 20–21).

The topics of the SCIS program reflect basic concepts in science and a Piagetian conception of intellectual development. Level I corresponds to the transition from preoperational to concrete operational thought in the child; level II reflects concrete operational thought; level III reflects the transition from concrete operations to formal operations; and level IV requires facility with formal operations.

Materials, activities, and concepts are compatible with the child's reasoning ability at each level, and science learning is seen as providing a bridge between personal explorations and interpretations of the world and an understanding of scientific concepts.

Units in the SCIS program are taught in a specific sequence. Each unit covers a number of topics and contains *invention* lessons and *discovery* lessons. Invention lessons allow the teacher to define new terms or concepts; discovery lessons permit the children to apply these new ideas. Optional activities are also provided.

In each lesson children are given specific sets of materials and asked to experiment with them. All the children in the class are usually working on the same experiments, either individually or in small groups. Some lessons in the program are left completely open-ended; others may terminate in classroom discussions. Teachers are often advised to guide discussions with open-ended questions such as, "Tell us what happened in your experiment," or "How did the objects change?" A range of outcomes could be expected from any of the experiences provided. Goals are to be achieved cumulatively over long periods of time.

ELEMENTARY SCIENCE STUDY

The Elementary Science Study (ESS) provides a set of instructional units, each of which can be used at several grade levels. David Hawkins, former director of ESS, defines three phases of science instruction in a program. In the first, children primarily "mess about," freely exploring the materials and making their own discoveries in an unstructured environment.

In the second phase, the work is externally guided but still highly individualized through the use of "multiply programmed" materials—materials that contain written or pictorial guidance for the student but are designed for the greatest variety and ordering of topics. Consequently, for almost any way a child may evolve, material is available to help him move along in his way.

The third phase of science instruction moves children from concrete perception to abstract conceptualization. This phase of theorizing must be built upon experience and experimentation, but abstraction does not develop without special attention. Although each of these phases is described discretely, actually they all represent central tendencies of the phases and each includes activities reflecting the other (Hawkins, 1965).

The "messing about" phase can be illustrated in the directions for getting started provided in the *Teachers Guide for Geo Blocks.* In the Geo Blocks unit, children are provided with a set of blocks smaller than the traditional kindergarten unit blocks. They are designed as units so that a number of small blocks equal the size of a larger one. Many small blocks and fewer larger ones are provided so that children are forced to develop equivalences. The blocks are used to build towers, ramps, three-dimensional maps, and other constructions. Specific problems are provided for the children to work through with the blocks. However, the teacher is advised not to structure prematurely.

Teachers are asked to observe but not intervene in these early explorations, although they may make informal suggestions for elaborating the use of the blocks. Later, more directed use can be developed by the children as a result of the teacher's questioning. Questions may deal with building, counting, shapes, slopes, grouping, surface area, and volume. In addition to Geo Blocks, a number of other units have been prepared by ESS. Some of these are appropriate for young children, others are designed for the intermediate grades. Units include *Small Things, Growing Seeds, Batteries and Bulbs, Mirror Cards,* and *Light and Shadows,* among others.

While the S—APA and SCIS programs tend by their structure to support whole class activity, the ESS units can be used by a small group. The ESS program also uses "discovery" techniques as an instructional strategy to a greater extent than do the others. Children are placed in direct contact with scientific phenomena with a minimum of prestructuring by the teacher. Teachers play an active role in helping children build scientific concepts. In the first phase of the learning situation, that role relates more to the organization of the environment to facilitate children's "discovery."

SELECTING A SCIENCE PROGRAM

These three programs represent only a few of the programs in science available today. The newer programs generally contain up-to-date science content. They also make provisions for active participation of the child in the learning process so that science instruction goes well beyond rote memorization.

The first decision that needs to be made is to include science in the classroom program. Too often at the kindergarten and primary levels, teachers are so concerned with teaching children to read and write that they use all their classroom time for academic skill instruction. The art program may then be relegated to Friday afternoons; physical education becomes a way of helping to rid children of their excess energy; and science and social studies may be offered only erratically and superficially.

Evidence has accumulated that the current science programs can have an important impact on children's thinking and academic achievement. Increases in scores on IQ and achievement tests have been noted as a result of children's immersion in a science program. Mary Budd Rowe (1976), who summarized a number of studies detailing these positive gains, suggests that too often those children who can benefit most from science programs, including the poor and the handicapped, are the ones who are denied them. If teachers could provide enriched educational opportunities for all children in these early years, perhaps there would be fewer learning difficulties in the upper grades.

Once teachers opt to include a science program, they need to decide which to include. Selection could be based on an analysis of available programs, their content emphasis (for example on facts, concepts, or skills) as well as assumptions made about child learning and development.

A science program should be compatible with the rest of the classroom curriculum. The S—APA program, for example, would fit into a more formal, behavioral-oriented classroom. The SCIS and ESS programs, derived from a Piagetian view of cognitive development, could be implemented by teachers who support this view. None of these programs would fit into a textbook-oriented classroom where children are expected to read books, listen to lectures, and watch demonstrations for their science activities. These programs all require children to "do" science, to engage in inquiry-oriented activities.

SELECTING A SCIENCE PROGRAM
FOR YOUNG CHILDREN

At the kindergarten and primary levels, a number of fully developed science programs are available that have the potential of providing significant science learning for young children in the classroom. Often the decision rests with a school system, which may adopt a single textbook series or program to insure continuity of learning through the grades.

A Program for the Nursery School

The nursery-school teacher has fewer guidelines to follow in selecting a science program. Some nursery-school teachers skim off a number of experiences from a science program intended for older children and offer these to their classes. However, such activities may be unrelated to each other and the intended meanings of the experience may actually be beyond the young child's capability for understanding. Other teachers use a nature study approach, creating displays of leaves, rocks, small animals, or other "science material" in the classroom, and also talk to the children about weather and seasonal changes. Still others provide children with scientific labels for everyday phenomena.

Observing and appreciating nature is important, but it is not enough. The key to science is helping children *do* something with what they observe of the natural world. The new science curriculum projects can provide guidelines for structuring a science program at the nursery-school level, since they all seem to have common prerequisites.

Each program requires that the children be able to make and describe observations of physical objects, know how to categorize objects by certain attributes, and discriminate between groups of objects that fit into a category and those that do not. A significant program could be built around experiences that help children to observe, describe, and categorize physical phenomena. These activities could be balanced with others in which children freely explore scientific materials and their use in a range of classroom experiences.

Exploring and Describing Attributes and Actions

Each person receives information about the external world through his five senses: sight, sound, touch, taste, and smell. This information can be identified and categorized. Visual properties of things can be differentiated in terms of size, shape, color, and other qualities. Sounds can be identified by pitch, intensity, quality, and regularity. Sounds can also be related to their producers. Touch sensations can be described as hard or soft, rough or smooth, warm or cold, sharp or dull. The qualities of taste and smell, although not as precisely identifiable, can also be differentiated. These properties are listed as examples and are not to be considered exhaustive.

For each sense there are manipulative activities and related language experiences that would help children identify, categorize, and differentiate experiences and begin to describe objects by their sensory properties. This is the beginning of scientific thought. Children must also learn descriptive language that allows them to symbolize and to communicate their sense experiences.

Examples of activities.   At snack time, the teacher might want to vary the traditional serving of milk or juice and crackers and bring in a variety of foods to taste. Children can eat these foods and talk about how they smell, taste, and feel. Fruits make excellent samples, as do many vegetables, including those seldom seen by children in their natural form and not often tasted raw, for example, carrots, potatoes, celery, turnips, and spinach. A variety of breads and crackers, as well as many other foods, can be included.

As the children taste these foods they should be asked to talk about their sense experiences, focusing on taste, texture, smell, and so on. Foods can be described as sweet or salty, or soft or crisp. Children often associate their current sense experiences with something in their past. A description of cookies as "like my grandmother used to make" should be accepted a a legitimate, vivid, description.

The teacher might wish to cook some of these foods, especially the raw vegetables, to show children the process of change that takes place when heat is applied. Cooked spinach looks different from raw spinach. Cooked carrots feel different from raw carrots. Even mixing foods together often makes significant differences in the way they look, taste, and feel. Sugar dissolved in water still tastes sweet, but no longer has a granular feel. Flour also changes consistency when mixed with a liquid. Foods can be used in an endless variety of ways.

Children should observe these actions and be asked to describe the changes they see taking place in foods. They can make charts of the descriptions to be mounted on the wall or the bulletin board and referred to later.

The children may arrive at generalizations as the result of their observations and descriptions (for example, when food is heated, it changes). A generalization that seems wrong to the teacher but fits the children's observations should be accepted. The teacher can later provide experiences that complicate the observations in the hope that a new and more accurate generalization will be forthcoming.

Experiences with many other materials can help children become aware of the attributes of things. Providing similarly shaped objects of lead and aluminum helps them differentiate between heavy and light objects. A touch board containing sandpaper, velvet, absorbent cotton, a piece of aluminum foil, and other such everyday items displays different textures. Setting up a "feeling box" containing an object hidden from view that can be touched by the children helps focus on tactile perception. Teachers can talk about the colors and shapes of a number of things, bringing in samples of primary colors and specific shapes and using everyday objects around the school. Block structures can be identified as larger or smaller, wider or narrower than other block structures.

Children can focus on the different elements of their perception in the free, less structured activities of play situations, or in more structured activities specifically designed to help them learn a particular category or name for an attribute. Once attributes are learned, children can be helped to make finer and finer discriminations and to begin to categorize things by their attributes. The same objects can be used to teach different kinds of categorization. A box of buttons, for example, might be given to a group of children to be separated by color, size, or on the basis of the material from which they are made.

Observing and describing the physical attributes of objects and organizing these observations in some meaningful way is just one part of an early childhood science program. Another part relates to observing and describing the actions of objects, and the interaction of objects with one another, under varying conditions.

Constance Kamii and Rheta DeVries, in their book *Physical Knowledge in Preschool Education* (1978), describe activities that can be used with young children to help them develop an understanding of such actions and interactions. Providing children with rollers and flat boards allows them to experiment with activities related to balance and motion. Equipping a water play area with various sizes and shapes of bottles, cups, tubes, and funnels offers them opportunities to explore the properties of water as it is transferred from one container to another or as it flows through a tube, as well as in other situations. Other play activities provided by the teacher could allow the children to explore additional aspects of the physical world as they develop descriptions and tentative explanations of what happens and as they test their ideas against one another, against the teacher, and against further encounters with similar phenomena.

Additional science activities.   An early childhood science program can go beyond those activities described above. Elements of nature study continue to serve the goals of early childhood education. Field trips to parks, wooded

FIGURE 6-1
Exploring the properties of water.

areas, and nature preserves are worthwhile, both as opportunities to learn and practice observations skills and as ways of helping young children learn to appreciate and develop a sense of wonder about nature.

Even trips through the school yard and along the streets surrounding the school can provide opportunities to learn about and come to appreciate nature. A wide range of plants grow unattended in many places, such as in areas around fences and in cracks in sidewalks. These are worth studying. Bringing plants, rocks, and other elements of nature into the classroom for closer observations is also helpful. These might be placed on science tables for continued observation. A terrarium could be made with some of the material collected, using a jar or large glass container. If each child makes a terrarium with different materials (using sand instead of soil, for example) and if different terraria are tended in different ways (some with more light than others, or with more or less moisture included, for example), children can observe the effects of different environmental conditions on plants.

Young children can also be helped to understand how scientific knowledge is applied to improve the way we live. Cooking activities such as those described above provide excellent opportunities for children to learn about nutrition. Field trips around the neighborhood can provide a springboard for lessons about ecology. Children may not be able to understand all the principles behind the exhortation to eat a balanced diet or to protect their environment, but they can be helped to know which foods are more nutritious than others as well as to appreciate the importance of protecting the physical environment and keeping it clean.

Including science materials in classroom activities. The teacher should be concerned with designing children's play activities so they can discover properties and relationships and use them. Setting up a pulley system in the block area for the children to use in building will help them learn about force and how it can be increased or changed in direction. The child should be allowed to verbalize the experience in his own way. It is less significant that he learn such terms as *friction, inertia,* or *mechanical advantage.* More important is that the child has intuitively learned through experience that a pulley will make it easier to lift things.

A doorbell and buzzer operated on batteries, included in the housekeeping area, can stimulate dramatic play as people come and go, and children see the effects of electricity and the need for a circuit in operating electrical devices. Battery-powered electric lights complete with switches could also be wired into a playhouse. A bulb, battery, and a couple of lengths of wire can be provided in a box for the children's free manipulations and discovery. Magnets, magnifying glasses, and other items can be made available to children for "messing about" or for inclusion in their play activities.

It would be helpful if the teacher asked children to explain what happened when they used these materials. The key to response is not its formal accuracy, but to provide explanations that reasonably explain their experience from their point of view. Teachers then know what they understand, and what confusions still exist. They must then determine whether to leave the adequate though erroneous explanation alone for a while, or to engage the child in other experiences that will lead him to discover his errors. Often group discussions allow a child the opportunity to test perceptions and understandings against those of other children.

Children might also be given opportunities to grow things from seeds, tubers, and cuttings. They should be able to describe things growing as well as what seemed to help them grow. Fish and small animals, in appropriate containers, can also be provided.

In all science inquiry children should be given opportunities to ask questions about what they see and to be able to find the answers. Sometimes the questions are unanswerable. "What is electricity?" might best be answered by, "I don't know, but we can see some of the things that electricity can do." It is better to answer questions honestly than to offer inaccurate or semimagical answers. Children need to become comfortable with the unknown.

In using everyday classroom activities to further the science program, we break down artificial barriers between subjects. Most problems that we deal with cannot be labeled "science problems" or "social science problems," but rather spill over into many areas. Ecological issues, for example, may have a biological base, but the tools needed to resolve them grow out of a knowledge of economics and politics also.

Science activities can enhance the language arts program. The observations and descriptions needed in science enable children to use words better. Their descriptions will be more accurate and vivid. Their vocabularies will increase and they will use more adverbs and adjectives. Measurement used in science can benefit the mathematics program as well. Even drawing and modeling as a way of recording observations tie science to the arts. Both science and

FIGURE 6-2
Models help children explore ideas beyond the here and now.

social studies units can provide themes to help integrate the early childhood program.

SCIENCE ACTIVITIES IN THE CLASSROOM

A teacher must organize the classroom so that science learning can take place in an area that is identifiable by the children and has a degree of isolation. The center should have within it or near by some closed storage space, such as a cabinet, in which science materials not currently in use can be kept. If these materials are readily available, the teacher is able to use the children's cues to move into a science topic that happens to interest them, thus exploiting their personal motivation for learning. If a range of materials is not available, the teachers may have to postpone an experience or even allow a critical moment for learning to pass right by.

In addition to storage, there should be some open shelf space that allows access to a range of science materials. Space should be available for children to work at problems. If the center is relatively isolated, a teacher can set up a problem and allow the children to work on it individually or in small groups. Since scientific inquiry is the important goal of science instruction, most of the science work ought to be done by individuals or small groups.

Using Displays

Simply *having* a display is inadequate for science education in the early years; the key to its effectiveness is how the display is used. Teachers should organize their displays for the children's use.

Bulletin boards can be organized to demonstrate a scientific concept. Leaves of the same kind of tree can be pinned up to show diversity of foliage. Pictures of a plant at different periods in its growth demonstrate the process of growth. Objects of varying size show the concept of "bigger than" or "smaller than."

Materials on a science table can be organized so that they can actually be used by the children. The children might organize a group of rocks by texture, color, or form. Different types of lenses allow children to look at objects and discover the effect on their apparent sizes. Children can discover the properties of magnets on both magnetic and nonmagnetic material.

Displays can be organized in many ways. The crucial element is that the child use the display in learning to develop modes of scientific thinking. Simply exhibiting materials for children to examine is inadequate.

Displays that are effective are changed regularly. If the content of a display reflects the children's concern with particular areas of scientific inquiries, it can be changed to keep up with shifts in the focus of science learning in the classroom.

FIGURE 6-3
Science displays can extend
children's thinking.

Providing Demonstrations

Actual experiments, in the traditional sense—including the use of laboratory controls—are seldom carried out in the classroom. Often little is to be gained from experiments that cannot be gained from freer experiences with the same materials. Teachers can also use demonstrations instead.

Demonstrations can be a way of *telling* or asking children about science. If the demonstration is performed and followed only by an explanation, it is an illustration.

Demonstrations lead to inquiry when followed by questioning and discussion sessions. Teachers can stimulate such sessions by asking questions such as, "What happened?" "Why did it happen?" "How do you know?" "Did you see anything else happening?" "Can you think of other ways we can explain what happened?" "How can we tell that our explanation is correct?" If these questions are a part of honest inquiry, the children must have access to the information that can be used to test their conclusions. If such information is not directly observable by the children, their responses may border on the magical rather than the scientific.

For example, a child who is told that the flame of a candle in a jar went out because it had used up all the oxygen has not been told anything useful, from a scientific point of view. There is no way the absence or presence of oxygen can be demonstrated to that child. The explanation must be accepted on faith, which is in itself unscientific. It is important that the explanations teachers provide be in keeping with the information available to the young child.

Demonstrations are ways of helping children focus their observations so that they can better see a phenomenon. If children can perceive a thing or action more clearly they can more easily abstract the ideas embedded from the physical world and thus understand them. If children are not able to answer the questions asked then it is possible that the demonstration did not serve its purpose. It might have been beyond the level of the children's understanding or the ideas might have been presented in a confusing or obscuring way.

Recording the Results of Inquiry

Scientific inquiry should be recorded and communicated so that ideas can be retested and the results of inquiries can be compared. Children in the upper primary classes can write with sufficient competence to begin to develop science notebooks which reflect their science activities. Teachers can devise many ways of helping younger children record their scientific activities.

Children can dictate materials into tape recorders or for the teacher to record on experience charts or in individual books; they can use paintings and drawings to record their experiences in some symbolic fashion. The teacher should set aside time for discussion and recording, because the language and symbolic aspects are important for the child's continued learning.

The records developed for science activities provide one way of interrelating subject areas. Helping children draw objects accurately or use words that accurately represent an observation can help them become more creative artists or writers. As they gain mastery over ways of recording and representing observations and experiences, they become able to do more with media. They also learn the uses of records so that the acts of reading and writing become more meaningful.

Providing Opportunities for Inquiries

This chapter has emphasized science instruction as a part of the curriculum that requires children to actively inquire. Science has been viewed not as a set of labels or concepts, but as a way of conceiving of the world—a way of thinking about things. This point of view makes it imperative that at every point in the curriculum children actively think about the experiences provided for them and that their thought processes about physical and natural phenomena parallel their acquisition of scientific information. The ramifications for classroom organization are that activities must be organized so that children can *act upon* materials and experiences and arrive at their own conclusions. This requires that most activities be organized for individuals and small groups. The teacher should not spend a great deal of time telling children about science, but instead continuously provide them with opportunities to find out on their own.

In this approach, the teacher must be both sensitive to the child's thought processes and an observer of what he does in class. The important element of science learning is not necessarily the product of scientific inquiry—the conclusions that children arrive at or the kinds of categories they develop—but rather the process by which these conclusions are generated and the reasons and methods of developing a set of categories. This approach should support a great deal of diversity in the classroom—diversity in achievement, goals, and activities.

A good early childhood science program requires more than a set of apparatus and some instructions for its use. It demands a climate of inquiry pervading the class. Lazar Goldberg (1970) defined the characteristics of such a climate as

> antiauthoritarianism and democracy; high tolerance for dissent, argument, error and failure; regard for aesthetic reward; absence of fear and humiliating measures; emphasis on cooperation rather than competition; respect for manual as well as intellectual effort; and above all interesting and significant activity. It is not a climate where "anything goes." Rather it is one which is humane and reasonable. It is a climate in which children cultivate valid criteria for choosing among alternative beliefs. (pp. 14-15)

Such a climate can support the achievement of "autonomy based upon reason" in young children.

REFERENCES

AMERICAN ASSOCIATION FOR THE ADVANCEMENT OF SCIENCE. *Description of the program: Science—a process approach.* New York: Xerox Educational Division, 1967.

BRANDWEIN, P. F., COOPER, E. K., BLACKWOOD, P. E., and HONE, E. B. *Concepts in science* (Grade I, Teacher's Edition). New York: Harcourt, Brace Jovanovich, Inc., 1966.

CRAIG, G. S. *Certain techniques used in developing a course of study in science for the Horace Mann Elementary School.* New York: Teachers College Press, 1927.

CRAIG, G. S. *Science for the elementary school teacher.* Lexington, Mass.: Ginn, 1958.

GOLDBERG, L. *Children and science.* New York: Scribner's, 1970.

HAWKINS, D. Messing about in science. *Science and Children,* 1965, *2* (5), 5-9.

HURD, P. D., and GALLAGHER, J. J. *New directions in elementary science teaching.* Belmont, Calif.: Wadsworth, 1968.

KAMII, C., and DEVRIES, R. *Physical knowledge in preschool education.* Englewood Cliffs, N.J.: Prentice-Hall, 1978.

KARPLUS, R., and THIER, H. D. *A new look at elementary school science.* Skokie, Ill.: Rand McNally, 1967.

ROWE, M. B. Help is denied to those in need. *Science and Children,* 1976, *12,* 323-325.

WATERS, B. S. *Science can be elementary: Discovery—action programs for K-3.* New York: Citation Press, 1973.

SUGGESTED READINGS

ABRUSCATO, J. *Teaching children science.* Englewood Cliffs, N.J.: Prentice-Hall, 1982.

GOODWIN, M. T., and POLLEN, G. *Creative food experiences for children.* (Rev. ed.). Washington, D.C.: Center for Science in the Public Interest, 1980.

HOLT, B.   *Science with young children*. Washington, D.C.: National Association for the Education of Young Children, 1977.

JACOBSON, W. J., and BERGMAN, A. B.   *Science for children*. Englewood Cliffs, N.J.: Prentice-Hall, 1980.

KAMII, C., and DEVRIES, R.   *Physical knowledge in preschool education*. Englewood Cliffs, N.J.: Prentice-Hall, 1978.

ROCKWELL, R. E., SHERWOOD, E. A., and WILLIAMS, R. A.   *Hug a tree and other things to do outdoors with young children*. Mt. Ranier, Md.: Gryphon House, 1983.

ROBINSON, B., and WOLFSON, E.   *Environmental education: A manual for elementary educators*. New York: Teachers College Press, 1982.

WANAMAKER, N., HEARN, K., and RICHARZ, S.   *More than graham crackers*. Washington, D.C.: National Association for the Education of Young Children, 1979.

7

Mathematics
for Young Children

Just as children enter school having learned much about the spoken language and the physical world, so they come to school with a broad background of experiences in mathematical learning. Children have been living in a world of quantity. They have experienced "too small," "too large," and "all gone." Their parents may have taught them to count before nursery school, although saying number names in order might have been taken for counting. The children probably have little experience with mathematical operations and much of their understanding is at an intuitive rather than an analytic level.

Robert Rea and Robert Reys (1971) studied entering kindergartners' knowledge of geometry, numbers, money, and measurement. A wide range of abilities was identified. Nearly three-fourths of the children correctly identified the numerals 1, 3, 4, and 5, and between 50 percent and 80 percent were able to point correctly to the appropriate numeral when the number names one through eight were presented. When a sequence such as 1, 2, 3 or 5, 6, 7 was presented, about 90 percent of the children could provide the next number in the sequence. Over half the children were able to form groups of three and seven discs, count up to five items on a card, identify the number of items in a group up to eight, and point to the first and last item in a sequence when asked. About three-fourths of the children could also compare the number of items in two groups containing up to four items each.

Rea and Reys (1971) also found that the majority of the children could identify penny, nickel, and dime coins and distinguish between one, five, and ten dollar bills. More than half knew that a penny bought the least and a half-dollar the most of all coins, and that ten dollars bought the most of all the bills. The children also possessed a wide range of geometric knowledge.

Such an inventory can only sample a limited range of children's knowledge. Some children know more than others about the items tested. Many things known by children may not have been sampled. But such a study points out that many children have much mathematics knowledge before kindergarten. It suggests that they are capable of mathematics learning.

Herbert Ginsberg (1980), in reviewing studies of young children's knowledge of arithmetic, concludes that children have gained a considerable amount of knowledge of arithmetic before entering school. These children are able to count and to solve simple addition problems. Ginsberg suggests, however, that once in school, children do not always do arithmetic as teachers wish, preferring their own intuitive strategies to standard algorithms.

DECIDING WHAT AND HOW TO TEACH

The work of Jean Piaget has been used to illuminate the capabilities of young children in mathematics more than in any other curriculum area. This is partly because of the close proximity of mathematics operations to the formal mental operations that have been studied by Piaget and his colleagues.

The operations that can serve as the basis of an early childhood program have been characterized by Constance Kamii (1973) as logico-mathematical and spatio-temporal knowledge. They are structured from the child's own actions and the logical sense of these actions. Thus, they are constructed by the child himself. The three areas of logico-mathematical knowledge include classification (finding similarities and differences among objects, and grouping and separating objects according to them), seriation (ordering things according to relative differences), and number (judging "same," "more," or "less," and conserving quantity). In relation to time and space, the child needs to structure time in sequence and develop topological structures at the representational level. These are essentially the mental operations needed by children as they approach mathematics instruction in school.

Douglas E. Cruikshank, David L. Fitzgerald, and Linda R. Jensen (1980) suggest that a beginning mathematics program should focus on an understanding of the concept of number as children explore the mathematical relationships among objects and among sets. Children must learn the meaning of number and the symbols for number. They should also be able to learn basic number facts and number operations. Children can also begin to understand concepts of space, including both topological and Euclidian geometry, and apply number to space through measurement. They can also develop problem-solving skills. Such a list of topics for children in the preschool, kindergarten, and primary grades is in keeping with the studies of young children's mathematical capabilities.

As important as the topics to be covered is the method by which children will be expected to approach these topics. In an attempt to ensure that significant mathematical learning will take place in school, many primary grades, kindergartens, and even preschools have adopted workbook-based and text-book-based programs. Unfortunately these programs often only give children an opportunity to approach mathematical concepts through words or, at best, when accompanied by pictures. Yet our knowledge of young children's thinking suggests that children must first have experiences with concrete objects before moving on to more abstract representations. Pictures are abstract representations, although less abstract than either spoken or printed words. Depending solely upon them to provide mathematical experiences places an added burden on young children.

In addition, a textbook-based or workbook-based program isolates mathematics from children's experiences and often makes it more difficult to apply what they already know about the quantitative world to a growing understanding of number, number relationships, and number operations. We need to help children learn to use their intuitive knowledge as a way of approaching more formal learnings.

Constance Kamii (1982) suggests that there are a great many situations that occur within the life of the preschool and kindergarten child that can be used to help teach about numbers and number relationships. She also suggests that a variety of group games can be used with children to this end.

Almost all areas of the early childhood program provide opportunities for children to group things and to count limited numbers of objects. In the block-building area, children can make comparisons and show one-to-one correspondence by matching two walls of a block construction. The woodwork area can provide experiences in comparing lengths of wood or counting nails, while arts and crafts activities also allow for comparing the volume of clay being used, or grouping the paper for collage by shape and other attributes. Sand tables and water play areas can be provided with a variety of containers so that children experience and compare different measures.

In addition, a great range of manipulative materials may be given children in a game setting so they can gain experiences with numbers, size, shapes, and the like. Various structured mathematics materials such as the Stern blocks, Cuisenaire rods, or Montessori beads may be used. Puzzles using geometric inserts, peg-sets, and sets of beads and strings can be used for counting, showing numbers, and patterning. The endless opportunities available in any classroom for counting, comparing, and measuring provide children with a wealth of opportunity to do mathematics.

Organizing a mathematics center in one section of the classroom supports their regular use. Directions for using manipulative materials should be available so that individuals or small groups can engage in activities independent of the teacher. Richard Copeland (1976) provides a fine set of suggestions for organizing and equipping a mathematics laboratory, which can be used in creating a classroom math center.

Experiences with real things in their environment, if used appropriately, can keep children from feeling that mathematics is alien to their lives. It is disheartening to see some young children labeled incapable of understanding mathematics when they go to the store each day, order groceries for their families, pay the grocer, and count the change, being sure to check the transaction along the way so that they are not cheated. Often it is the way mathematics is taught rather than the nature of mathematics that creates learning difficulties.

TEACHING BASIC MATHEMATICS CONCEPTS
IN THE EARLY YEARS

Although it is simple to order the range of mathematics learning for the early years and to assign grade placements for each topic, such an exercise is not productive. One might approximate the age at which concepts can be taught, but teachers should respond to individual differences in a class. It is important to note also that concepts are not learned in an all-or-none fashion. Starting with intuitive responses to the environment, children go through a series of successive approximations of mature concepts. Continued experiences with an idea and its various manifestations and examples help children understand the concept in greater depth. Therefore, no age or grade placements are suggested for topics discussed in this chapter. Teachers need to be sensitive to the children's level of understanding and to the prerequisites for understanding a particular concept.

Assessing children's levels of understanding is more difficult than assessing the ability to produce specific responses. One way of assessing their level of understanding is to see if they can use what they have learned in other situations. Important clues can be gained by listening carefully to responses to questions. Incorrect responses may be a result of inattention, but more often they reflect an inability to grasp concepts. Teachers can diagnose children's difficulties and either present activities that will clarify misconceptions or gear their teaching more closely to children's ability to understand.

Grouping

In developing young children's concepts of quantity, the teacher can begin by having them group things. Children could group all the pencils in a box, all the red beads in a bead set, the pieces of a puzzle, containers of milk, or the children in a class. Such a group may be called a *set*. Sets can be made up of dissimilar things, but it is less confusing for the children in the beginning to use objects with common elements.

Young children can also begin to compare the number property of sets by matching the members of a set. As the children set the table for snack time, for example, they can compare the set of napkins with the set of straws laid out. In matching, they might discover that the two sets have the same number of elements, or that one set has more elements. Learning the concepts of *more, fewer,* and *same* precedes knowing *how* many more or *how* many fewer there are. Such a use of sets and the comparison of sets has practical application for the children, making the uses of mathematics obvious to those who may now have to modify their environment on the basis of increased mathematical knowledge (provide more napkins or more straws).

The matching of sets to teach one-to-one correspondence may also be done with pictures and charts. However, it is helpful for children to have real objects to manipulate in the beginning. With manipulative objects, they can line up two sets of objects, matching a member of one set with a member of the other, even before they can count.

Counting

Children often come into nursery school or kindergarten "knowing how to count." What too often passes for counting is the ability to recite the names of numbers in sequence without any understanding of the idea of the number that corresponds to a given name or numeral.

Young children need experiences that help them associate names or symbols with the numbers they represent. They see little difference between a physical representation of number and the idea of number. They can be helped to make these associations through the experiences described above. At first, children can be given manipulative materials and asked to build sets of two and three. It is easiest for them to begin to match their constructed sets with models. The spoken symbol for the number can be learned immediately; the written symbol may be learned later. Although much has been made about the differentiation of number and numeral, emphasizing such a differentiation may be confusing to young children.

Many experiences allow children to build sets of two, three, four, and so on. They can match these sets to other sets, matching either groups to other groups, or groups to pictures of groups. They can also match sets of objects to symbols of these sets. As children begin to write—numerals as well as letters—they can begin to match the numerals they write with the correct number of objects in a set.

From this point, children begin to construct new sets by adding one more object to a set already constructed. They can also be given opportunities to order sets in relation to the number of objects in each group. Through a series of such experiences, children will learn that the numbers one to ten fit into a special order from smallest to largest quantity. This is the beginning of counting and understanding ordinality. A range of materials may be used to move children along, and a number line with numerals written from 0 to 10 may help them in their final ordering.

FIGURE 7-1
Counting objects helps
develop a concept of num-
ber.

The Number System

Once children begin to count beyond nine and record these numbers, they must become aware of our numeration system. The children are already aware of the number named by each symbol or digit, 0, 1, 2, . . . 9. They must now learn that the numeration system has a base of ten and that the place of each digit in a numeral represents its value. A whole range of activities in which children learn to substitute ten unit elements for an element valued at ten using rods, beads, chips, or markers can help them develop this concept of equivalence. Then, working with columned paper or pocket charts, they can study the role of position in relation to value. The notation of two-place numerals can be presented at this time.

Three-place numerals and other ways of representing numbers would be taught next. One-place numerals are easily represented by squares and sets of squares lined up to ten, or by a variety of three-dimensional rods or sets of beads. Two-place numerals can be represented in like fashion. A set of ten rods of ten values each equals one hundred.

Larger numbers become rather cumbersome in concrete representation. The Montessori golden beads represent one thousand as a cube—ten beads long, ten beads wide, and ten beads deep. Children soon become aware of the need for more efficient representation of numbers, especially large numbers, and are ready to represent and read large numbers in the arabic notation system.

Number Operations

Children can go from counting, comparing, and noting numbers to the basic operations on numbers: addition, subtraction, multiplication, and division. By counting up or down, the child can develop the basics of addition and

FIGURE 7-2
Number charts can teach ordinality.

subtraction. For centuries people have used counting up and down as the basis for addition and subtraction, as evidenced in the use of the abacus. With this rather sophisticated yet simple device, counting beads allows a person to go through complicated mathematical procedures.

Similarly, beginning addition- and subtraction-type problems can utilize the process of counting objects. Only later, when children have developed an understanding of the process, do they move to the use of shortcuts, or *algorithms.* After understanding is developed, practice activities can be offered to improve computational skills.

Children should be provided many situations in which they can put together sets of objects to establish the facts of addition, and gain an intuitive understanding of it. At this point, the process can be formalized and the appropriate language of mathematics introduced. Too early an emphasis on the formal aspects of arithmetic may thwart the children's intuitive acquisition of concepts and operations. Continued practice with the operations will lead to their mastery.

Similar approaches can be used in teaching subtraction, beginning with the opportunities to actually "take away" members of a large group and see how many are left. The children can then count down on an abacus or similar device, moving objects over, then comparing larger sets with smaller ones. The proof of the correctness of response is immediately available.

If children have already learned the concept of place and understood the equivalence of one ten to ten ones, for example, it becomes relatively simple to move from addition and subtraction of one-place numbers to two-place numbers, since the readiness for this learning has already been developed.

Multiplication and division are usually introduced in the primary grades. These processes, too, can be approached by the use of manipulative materials and by recourse to prior mathematics learning. Children have probably already learned to count by twos, fives, and tens before multiplication is introduced.

They have also learned to add. If they are asked to put together five groups of two blocks each, for example, they can visualize the process of multiplication. Many experiences such as these are helpful to begin with. Later the multiplication facts can be organized into tables.

Asking such questions as, "If I want to make groups of three out of this pile of twelve beans, how many groups will I have?" or "I want to give the same amount of pretzels to each of the five children here. I have ten pretzels. How many will each child receive?" is an appropriate beginning of division. Using real situations, involving the children in the manipulation of concrete objects, and having them act upon their environment provide the basis for later mathematics learning.

Geometry

Almost from birth, children have been developing an understanding of spatial relationships. They are beginning to grasp the basic concepts of topological geometry in their intuitive constructions. Copeland (1979) suggests that this form of geometry might best be presented to children informally prior to Euclidian geometry. Among the basic topological concepts that can be taught are *proximity,* the distance of objects from one another; *separation,* the lack of nearness; *order,* the arrangement of objects in space; *enclosure* or *surrounding;* and *continuity.* Any number of experiences with blocks, beads, or other manipulative materials could be used to illustrate these concepts. Children separate blocks or beads as they move them away from one another. They often talk about objects or persons being far and near. The ongoing activities of the class help provide the basis for teaching these concepts if the teacher is aware of them and makes them explicit.

Copying the pattern of beads, blocks, or other manipulative materials or placing objects in a pattern can help the children understand the concept of order. Dealing with the idea of in and out ("Put the crayons *in* the box; put the box *between* the other two on the shelf.") can help the child use the concept of surrounding or enclosing. It is important that children operate on these materials and that teachers ask them questions about the objects' relationships to one another, to help them formalize their understanding of these concepts.

In the geometry program young children can also learn to identify and compare basic shapes: square, circle, and triangle. Rectangles and other shapes, more difficult to identify, can be introduced at whatever point children are able to compare the measurements of sides and angles of objects. In identifying these shapes, the children learn to count sides and angles, or "corners." They can later compare sides, as well, so that they can differentiate between a square and a rectangle.

Later, as the children learn to measure, they will begin to compare perimeters and areas of different objects and shapes. Problems such as which shape of several has the greatest perimeter or how many things it takes to cover

FIGURE 7-3
A geoboard is helpful in exploring problems of shape.

the top of a table (a problem in area) can be worked out by children who have been provided with the proper manipulative material and learned how to set out to solve problems of this nature. Children can also learn to classify objects by shape and to find geometric shapes in familiar objects around them. The concrete presentation of geometry makes it a natural part of the program since they can handle things, ask questions, and test their ideas on elements of physical reality. Although proper vocabulary is important in teaching geometry to children, the language should be an outgrowth of experience. Otherwise, the content becomes abstract and, unfortunately, meaningless.

DEVELOPING MEASUREMENT SKILLS

One way to integrate the mathematics learning and to concretize quantitative and spatial concepts is to use measurement. This allows young children to use their developing mathematical knowledge as a vehicle for understanding the immediate world. Measurement can be approached simply and intuitively by young children. Teaching measurement begins with teaching the comparison of things to one another, and moves to comparisons of things to a common arbitrarily established standard, to comparison and quantification in relation to commonly established standards. Each area of measurement has its unique set of problems.

Linear Measurement

Young children come up against problems of linear size early in life. The problems of matching the heights of two sides of a block structure or of finding a piece of wood that fits in a woodwork construction are examples of children's experiences with problems of linearity. It is a simple matter to give children sets of wooden rods and ask them to find the longer one or the shorter one, or even to have them stand beside one another and judge who is taller. The words "tall," "taller," "short," "shorter," "long," and "longer" can be taught in this connection.

A somewhat higher order of linear comparison is reached in asking children to compare things that cannot be placed next to one another: block structures on two sides of the block area, or the heights of the sink and the woodwork bench. In this case, they have to somehow record the measurements and compare the recording of one object with another. A length of wood might be marked to record the height of one block building and later moved to the other block building so visual comparison can be made. After many such experiences, regular measuring devices can be introduced, such as primary rulers and yardsticks. As children learn to count they can be taught the numbers on the ruler and the unit "inch." Before fractions are introduced, length can be reported as "between _____ and _____ inches long."

After working with inches, children may be taught the concepts of "foot" and "yard." Unfortunately, our measurement system is still not metric and the relationships between various units of measure are nonregular (for example, there are twelve inches in a foot, three feet in a yard, and thirty-six inches in a yard). These relationships may take some time for children to master.

Once children have learned to measure objects there is no end to the amount of measuring they can do and, with these measurements, no end to the amount of practice in addition and subtraction that can result. Floors, walls, furniture, materials, and people are all objects to be measured. Children can compare the measurements and make spoken and written statements about them.

Measurement of Weight

Weight is somewhat less directly perceivable than length. Placing an object in each hand and comparing weight is tricky, for the volume of the object distorts our perceptions. A pound of feathers, for example, does not *feel* as heavy as a pound of lead. External aids to judgment are most necessary in teaching children about weight comparisons.

A simple balance is a useful tool in helping young children make weight comparisons. This can be either purchased from an educational equipment company or made by using a length of wood, some string, and a couple of pie tins. If the teacher makes such a device she should be certain that the two ends do indeed balance when empty.

Again, the measurement of weight begins by comparing objects. When children place two objects in the balance pans they make a visual judgment about which is heavier and which lighter by noting which pan is lower. The next step is to make comparisons with arbitrary standards with which the weights of objects can be measured. These standards might be anything—large metal washers, fishing line sinkers, or rocks. Later metal weights representing units of measure can be introduced—one-ounce weights, half-pound weights, and one-pound weights.

Young children find the relationships between units complicated; they simply have to be learned arbitrarily. It is helpful if the children first have the experience of direct measurement before moving on to indirect measurement. A limitless number of objects in the environment of the school can be weighed. These weights can be added up, subtracted from one another, or compared. Statements about these activities are communicated orally and in writing. The language of measurement, including concepts such as "lighter than," "heavier than," and "the same weight as," becomes important.

Measurement of Volume

In learning to measure volume, children can be provided with containers of various sizes and shapes to fill and to transfer the contents from one to another. It is a good idea to include containers of the same volume, but different shapes to show children that volume is not simply a function of the height or width of a container. In time, containers of standard volumes should be introduced: one cup, half-cup, pint, quart, and gallon. The sand table and water play area are excellent places to introduce measurement of volume.

One of the complicating factors in teaching measurement at this particular time is the movement toward the metric system. We are using more metric measurements in our lives while we continue to use the more familiar traditional units. States are presently mandating the teaching of the metric system in schools while children are being overwhelmingly confronted with pounds, feet, and Fahrenheit degrees of temperature in their everyday lives. They may not care that their milk was poured from a container that holds .95 liters, or that the cottage cheese was scooped from a package weighing 227 grams, or that their fathers must drive no faster than 88.7 kilometers per hour (one quart, one-half pound, and 55 miles per hour respectively). Although the interactions of the two systems during this interim period will require that people learn to convert from one system to the other, it is probably best to teach metric measurement directly, parallel to teaching measurement with traditional units.

When children engage in measuring activities using metric units, they need meter sticks as well as yard sticks, weights for the pan balance in grams as well as ounces, thermometers showing the Celsius scale and the Fahrenheit scale, and containers based on liters as well as quarts and pints. Since units in the metric system are based on the decimal system, conversion from smaller to larger (as from millimeters to centimeters to meters) or the opposite should be easier than in our present system with its irregular set of relationships. The fact that time units will not be going metric means that children will still have to learn complicated time units, but at least there will be no need for conversions here.

Measurement of Time

Much attention in the early years is given to the measurement of time. Time is measured indirectly, making it a difficult dimension for young children to measure. Teachers do a lot of classwork with calendars and clocks.

There are two processes involved in learning to measure time that need to be addressed separately. One is reading clock faces and calendars; the other is measuring something that cannot be seen or felt. The passage of time is perceived subjectively. All of us have experienced periods of time that have dragged on interminably and others that have moved too quickly. Time is a difficult concept for children to grasp. Until entrance to school, they seldom have much awareness of time, except for the passage of day and night and the regularity of daily occurrences, including viewing television programs. There have been few expectations to be "on time," or to do things at a particular time. They have also experienced few cycles of seasonal change. With the beginning of school, the child's life suddenly becomes ordered in time, and time takes on increased psychological importance.

Many of the problems that children face in clock and calendar work stem from the fact that they are being asked to read fairly sophisticated material on the clock or the calendar without being taught the symbols and systems by which they are ordered. Other problems stem from the complicated relations of time segments to one another, as well as from the child's lack of knowledge of the benchmarks needed for the measurement of time. Often the only alternative left to the child is to memorize the material offered without ever really understanding it. It is amazing how few curriculum guides ever take the time to analyze and identify the elements needed to insure successful learning in this area of measurements.

One of the ironies of modern technology is the availability of digital clocks and watches. Direct reading of hour and minutes may be easier, but the passage of time is more evident with an analog clock than with a digital clock.

OTHER TOPICS IN MATHEMATICS

A number of additional topics will be touched upon in a mathematics program for the early years. Although generally not treated as extensively as the ones described above, they are still important elements. Included are the study of fractions, the use of graphs and charts, and money.

Fractions

Once they understand whole numbers, young children can also be helped to understand simple fractions as equal parts of a unit. They can learn the meaning of one-half, one-fourth, and one-third. Their first understanding is of the number of parts of a unit, without concern for their equality. The teacher will find many opportunities to use fractions in the classroom: sharing snacks, giving out materials for craft work, and children's work in the block area or at the woodworking bench.

Understandings in this area, as in other areas, grow slowly in young children. A nursery school child's concept of "half" comes from seeing objects divided into two parts. The fact that the parts must be equal to be considered halves is a part of the definition that comes later. Children's understandings, however, grow as a result of many encounters with their environment, beginning long before they are able to grasp complex sophisticated meanings.

Graphs and Charts

As children learn to communicate in writing they may become aware that some things are communicated in ways other than through the use of words. Geography requires written communication of topographical information through maps. Quantitative information, similarly, might best be communicated using graphs and charts. A variety of graphic representations can be used in the early years. They might start simply as ways of comparing children in the class in just two columns, such as the number of boys versus girls, those who go home for lunch versus those who stay at school, or those who live in houses versus apartments. Beginning graphs can be three-dimensional representations. A line of building blocks or wooden cubes representing each group, with each block or cube standing for one person, can be used at first; later, two-dimensional representations can be added.

The children can then move on to more complicated graphs: of children's birthdays (by months), heights, weights, color of hair, interests. Line graphs can be made of the morning temperature of the room or the outdoors over a period of time, of the number of children absent each day, or of the number of cars passing the school in a five-minute interval. This will require the collection of information from which the graphs will develop and will often be a part of a more extensive study. Using graphs in this fashion demonstrates that they are a practical way of recording and communicating information.

Money

Another topic often included in the primary mathematics program is the study of money and money equivalence. Our monetary system is based on the unit of ten, just as our system of numeration. Once the relative value of coins and paper money is learned, little new knowledge or skills are required for children to develop skills of monetary computation. As a matter of fact, the use of real or fake money is a helpful resource in teaching the numeration system itself to the very young.

In the early years, the main concern is teaching children to recognize coins of different values and to exchange coins properly. Manipulations with real coins are necessary to some extent, although play money can be used. Opportunities for using coins in play, as in a mock supermarket, or in real situations, such as shopping trips, and experiences in purchasing, making, and selling objects are helpful.

USING A MATHEMATICS VOCABULARY
WITH YOUNG CHILDREN

Psychologists and educators have become very much aware of the importance of language development in children and the relationship of language to thinking. In the area of mathematics, there has been an increased concern with language because the vocabulary used in many new mathematics programs is so different from that in older programs.

It is important that children learn to use the language of mathematics with some degree of precision. It is also important that they find mathematics meaningful. Children use new words appropriately if they understand them and know when to use them.

Mathematics is a language system. The symbols of mathematics allow people to write rather complex statements in a simple form with a degree of clarity and specificity that would be difficult to match with words alone. As children become appreciative of written communication, they can be helped to become appreciative of the language of mathematics and learn to use it appropriately.

USING REALISTIC EXPERIENCES

Nursery schools and kindergartens are replete with opportunities for infusing mathematics learnings into the day's activities. Children can tally those in attendance; marks can be made for each boy and girl and these can later be grouped and added. Other routine activities also hold similar promise. Setting up for snack time provides opportunities to see one-to-one relationships and to count. Work in the block area requires a mathematical sense, as do woodworking and crafts activities. Music, dance, and games all allow counting and matching. Dramatic play activities can offer other experiences: playing store or driving a bus, using money, counting, and measuring.

As children move into the primary grades, less fanciful activities are available in the classroom. Most classrooms are full of things that can be compared, counted, added, weighed, and measured. It is important to give children both the chance to involve themselves in these operations and direction in doing it. Task cards, or assignment cards can help.

Assignment cards have written simple problems or activities in which children can engage. These cards allow individualized instruction and provide many learning activities without constant teacher supervision. A small file box can contain a large number of assignment cards, numbered in order of difficulty and coded by topic. Such things as weight, linear measure, clock work, counting, writing equations, measuring volume, and geometry can all be taught through assignment cards. Teachers can set up a chart for each area of assignment cards on which children can check off those they are using. This simplifies record keeping. The teacher also needs to devise a way to check the accuracy of the completed assignment.

Some assignment cards may list closed-ended tasks; others may be open-ended, allowing opportunities for creativity and discovery in mathematics. The key to developing good assignments is to analyze the environment in which the children live and work and the activities in which they and others around them engage. Teachers should look for areas in which children can practice and extend the mathematical skills and concepts they have gained in the more formal parts of the school program. Such assignments can also allow for opportunities to relate mathematics tasks to other subjects. Thus a child could use a graph for quantitative representation, then represent the idea in another way, writing a story or drawing a picture. Examples of assignment cards follow.

WEIGHT

Place a cup of rice in one pan of a balance and a cup of beans in the other. Which is heavier? Write a story about these.

Choose two things that look the same size and weigh them. Do they weigh the same? Now choose two things that seem to feel the same weight, but are different in size. Weigh them. Are they the same in weight? Which is easier to guess, equal weights or equal sizes?

Take your shoe and place it in the scale. Weigh it to the nearest ounce. Record the weight. "My shoe weighs _____ ounces."

LINEAR MEASURE

Measure the length of your desk. Measure the length of the teacher's desk. Which desk is longer?

Measure the heights of all the boys in the class. List the boys in order of height, starting with the tallest.

VOLUME

Using a one-cup measure, fill up a quart container. How many cups does it take?

COUNTING

Count the number of windows in the room. How many can be opened? How many must remain closed? Do more windows open or close?

Count the number of books with blue bindings in the library.

GRAPHS

Make a graph using unit blocks for each person. Show the number of persons in the class that have a birthday during each month of the year. Write a story about it.

AREA

Cover the top of your table with index cards. How many are needed?

SHAPES

How many things can you find in the room that have circles in them? List them. Draw a design using ten squares. How many different designs can you make?

Such assignments allow the children to grasp mathematical relationships in the world around them. They will gain new mathematical insights and be able to practice the knowledge they have already acquired. In the area of measurement, dual assignment cards can be constructed reflecting metric units and conventional units used in the same problem. Assignment cards can point out the learning opportunities in the surrounding world. The use of the environment as a resource of learning mathematics opens up new vistas for children's mathematical understandings.

Using Materials

Although many opportunities exist for learning mathematics in the environment, teachers cannot depend on natural occurrences as the only source of mathematics learning.

In the primary grades, one usually finds a dependence upon mathematics textbooks and workbooks. If used flexibly, these provide an excellent source of learning activities. Textbooks may offer the teacher as well as the children a guide to learning. The selection of a single textbook series can assure a degree of continuity of learning from grade to grade and provide a number of instructional and practice activities.

Mathematics instruction must go beyond the textbook, however.

FIGURE 7-4 Children need manipulative material in exploring numerical concepts.

Manipulative materials help the children understand concepts and processes through practical application with concrete examples of the ideas taught. A large number of these materials are commercially made. Many teacher-made materials should be included. Although the quantity and type of materials provided depends on the needs of the class at any time, it is helpful to have a mathematics center available in the classroom where mathematical material can be kept and used. The materials should be easily accessible and well organized so that cleanup is not cumbersome.

No matter how much material and supplies are provided, it is still the teacher who remains the key to the success of the program. Teachers need to be knowledgeable in mathematics and methods of teaching mathematics, but sensitivity to children is also important. For within the framework of their knowledge teachers are constantly planning activities, assessing progress, diagnosing difficulties, and providing additional sources of learning for some while looking for enrichment activities for others. It is the teacher who can make the subject of mathematics a vital and meaningful area of inquiry in the early years of schooling.

REFERENCES

COPELAND, R. W.   The mathematics laboratory—An individual approach to learning. In *Mathematics and the elementary teacher* (3rd ed.). Philadelphia: Saunders, 1976.

COPELAND, R. W.   *How children learn mathematics* (3rd ed.). New York: Macmillan, 1979.

CRUIKSHANK, D. E., FITZGERALD, D. L., and JENSEN, L. R.   *Young children learning mathematics.* Boston: Allyn & Bacon, 1980.

GINSBERG, H. P.   Children's surprising knowledge of arithmetic. *Arithmetic Teacher,* 1980, *28*(1), 42-44.

KAMII, C.   A sketch of a Piaget-derived preschool curriculum developed by the Ypsilanti Early Education Program. In B. Spodek (Ed.). *Early childhood education.* Englewood Cliffs, N.J.: Prentice-Hall, 1973.

KAMII, C.   *Numbers in preschool and kindergarten.* Washington, D.C.: National Association for the Education of Young Children, 1982.

REA, R. E., and REYS, R. E.   Competencies of entering kindergartners in geometry, number, money and measurements. *School Science and Mathematics,* 1971, *71,* 389-402.

SUGGESTED READING

COPELAND, R. C.   *How children learn mathematics* (3rd ed.). New York: Macmillan, 1979.

COPELAND, R. C.   *Math activities for children.* Columbus, Ohio: Chas. E. Merrill, 1979.

CRUIKSHANK, D. E., FITZGERALD, D. L., and JENSEN, L. R.   *Young children learning mathematics.* Boston: Allyn & Bacon, 1980.

KAMII, C. *Numbers in preschool and kindergarten.* Washington, D.C.: National
  Association for the Education of Young Children, 1982.
MAFFEI, A. C., and BUCKLEY, D.   *Teaching preschool math.* New York: Human
  Sciences Press, 1980.
RICHARDSON, L. I., GOODMAN, K. L., HARTMAN, N. H., and LePIQUE,
  H. C.   *A mathematics activity curriculum for early childhood and special educa-
  tion.* New York: Macmillan, 1980.

8

Social Studies for Young Children

Schools for young children help them understand themselves, the world around them, and their relationship to it. Children learn about themselves through feedback from the outside world as they test their powers on the physical and social worlds. They become aware of the context in which they live and strive to understand it, becoming more a part of that context as they define the boundaries between themselves and the surrounding world.

Young children develop knowledge and skills that are useful both for everyday life and as a prerequisite for future learnings. Their approach to the physical world is direct, testing what they know about physical things by touching, listening, or viewing. Although children have direct contact with people and can observe their behavior directly, it is the *meaning* of behavior that is important rather than the observable behavior alone—and the meaning is not directly accessible. The products of social behavior and the context in which behavior takes place, however, are more accessible.

ELEMENTS OF A SOCIAL STUDIES PROGRAM

Francis P. Hunkins (1982) suggests that social studies involves learning about ourselves and others and how we interact with people and places. It draws on those fields that deal with investigating humankind. Thus, we learn about our backgrounds through history, the social groups to which we belong through anthropology and sociology, the values we consider essential through philosophy and religion, where we live and how we relate to our environment through geography, how others influence and are influenced by us through political science, and how we satisfy our basic needs and wants through economics.

In studying various social studies topics with young children we need to be concerned with helping children develop the intellectual processes that enable them to understand the world. We must also be concerned with their developing an understanding of social roles and institutions and finding their places within them as well as understanding and developing a set of values. We can also help children develop and understand their inner world as well as the world surrounding them.

Intellectual Processes

Using the Piagetian construct of knowledge presented in chapter 3— including physical knowledge, social knowledge, logico-mathematical knowledge, and representation—one can identify the intellectual elements in a social studies program. Physical knowledge includes knowledge of physical elements in the world. This can probably best be gained by direct experience through field trips, observations, and interviews. Texts, audiovisual material, and simulations are also useful. Social knowledge includes the knowledge of social conventions, symbols, values, rituals, and myths; it is knowledge of what is considered right or proper and what is taboo. This can be told to children directly or indirectly.

Logico-mathematical knowledge requires that children use their thought processes to process information. Categorizing and ordering objects and events, observing and stating relationships, and putting things into the proper time/space context are included in this. Representing ideas and feelings is done through pictures, maps, charts, play activities, and stories (Spodek, 1974).

Socialization

Socialization is one of the prime goals of early childhood education. The social studies contribute to the socialization process, as do many other learning opportunities in the school day. The classroom teacher is concerned with helping children find their role in the school community and in the larger community. While there is some transfer in learning socialization strategies from one area to the other, there are enough significant differences in these two forms of socialization to warrant their separate treatment.

Within the classroom, teachers create conditions that help children learn the pupil role and teach the rules, expectations, mores, and values of the school. Developing an awareness of the way the class is organized, rules are made and enforced, the amount of freedom provided, the kinds of activities rewarded, and the rituals of daily life all lead to this socialization. But there is more to socialization. At times group efforts are allowed in the classroom; at other times children are expected to work alone. They soon learn the need for sharing, and that physical conflict is frowned upon. Children also learn that there are appropriate ways of interacting with and addressing teachers. The lessons of the socialization process are sprinkled throughout the entire program.

The social studies program can play an important part in helping children find their roles in the larger community. Children need to understand how society is organized, to learn the shared values, rituals, symbols, and myths. The school's attention to holidays, to stories of historic figures and heroes, to the reading of traditional stories and the singing of traditional songs all contribute to the process. Activities that allow children to inquire into social phenomena can help them better understand the organization of society and thus be better able to act out their roles in appropriate ways.

Values

All education is concerned with values. The basic social values that we wish to communicate to children include concern for the worth of the individual, concepts of freedom and responsibility, the importance of democratic decision making, and concern for the safety of persons and property. These cannot be taught as a separate subject, for they are communicated as much by the way the teachers organize their classrooms and deal with individual children as through separate lessons. If children from minority groups are not respected and valued for the contribution they make in the classroom, then patriotic exercises take on little meaning. If rules of behavior are arbitrarily set by the teacher, children learn not to value rational decision making as a basis for developing behavior controls.

Children learn what to value from inferences drawn from the behavior of significant adults in their lives, by imitating their behavior and assimilating perceived values. Values are learned constantly, not just in single segmented subject-oriented periods. Teachers transmit their values to children all day long. The social system within the classroom and the school operates as an educative force that may be more powerful than any curriculum in developing values.

Bernice Wolfson (1967) suggests that values can be learned by young children through role playing, creative dramatics, literature, and art experiences. She concludes that value development is promoted by providing a wide variety of opportunities for individual selection of goals and activities, by allowing children to consider alternatives and possible consequences of acts and of their own feelings.

In addition to teaching values schools have often been concerned with moral education—helping children distinguish right from wrong. While there is a common moral code, the sources of morality are varied in our country. The home and church are also concerned with the moral education of children. Nor are we at all sure how effective schools can be in teaching morality.

We must also be concerned with children's readiness to learn. Lawrence Kohlberg has identified three levels, with two stages at each level, of moral development in children.

I. PRECONVENTIONAL LEVEL. The child is responsive to cultural rules and labels of good and bad, right and wrong, but interprets them in terms of either the physical consequences of action (punishment and reward, for example) or the physical power of those who enunciate the rules. This level is divided into the punishment and obedience orientation stage and the instrumental orientation stage.

II. CONVENTIONAL LEVEL. Maintaining the expectations of the individual's family, group, or nation is perceived as valuable regardless of immediate and obvious consequences. The attitude is one of conformity, of loyalty, of actively maintaining the order. This level is divided into the interpersonal concordance of "good boy—nice girl" orientation stage and the authority and social order maintaining orientation stage.

III. POSTCONVENTIONAL, AUTONOMOUS, OR PRINCIPLED LEVEL. There is an effort to define moral values and principles apart from authority and apart from the individual's own identification with a group. This level is divided into the social-contract legalistic orientation stage and the universal ethical principle orientation stage (Turiel, 1972).

Kohlberg's framework provides a way of identifying the levels at which children judge moral dilemmas. Most children in their early years would be operating no higher than stage two or three, that is, not beyond the early stage of the conventional level. They can be helped to see what is proper behavior but their discourse about why it is proper will not be related to higher-order ethical principles. Discussions about the reasons for moral judgments might help the teacher identify the children's present stage. Questioning children about their reasons might help move them up to the next stage.

Self-Awareness

All programs, but especially those at the early childhood level, should concern themselves with affective development. Children can be helped to explore their self-concepts, deal with feelings about themselves and others, and develop appropriate means of expressing themselves and interacting with others. Such goals can be achieved through discussions, role playing, storytelling, and other techniques by which children are stimulated to express their feelings or concerns with the teacher, alone, or in a group.

It is important that children learn ways of dealing with their emotions and develop a heightened awareness of themselves, but teachers should be cautioned not to go beyond their own capabilities in exposing feelings with which they themselves might have difficulty in coping. The key to success in these programs is to focus on educational outcomes rather than on cathartic effects.

APPROACHES TO SOCIAL STUDIES

Over the years, many approaches to teaching social studies to young children have been used in schools. As educators became aware of the concrete nature of young children's learning, it was proposed that they deal with elements of the immediate world as a basis for social studies education. The same areas of human activity could be studied within a more expanded concept of humanity as children matured.

Unfortunately, this "here and now" approach was distorted in time so that although the *topics* for study (home, school, and neighborhood) remained in the tradition of early childhood education, the *method* of study (through direct experience) disappeared. The "here and now" approach was divorced from the child's life and treated in the most remote way possible in books.

A number of curriculum development projects in the social studies have been mounted in the past decade, including some at the kindergarten-primary level. Many were designed to make school programs social science oriented. Some projects looked at the social studies as a total field, integrating ideas from the various social sciences. The University of Minnesota *Project Social Studies* and the Taba *Elementary Social Studies* program are examples. Other projects like the *Anthropology Curriculum Project* of the University of Georgia and the *Developmental Economic Education Program* of the Joint Council for Economic Education concerned themselves with only a single discipline. Some concentrated primarily on developing resource units—outlines that could be disseminated to teachers and schools—while others, such as *Materials and Activities for Teachers and Children (MATCH)*, developed boxes of multimedial materials, including books, films, and manipulative materials to be used in carrying out teaching units.

Some programs were primarily cognitive in orientation, such as Lawrence Senesh's *Economic Education Program,* while others, like the *Intergroup Relations Program* of the Lincoln Filene Center for Citizenship and Public Affairs, concerned themselves with the affective domain (Taylor & Groom, 1971).

Each project had its own rationale. In all the projects there is greater recourse to social science materials than had been the case earlier. Many of the materials are still available from the projects or have been published.

Programs of affective early childhood education also exist. The teacher's selection of a program should be determined not only by their worthiness but by the ability to use them to achieve the program's goals. Teachers who are new to an approach might need the security of prescribed materials. Using the program becomes a form of teacher self-education.

A number of programs have been designed to help young children deal with their personal feelings and concerns. The *DUSO: Developing Understanding of Self and Others* program (Dinkmeyer, 1982) contains a teacher's manual, two story books, a set of posters, puppets, recordings and related activities cards and props, role-playing cards, and group discussion cards. The cycles of activities are organized into units to support understanding of self, feelings, others, and attributes of motivation. The *First Things: Values* (1972) program is a collection of filmstrips, records, and teacher's manual that focus on moral dilemmas; children discuss, arrive at a position, and justify it. The *Human Development Program* (Bessell, 1972) contains a theory manual, a curriculum book, and a set of daily instructional strategies focused on "magic circle" discussions related to awareness, mastery, and social interaction. The *Dimensions of Personality* (1972) program includes students' and teachers' manuals, group activity sheets, and a set of ditto masters. Work activities and group discussion are used to build positive self-concepts, competency in work in noncompetitive supportive groups, and basic social competence skills.

Peter Martorella (1975) compared these four programs in relation to teaching models, affective themes, and key roles expected of students and teachers. Martorella warns teachers about using the various programs, suggesting that basic issues related to each program are confused by the absence of any explicit and thorough examination of their theoretical bases and their failure to consistently operationalize program objectives. The lack of teacher-training also presents a problem.

DECIDING WHAT TO TEACH

When young children enter school they have already developed some knowledge of the social and personal world that is related to social studies. Kathy R. Thornberg (1983) found that young children have some understanding of what comprises their family and their own relationship within that family. This knowledge varied with the age of the child but not with the child's sex or family size. Thornberg suggests that the limits of young children's knowledge at the nursery, kindergarten, and first-grade level calls for a social studies program that is concrete and related to children's immediate lives.

Karen F. A. Fox (1978) suggests that children bring to school a "knapsack" of economic knowledge consisting of economic attitudes, unprocessed direct experiences, and cognitive capacities. These capacities place limits on young children's abilities to understand the abstract. Learning words and labels is not the same as developing understandings. Misconceptions may exist that should be clarified; but teachers can develop flexible programs that use children's unprocessed economic experiences.

The same could be said for children's knowledge of other areas of social studies. Children's prior experiences and concrete perceptions of the social world provide a foundation from which children create understandings. What they know about their immediate life also provides a basis for understanding more remote aspects of social life. Through understanding oneself each child can come to understand others.

Goals for the social studies must be related to overall goals of early childhood education. Instructional programs should be based upon concepts of readiness. Children should be given material that is appropriate, in a way that is consistent with their specific level of development.

Children at the nursery school level, for example, can begin to deal with sociological concepts such as *self* or *group* as they explore themselves in relation to others in school and at home. Their understanding of these concepts will be different from that of primary-grade children. Similarly, young children can deal with historical events before they can deal with chronological time and the periodicity of history.

Identifying Goals of Instruction

The process of deciding what and how to teach in an early childhood class involves setting goals, identifying topics, and developing instructional units or programs based upon these goals and related to the topics. Materials and resources need to be gathered; activities need to be planned and implemented. Some ways of judging the program's effects should also be identified.

Kindergarten-primary teachers can adopt a total program—either one from a textbook publisher or one from a curriculum project. However, no one program serves all the purposes of social studies.

In many social studies curricula, the relationship of social studies to the social sciences has been emphasized. The goals of instruction are concerned with understanding basic concepts, generalizations, or conceptual schemes. Such a scheme might be identified for the social studies as an integrated field. Paul Brandwein (1970) has identified the following "cognitive scheme" in the social sciences:

1. Man is a product of heredity and environment.
2. Human behavior is shaped by the social environment.
3. The geographic features of the earth affect man's behavior.
4. Economic behavior depends upon the utilization of resources.
5. Political organizations (governments) resolve conflict and make interaction easier among people (pp. T–16–17).

Other conceptual schemes have been developed that underlie a number of curriculum guides or programs in the social studies.

Such a scheme provides unity to a set of diverse activities. It also helps the teacher fit unplanned learning opportunities into the program. The scheme itself is never learned by children, but becomes a tool for the teacher's use.

Social studies goals cannot be conceived in terms of concept attainment alone. Hilda Taba (1967) identifies four categories of objectives: (1) basic knowledge, (2) thinking, (3) attitudes, feelings, and sensitivities, (4) skills. Basic knowledge includes basic concepts, main ideas, and specific facts. Thinking includes concept formation, the inductive development of generalizations, and application of principles and knowledge. Attitudes, feelings, and sensitivities include the ability to identify with people in different cultures, self-security, open-mindedness, acceptance of change, tolerance of uncertainty and ambiguity, and responsiveness to democratic and human values. Skills include both academic skills, such as map-reading, and research and social skills, such as the ability to work, plan, discuss, and develop ideas in groups.

Identifying Topics for Study

There have traditionally been a limited number of topics for early childhood social studies programs. No topical themes are identified in the literature for the nursery school social studies. At the kindergarten-primary level, these have usually revolved about the immediate environment of the child in school: home and family, the school (including the classroom), the neighborhood (stores, supermarkets, filling stations), and the community (community services, agencies, and workers), as well as transportation and communication. Sometimes comparative studies of communities are suggested, such as the urban community versus the rural or suburban community.

Recent curriculum guides, textbooks, and curriculum projects have widened topics for study by young children. These include family life in far-off countries such as Israel or Japan, broader comparative community study, and the study of concepts from the social sciences, such as *consumers* and *producers* and how they are related—derived from economics—or an understanding of *actions* and *interactions* among people—derived from sociology.

There is a danger that concepts related to these themes will be learned shallowly by rote because of a lack of direct data sources available for the children's inquiry. When topics dealing with the remote in time and space are offered to young children, care must be taken that they have the requisite learning necessary to establish their own meanings and that they have access to appropriate data sources. A program focused on inquiry skills requires that opportunities be provided for collecting and acting upon information. Concepts and generalizations abstracted from such inquiry can later be applied to more remote topics, having few or no opportunities for direct collection of information.

A unit on families in a foreign country can provide meaningful study if the children have some understanding of family structures, roles, and relationships. This might be achieved through studying families in the immediate environment. Teachers can alternate topics dealing with the immediate environment with related topics dealing with the remote in time and space, giving the children an opportunity to apply concepts and generalizations to new situations and to broaden their already developed conceptual schemes. A broad range of resources should be available for this study, including books, audiovisual materials, and collections of artifacts and simulated materials.

Teaching Social Competence

Social competence has been identified as one of the major goals of early childhood education. Social competence includes the behavior and thought processes that result in effective interpersonal relations. Four types of skills have been studied in relation to early childhood programs: situation-specific behavioral repertoires (for example, actions that build friendships), interpersonal solving, role taking, and verbal self-direction and impulse control (Price, 1982). Programs have been developed by Shure and Spivak (1971, 1978) to teach interpersonal skills to four-year-old and five-year-old children by generating alternative social strategies for solving given problems and by helping children think of the consequences of their actions. Similar strategies could be used by teachers as they observe children in class having particular social problems.

Early childhood programs often help children develop role-playing and fantasizing skills primarily through dramatic play activities. It is believed that children's social competence will increase as they gain these role-taking skills. Through assuming another role, children are able to understand and appreciate the perspectives of others.

Children can also be helped to develop greater control over their impulses and their aggressive behavior through early childhood activities. Having children think aloud and verbalize what they intend to do helps children gain control over their impulses. By using this articulated "private speech" they come to know and understand their behavior and thus gain control over its aggressive aspects. Such strategies for teaching young children prosocial behavior have an appropriate place in the kindergarten and primary grades as well as in the preschool.

USING RESOURCES IN PRIMARY SOCIAL STUDIES

Once decisions about goals and topics are made, teachers must organize for instruction. Planning at this point includes deciding about classroom activities, and identifying and organizing resources.

Teachers are the single most important resource in the classroom. They serve as models for teaching values and behaviors. The types of questions asked by teachers can either further inquiry or lead to stereotyped responses. In addition, they set up the classroom, decide on the activities to be included and the range of behavior permitted. They use their knowledge of the children, the resources available, and the topic under study to further children's learning.

Inquiry is important in early learning, but exposition still plays an important role. The teacher's role as teller—as source of information—is never to be underestimated.

Books also provide information not directly accessible to children. Children's information books are available that are well written, understandable, and accurate. Fictional books also reflect the social world, often with greater insight than many informational books. Children need to learn to use these important sources of information.

The oral tradition is important in social studies. Verbal descriptions offered by children and adults are useful sources of information. Group discussions help clarify ideas, and provide teachers with feedback about the concepts and the misconceptions the children might have. A group discussion cannot determine the truth of a child's statement. Having a child check his assertions against those of others, however, can help him become less self-centered and more aware of the external criteria of truth.

Although language is the most often-used symbol system in the social studies area, nonverbal symbols are also used, providing a useful resource for children as both a source of data and a way of recording and communicating data. The most used nonverbal symbol systems are the map and the globe. Primary globes that show the world represented in simple form should be introduced early in school. The globe is a more accurate representation of the world than a flat map. Charts and graphs are other nonverbal symbols children must learn to use.

Maps are important in the social studies. Children can learn to understand maps by developing their own, mapping field trips and other experiences. Children might begin mapping with three-dimensional representation—blocks—and later use pictures, and finally pure symbolizations. They could even invent their own symbol systems as they move to higher levels of abstraction (Richards, 1976).

Using Concrete Materials

The concrete materials of the social studies are representations of social science phenomena, either artifacts out of which we must infer behavior or symbolic representations. For instance, a teacher may bring a map into the

FIGURE 8-1
Maps and globes enable children to conceptualize the physical characteristics of our world.

classroom, or a three-dimensional model. Slides or a movie can help make the children familiar with geographical areas which they cannot visit and explore.

The earliest development of concrete materials for use by young children in social studies education was by Montessori who designed tactile globes and devised map puzzles. By playing with the map pieces, children became familiar with the names of countries and their boundaries. Each puzzle piece had a small knob attached to it to facilitate the children's handling. Similar geographic puzzles are available today.

With the development of the reform kindergarten movement in the United States during the first third of the twentieth century came the development of new educational materials. One of the most useful and flexible of these is *building blocks* (Hirsch, 1974). Two basic variations were developed. Patty Smith Hill devised a set of large floor blocks. Long blocks could be fastened to corner posts with pegs to create structures for children's dramatic play. These were large enough to allow children to play within them, and sturdy enough to take the occasional knocks of five-year-olds. Several variations of this type of block are available today, including hollow blocks, variplay sets, and Sta-Put blocks.

Unit blocks were developed by Caroline Pratt about the same time. The unit block, looking much like a length of two-by-four-inch lumber, is based upon a unit of measure. Each block is either the size of the unit, a multiple, or a fraction of that unit. Thus there are half-unit, quarter-unit, double-unit, and quadruple-unit blocks. Various shapes are added, such as columns, wedges, curves, and semicircles, to make a set. A good set of unit blocks is constructed of hardwood that will not splinter or wear excessively, and is finished so that each block is in exact proportion to the unit. This allows the children to construct complicated buildings that will stand securely for a time.

Because unit blocks are much smaller than the floor blocks, they cannot be used for dramatic play. With unit blocks, the child miniaturizes the world and plays with, not *in,* this miniature world. In the early stages of block play the young child is content to build abstract structural designs. This type of block-building gives way to building individual structures, then large, elaborate, interrelated structures. These may represent either the child's fantasy world or the real world, depending upon the guidance that has been offered, as well as the child's present moods or needs.

Block constructions can represent a home, a school, a shopping center, a neighborhood, a harbor area, or an airport provided there are enough blocks, freedom of ideas, and time available to the children.

Children can incorporate other materials in block construction. Miniature wooden or rubber people representing different family or community roles can be utilized, as can toy cars, trucks, boats, and airplanes. Traffic signs and street lights add to the reality orientation of a construction. Signs written by teachers or children can identify places; strips of paper or plastic represent streets or rivers. A ball of twine can help the children build a suspension bridge.

Imaginative use of many everyday materials enhances the building and provides an outlet for the children's creativity.

Blocks become arbitrary symbols to be used in representing portions of the world. A block construction as a concrete representation provides a good transition to the children's use of maps and other forms of symbol learning in the classroom.

Other forms of concrete material can be used to make models of places. Cardboard cartons, papier-mâché constructions, or other kinds of materials work well. Also available are commercial sets such as *Kinder City, Playschool Village, Lincoln Logs,* and *Lego.*

The dramatic play area of the nursery school and kindergarten with its props can encourage the exploration of family roles and relationships. Dress-up clothes and play props can suggest many situations; hats representing different occupations, in particular, are helpful. A ladder and a length of hose inspire children to work as firemen. A table, cash register, some paper sacks, and empty food containers suggest a supermarket. Sometimes the article in play does not even have to look like what it is representing. A bicycle pump, for example, can be a gasoline pump in a service station, or a fireman's hose. If the teacher is imaginative in the use of materials, the children will soon match, if not surpass, this imaginativeness in play.

Audio and Visual Representations

A range of audiovisual representations can also provide resources for social studies teaching. Still photographs stimulate discussions and provide information. Sets of pictures for use in developing discussions are available. Pictures should be large enough to be viewed by a group of children and contain enough detail without clutter so they can focus on what is important. Pictures can be shown to children in a group discussion setting or placed on bulletin boards. If bulletin boards are used, care should be taken that the arrangement helps the children see what is important. Pictures may also be combined with other display materials.

Magnetic and flannel boards allow the children or teacher to manipulate the materials and change the organization, thus allowing a more active use than simple picture displays provide. Commercial flannel board and magnetic board materials can supplement what teachers develop.

Commercially produced pictures may not contain the specific elements needed to study a particular environment. These materials can be supplemented by locally developed and teacher-developed materials. Fortunately, audiovisual technology is at the point where much good material can be produced by persons having little technical skill.

Instant cameras allow teachers to take still pictures that are immediately available. A range of cameras with automatic features can help teachers produce high quality color slides that can be projected on a screen or placed in a

FIGURE 8-2
A puzzle map helps children
learn about states.

viewer. Eight-millimeter movies and videotape cassettes can be made just as easily.

Sound recordings also provide a good resource for learning. Commercial recordings of songs and stories can be an authentic mirror of a culture. Children can supplement these with tape recordings of their own songs and stories. A trip is recaptured in a classroom through the sounds and pictures recorded. Upon return from an airport visit, for example, children could listen to the announcements of flight arrivals and departures and the roar of the jet engines as a plane taxis to the runway and takes off. Tape recordings can also be made with resource persons or of class discussions. Audio and visual resources combine very effectively.

Exhibits of materials are often useful in communicating information. Studying a service station, for example, might suggest an exhibit of things used and sold there, or an exhibit about petroleum and petroleum products. The first exhibit might include containers for products sold for automobiles, collections of small spare automobile parts, road maps, and simple hand tools used by mechanics. The petroleum exhibit could include a chart of petroleum products and refining processes. Containers of crude oil, lubricating oil, diesel fuel, home heating oil, kerosene, petroleum jelly, and paint thinners could be brought into the room for exhibition. Care should be taken with these materials since they are flammable and dangerous if swallowed. Pictures of these products or their uses can be substituted if deemed wise.

Teachers generally collect materials and arrange displays by themselves, but children and their parents can profitably be involved in this enterprise. Sometimes commercial sources provide display materials for school use. A survey of resources available in a community is wise. Care must be taken that commercially available materials are not distorted by advertising messages, however.

In some areas, local museums lend displays of social studies materials to schools. Dioramas or artifacts may come in kits, some of which are commercially available.

Using Community Resources

Teachers need to look beyond the classroom for learning resources. Resource persons are often quite willing to come to school: representatives of community workers (such as a garbage collector or a fireman), or persons with a particular skill or area of knowledge (a weaver or an anthropologist). A hobbyist, a visitor from a foreign country, a member of a particular ethnic group under study, or an older person who has first-hand historical knowledge might be of great interest.

In using resource persons, the teacher should be sure that both the children and the visitor know the purpose of the visit and that basic ground rules for participation are laid down. Children enjoy acting as hosts in their classrooms.

Field trips into the community need to be properly planned. In addition to the technical planning, the children should be aware of the purpose and focus of the trip. Although chance occurrences can enhance a trip, it is not wise to leave its organization to chance. Field trips need not be elaborate; often the simplest are the most meaningful. A walk to the corner to watch the traffic control operations or a visit to a local supermarket can provide a fruitful experience. Even though children may have had the same experience outside of school, the focus and preparation provided by the teacher can open new learning opportunities as new aspects of a familiar situation unfold.

Using Textbooks and Curriculum Guides

Social studies textbooks are available at the kindergarten-primary level. Often a textbook at this level takes the form of workbooks with pictures for the earliest units, and become a social studies reader at later levels. While many texts follow a story line, newer ones present social science materials directly to young children.

A textbook can provide only a limited amount of information; it should not be the only resource used. Textbooks can provide common knowledge, or pull together knowledge from a variety of sources. A good teachers' manual may also offer helpful suggestions for resources and instructional procedures. Rather than reading about concepts from a book, the children should actively inquire about and develop concepts on their own. Teachers may not want to order a single set of textbooks for an entire class, but have available several copies of many textbooks for children's use.

Curriculum guides can help a teacher develop significant instructional activities. Curriculum guides vary in scope and organization. Some provide a generalized scheme of the subject matter area and are more suggestive; others are highly prescriptive, describing in detail the work that is to take place. Still another kind of guide takes the form of resource units, containing outlines for study and information for planning activities. Often resource units contain more information than a teacher can use at any one time, thereby allowing freedom and flexibility without imposing too great a need to seek out materials and instructional ideas.

In most states and large local school systems, curriculum guides and resources are developed and made available to teachers. Where such materials are not available, teachers must use their own resources. Teaching units are available commercially and can also be found in such magazines as *Early Years* and *Instructor*. Teachers need to assess the worth of available units in terms of the significance of the goals, the practicability of the suggested activities, the availability of resources, and the applicability of the program to the particular class of children. At the preschool level, few resource units are available and teachers must generally rely on their own ingenuity for developing classroom activities.

Insuring Significance in the Use of Resources

Classroom activity can take place that does not produce learning or that causes children to learn the wrong things. Amassing resources and materials and providing children with activities does not insure learning. Although children's involvement is important, the achievement of instructional goals is the prime criterion by which we judge success. Teachers need to select carefully from the resources available, using only those that help children achieve significant and worthwhile goals.

Teachers frequently use free and inexpensive materials because they are readily available, but they should judge the worth of materials as much by the benefits that accrue as by their cost. Criteria for selecting resources include the material's usefulness for achieving instructional objectives, its possible effectiveness compared to other resources, and its appropriateness to the maturity level and background of the particular children. In addition, teachers need to consider the ease of use of the resources and the cost of the materials in relationship to gains, in terms of both initial expense and time and effort expended by children and teacher.

INTEGRATING SOCIAL STUDIES
WITH OTHER ASPECTS OF THE CURRICULUM

Social studies programs often lose their distinctiveness as they become merged with other portions of the program. In the nursery school and kindergarten, portions of the social studies program should be integrated into a general activity period. Children can build with blocks, act out social roles, and look at pictures as a part of the social studies program at the same time other children are busy in other curriculum areas. Even in the primary grades, social studies can integrate a wide range of learning so that the school day is not made up of distinct disparate activities. Other parts of the early childhood programs have much to offer the social studies.

Social studies activities often include constructing models or dioramas. Many arts and crafts activities can be related to social studies, providing children with opportunities to develop expressive skills. At the same time, the products become useful tools for social studies education. Drawing a picture of a supermarket, devising a decorative chart, or making Indian handicrafts are examples of how this can be done. The children can also use paintings, drawings, and constructions to tell what they have learned.

Music and literature of a culture can provide a key to understanding its symbol system and values. Ethnic music, songs, stories, and poetry have an important place in the social studies program. Good literature for children (and adults) provides insight into people, institutions, and social relationships that are hard to describe in straight exposition. Children can empathize with persons by sharing their feelings long before they can intellectually understand them.

The basic concepts of topological geometry, discussed in chapter 7, are just those concepts necessary to understand geography and maps. Being able to locate places and to determine proximity and separation are needed in map reading.

Language arts provide an excellent resource for the social studies. Children can create dramatic presentations or puppet shows in relation to social studies units. They can use dramatic play to act out roles and relationships, and tell or write stories that express the insights gained in a program. They also need to develop command of language skills to be effective in gathering information and communicating the fruits of their learning to others.

Example of a Social Studies Unit
For Young Children

The following is an example of a social studies unit that could be taught. It is an example of what is possible for teachers to do; however, it is not the only way or necessarily the best way to organize a social studies unit.

UNIT FOR FIRST GRADE ON CHILDREN
OF THE PEOPLES' REPUBLIC OF CHINA[1]

Overall Goal

To present to the children activities which will provide a positive and realistic picture of Chinese children and to develop in the children an appreciation and respect for the life-style of Chinese children.

[1]Developed by Prudence Debb Spodek, primary teacher.

Part I

Objective

1. To develop an understanding that children in the United States and China have similar daily activities.

Content Outline

1. Common activities:
   a. interacting with families
   b. going to school
   c. playing with friends
   d. marketing with parents
2. Common social structures:
   a. all belong to a family unit
   b. all engage in some type of work; for children, it is school
   c. all engage in gathering food
   d. all engage in leisure activity; for children, it is play

Teaching Procedures

1. Discuss with children those activities they engage in during the day; list these on a chart. Continue the discussion until the following activities are listed:
   a. going to school
   b. working at school
   c. playing with friends
   Be sure that meaningful activities are discussed and listed.
2. Show pictures of Chinese children engaged in activities in the same areas as those noted by the children. Discuss pictures, focusing on similarities between two life-styles. Students should be encouraged to relate their experiences to those pictured.
3. Picture magazines from China should be available for the children to look at during their free time.
4. Read stories about what children do at school in China.
5. Display a world map and maps of both the United States and China. Point out where we live and where the children in the slides live.

Materials

1. Pictures of Chinese children:
   a. interacting with adults
   b. walking to school
   c. engaged in kindergarten activities
   d. engaged in first-grade activities
   e. playing in the street and in the school yard
   f. shopping with adults in food market and department store

2. Picture magazines from China:
   a. *China Reconstructs*
   b. *Women of China*
   c. *China Pictorial*
3. Story books:
   a. *Pu Hung At Kindergarten.* Beijing, PRC: Foreign Language Press, 1978.
   b. Miao Yin-tang, *Good Children.* Beijing, PRC: Foreign Language Press, 1979.

Part II

Objective

1. To develop an understanding that languages are different, but all are used to communicate.

Content Outline

1. Introduce spoken Chinese words for:
   a. hello — ni hao
   b. goodbye — zai jian

   c. one   — yī   一   six   — liù 六

   two   — èr   二   seven — qī   七

   three — sān 三   eight — bā   八

   four — sì   四   nine — jiū 九

   five — wǔ   五   ten   — shì 十

2. Introduce written Chinese characters for numbers 1 through 10.
3. Use Chinese numbers in simple math activities orally, nonverbally, and in writing.

Teaching Procedures

1. Introduce the Chinese words for hello and goodbye. Use these phrases as often as possible in daily activities. Encourage the children to also use these phrases.
2. a. Introduce the numbers 1 through 10 in Chinese and English, orally.
   b. Use the Chinese numbers in action sentences in which children participate.
   c. Have children make up action sentences using Chinese numbers.

   d. Use charts, flash cards and chalkboard for transition from verbal language to written language. Use activity cards with action sentences for tasks for independent work.

Materials

1. Charts and flash cards with English and Chinese characters for numbers.
2. Set of activity cards on simple math activities using Chinese characters for numbers.
3. Number book: Lew, Gordon. *Little Ming's Number Book.* San Francisco: East-West Publishing Co., 1974.

Part III

Objective

1. To develop an appreciation of different foods and different ways of preparing and eating foods.

Content Outline

1. We need food to live.
2. The Chinese eat many foods that we do. They prepare these foods differently, using different utensils. (Provide experience cooking one of these dishes.)
3. There are some foods the Chinese eat that we do not eat. (Provide experience eating some of these foods.)
4. The Chinese eat with chopsticks and spoons in the "family style" of sharing common dishes. (Provide experiences with chopsticks.)

Teaching Procedures

1. Show pictures of Chinese Food. Have displays of Chinese cooking and eating equipment. Through discussion, have children list what similarities and differences exist between the Chinese cooking equipment and our equipment.
2. Teach children to use chopsticks. Practice picking up objects. Set up an activity center for using chopsticks.
3. Make rice with children and eat it with chopsticks. Add some vegetables and soybean products (for example, snow peas, Chinese cabbage, black mushrooms, bean curd) for a tasting party. (Check what is available at the local supermarket or specialty shops.)

Materials

1. Magazine pictures of children eating with chopsticks.
2. Chopsticks and bowls for children to use.
3. Display of cooking implements: wok, steamer, cooking tools, picture of cleaver, chopping board, boiling pot.
4. Picture of Chinese table setting for family-style meal.
5. Chart illustrating how to use chopsticks. Small objects for children to pick up with their chopsticks.
6. Materials and equipment for tasting party of Chinese vegetables and soybean products.

Part IV

Objectives

1. To develop skills in doing art projects that children in China might do.
2. To develop an appreciation for the art projects.

Content Outline

1. Introduce paper cuttings.
2. Experiences with cutting and making designs using paper and scissors.
3. Introduce watercolor paintings.
4. Experience with watercolors and Chinese watercolor brushes.
5. Introduce paper folding and experimentation in making different shapes and/or objects out of paper by folding it.

Teaching Procedures

1. Present display of Chinese paper cuts. Have children describe them and express their thoughts and feelings about them.
2. a. Demonstrate how to make a rooster cut-out. See Tempko, Florence, *Folk Crafts for World Friendship.* New York: Doubleday, 1976, pp. 42–43.
   b. Using lightweight red construction paper, have children draw designs on them. Encourage large and simple designs. Have the children cut the designs out, giving help as needed. Place designs on windows as silhouettes. (This may be a difficult project for some.)
3. Present watercolors. Have children describe them and express their thoughts and feelings about them and the content.
4. Introduce Chinese watercolor brushes. Set up independent ac-

tivity for children to experiment freely with the watercolors and brushes.

5. Introduce making simple shapes with squares of paper and have children make their own. See Soong Ma-ying. *The Art of Chinese Paper Folding for Young and Old.* New York: Harcourt, Brace Jovanovich, Inc., 1948.

6. Display all art work.

7. Share book on Chinese children's art work. Encourage free discussion about the pictures.

Materials

1. Display of Chinese paper cuts depicting children in different sports and flowers.

2. Watercolors of Chinese landscapes by contemporary Chinese artists.

3. Red and black lightweight construction paper, scissors, chalk, nine-by-twelve-inch watercolor paper, watercolors, conventional brushes, Chinese watercolor brushes, and eight-inch square origami paper.

4. Book: *Selected Drawings by Chinese Children.* Edited by the Chinese People's National Committee for the Defense of Children. Beijing, PRC: Foreign Language Press, 1979.

Part V

Objective

1. To introduce children to games that Chinese Children play and to develop an appreciation for these games.

Content Outline

1. Introduce the following games:
    a. football
    b. skipping rope
    c. "well rope" (string figures)
2. Experience in making some of the equipment needed to play the games.

Teaching Procedures

1. Introduce rules for each game and necessary equipment and have small groups play the games. Encourage playing the games during recess and other free times.
    Football: Make a "ball" about four inches in diameter by wadding newspapers together. Stick several long feathers in the ball and

strengthen by winding string around the ball. Children kick the ball to one another with their feet. It should not touch the ground or be hit with the hands. If the ball does touch the ground, start again.

Skipping Rope: Two children hold an elastic rope made of rubber-bands and pull, wiggle it and raise it; one child jumps over the rope at a time without touching the top. Have children save news-paper rubberbands and link them together to make a rope about six feet long.

"Well Rope": These are string figures that we know as "cats cradle." Two persons and one loop of string are needed. Four hands are needed to show the figures that the children can make. They do look difficult, but once string is in hand, the children will be able to follow the teacher's directions. Be sure the teacher has mastered the figures! Diagrams and instructions can be found in Jayne Caroline Furness. *String Figures and How to Make Them.* New York: Dover, 1962, pp. 324–336.

Materials

1. Newspapers, feathers, string, rubberbands.

Part VI

Objective

1. To expose children to children's stories written and illustrated in China.

Content Outline

1. Read Chinese Children's stories in English.
2. Discuss stories and children's reactions to them.
3. Individual projects based on stories.

Teaching Procedures

1. Read stories to children. Discuss the story content.
2. Have books available for independent reading and browsing.
3. Have individual children retell a story, describe a character, extend the story line, or speculate about the story.
4. Have children illustrate a favorite story.

Materials

Books (These books are published by the Foreign Language Press in Beijing, Peoples' Republic of China.)

Chang Mao-chiu, *The Little Doctor.* 1965
Chao Fu-hsing, *Hunting with Grandad.* 1965
Chiang, Mi, *Gold Flower and the Bear.* 1979
Chin Chin, *Fun in the Garden.* 1965
Ho Yi, *Adventures of a Lead Pencil.* n.d.
Hsieh Chi-kuei, *Hello! Hello! Are You There?* n.d.
Hung Hsun-tao, *The Magic Brush.* n.d.
Kuan Hua, *The Fox.* n.d.
Miller, Grambs, and Zhao Long-yi, *Xiao Ming and Katie Visit the Beijing Zoo.* 1980
Sun You-jin, *The Adventures of a Rag Doll.* 1980
Wang To-ming, *Duckling Goes A-Sailing with His Friends.* n.d.
Xu Guang-yu, *Why Do Rabbits Have Short Tails?* 1981
Little Chen and the Dragon Brothers. Adapted by Can Xi and Jian Wen from *Folktales from Guilin,* 1980
Looking after Myself. 1979

Evaluation

1. Did the Unit provide experiences and activities which would enable the children to understand and appreciate the life-style of Chinese children?
2. Did the children demonstrate this understanding?
3. What skills did the children develop? How were these demonstrated?

Additional Books

Fawdry, Marguerite. *Chinese Childhood.* Woodbury, England: Barrons, 1977.
Lonsdale, Anne. *Oxford Children's Reference Library: China.* London: Oxford University Press, 1971.
Lo Hui-min. *The Story of China.* Sydney, Australia: Angus and Robertson, 1970.
Qi Wen. *China: A General Survey.* Beijing, PRC: Foreign Language Press, 1979.
Tian Yuan. *Chinese Folk Toys and Ornaments.* Beijing, PRC: Foreign Language Press, 1980.

This unit is designed to help children use what they already know about themselves, their friends, and their families in American culture to understand something of another culture. There are other ways that children can use what they understand about their own social experiences to extend their knowledge beyond the immediate. This is not only important for developing multicultural understanding but for providing a way in which children can develop an understanding of a broad range of social activities and social structures, whether they are directly accessible or remote.

A study of the families of the children in class (done carefully and with permission) can help children see that there is a range of social structures within the community and that there are similarities and differences in the functions of family units. A study of community workers can help children understand what people do at work, whether they produce goods or services, for example. This can help children to see the relationship between what workers do and what people want and need in a community.

For each topic the teacher must view social studies as a method of inquiry rather than as a body of information to pass on to children. Additional topics can also be used, such as a unit on Mexican-Americans or on Black Americans, taught within a framework of anthropology, that presents significant learnings from both a social science and human relations point of view. A Black Studies curriculum has been developed with units in social studies—as well as language arts, art, and music—that could be easily integrated into a social studies program (Spodek, 1976). Studies of other ethnic groups are also worth including in the early childhood program. Ours is a multicultural nation. While the social studies program must deal with elements of the majority culture, elements of other cultures impact on children of both minority and majority groups and should be included. These provide opportunities for children to cope with a multicultural existence and to enjoy the benefits of this diversity.

A social studies program in the early years might not help children learn the names of presidents in order or the capitals of countries throughout the world. It should, however, help them gain a better understanding of themselves in relation to the social world in which they live. In addition, it should provide children with reasonable and verifiable ways of finding out about their social world. Linked with an understanding of the physical world, such knowledge helps them begin to make reasonable decisions about some of the things that happen to them.

REFERENCES

BESSEL, H. *Human development program.* San Diego: Human Development Training Institute, 1972.

BRANDWEIN, P. F., et al. *Principles and practices in the teaching of social sciences: Concepts and values.* New York: Harcourt, Brace Jovanovich, Inc., 1970.
Dimensions of personality. Dayton, Ohio: Pflaum/Standard, 1972.

DINKMEYER, D. *Developing an understanding of self and others (Duso-1)* (Revised). Circle Pines, Minn.: American Guidance Service, 1982.
First things values. Pleasantville, N.Y.: Guidance Associates, 1972.

FOX, K. F. A. What children bring to school: The beginnings of economic education. *Social Education,* 1978, *42,* 478–481.

HIRSCH, E. S. (Ed.). *The block book*. Washington, D.C.: National Association for the Education of Young Children, 1974.

HUNKINS, F. P., JETER, J., AND MAXEY, P. *Social studies in the elementary schools*. Columbus, Ohio: Chas. E. Merrill, 1982.

MARTORELLA, P. H. Selected early childhood affective learning programs: An analysis of theories, structure and consistency. *Young Children*, 1975, *30*, 289–301.

PRICE, G. G. Cognitive learning in early childhood education: Mathematics, science, and social studies. In B. Spodek (Ed.). *Handbook of research in early childhood education*. New York: Free Press, 1982.

RICHARDS, B. Mapping: An introduction to symbols. *Young Children*, 1976, *31*, 145–56.

SHURE, M. B., AND SPIVACK, G. *Solving interpersonal problems: A program for four-year-old nursery children*. Philadelphia: Department of Mental Health Sciences, 1971.

SHURE, M. B., AND SPIVACK, G. *A mental health program for kindergarten children*. Philadelphia: Department of Mental Health Sciences, 1978.

SPODEK, B. Social studies for young children: Identifying intellectual goals. *Social Education*, 1974, *38*, 40–45.

SPODEK, B., AND OTHERS. *A black studies curriculum for early childhood education* (Rev. ed.). Urbana, Ill.: ERIC/EECE, 1976.

TABA, H. *Teachers' handbook for elementary social studies*. Reading, Mass.: Addison-Wesley, 1967.

TAYLOR, B. L., AND GROOM, T. L. *Social studies education projects: An ASCD index*. Washington, D.C.: Association for Supervision and Curriculum Development, 1971.

THORNBERG, K. R. Young children's understanding of familial concepts with implications for social studies units. *Social Education*, 1983, *47*, 138–141.

TURIEL, E. Stage transition in moral development. In R. Travers (Ed.). *Second handbook of research on teaching*. Skokie, Ill.: Rand McNally, 1972.

WOLFSON, B. J. Values and the primary school teacher. *Social Education*, 1967, *31*, 37–38.

SUGGESTED READINGS

JAROLIMEK, J. *Social studies in elementary education* (6th ed.). New York: Macmillan, 1982.

MICHAELIS, J. U. *Social studies for children in a democracy* (7th ed.). Englewood Cliffs, N.J.: Prentice-Hall, 1980.

MITCHELL, L. S. *Young geographers*. Orig. pub. The John Day Co., 1934. New York: Bank Street College of Education, 1971. (Distributor: New York: Agathon Press.)

PAGANO, A. L. (Ed.). *Social studies in early childhood: An interactionist point of view*. Washington, D.C.: National Council for the Social Studies, 1978.

ROBISON, H. F., AND SPODEK, B. *New directions in the kindergarten*. New York: Teachers College Press, 1965.

SARACHO, O. N., AND SPODEK, B. (Eds.). *Understanding the multicultural experience in early childhood education*. Washington, D.C.: National Association for the Education of Young Children, 1983.

SCHMIDT, V., AND MCNEILL, E. *Cultural awareness: A resource bibliography*. Washington, D.C.: National Association for the Education of Young Children, 1978.

SEEFELT, C.   *Social studies in early childhood education.* Columbus, Ohio: Chas. E. Merrill, 1977.

SPODEK, B., ET AL.   *A black studies curriculum for early childhood education* (Rev. ed.). Urbana, Ill.: ERIC Clearinghouse in Elementary and Early Childhood Education, 1976.

WALSH, H. M.   *Introducing the young child to the social world.* New York: Macmillan, 1980.

9

The Expressive Arts

The expressive arts have traditionally held honored positions in early childhood education. The early Froebelian kindergartens included music and art activities in the form of the *Occupations* and the *Mother's Songs and Games.* Both of these were carefully patterned according to explicit directions and gave children opportunities to be actively involved in making and doing, though not on being creative.

Such is the case in the art activities found in many contemporary programs for young children. The kindergarten that gives every child exactly the same paper construction leaves no room for the child's interpretation of reality or their outpouring of ideas and feelings. Music, movement, and art can serve as vehicles for creative expression, and can enhance individuality and creativity.

There are those who believe that creativity flourishes only when children are given free rein with material, and that any requirement for their activity is an unnecessary and stifling imposition. Others feel that children left unbridled cannot develop the inner discipline and self-reflection necessary for creative activity. In reality, children can benefit from a variety of structures and degrees of adult intervention. Formal relationships between teacher and children do not necessarily lead to stereotyped activity. Involvement in a Froebelian kindergarten and training in the prescribed use of blocks—one of the Froebelian *gifts*—is seen as having a major formative influence on Frank Lloyd Wright, one of the most creative of American architects (Clements, 1975).

The arts are to be valued in school as a way of using feelings, sensitivities, and understandings that require expression in a nonrational, often nonlinear form. Shaping the child's expression into two- or three-dimensional constructions, into sound patterns, or into the deliberate development of movement patterns extends his way of understanding the world in a manner not possible through the sciences or conventional verbal description. This is a personal way of knowing, but one that can be shared with others.

According to Nancy R. Smith (1983), children build basic concepts of the world of objects and how they work, and of their own effectiveness within it through their experiences. This world of materials lends itself to representation. It is through representation that children create meanings. Artistic representations have a narrative strand (the idea or the story), an emotional strand (the feelings communicated), and a compositional strand (the interest and unity created by the arrangements of elements). The aesthetic qualities of artistic work are rooted in the quality of the meanings and the organization of each strand and the whole.

CREATIVITY

"Usually creativity is thought of as being constructive, productive behavior . . . a contribution from the individual" (Lowenfeld & Brittain, 1982, p. 69). Mary L. Marksberry (1963) identifies three types of creative products: unique communications, plans or proposed sets of operations, and sets of abstract relations. Music, movement, and art activities generally produce creative products in the first category. A painting, a piece of sculpture, a musical selection, or a series of movements are of this nature. Other areas of the curriculum, such as language arts—including the child's own stories, poems, or special descriptive phrases—are unique communications. Personal interpretations of other people's works might also be so considered.

The other two types of creative products can be found throughout the program. The techniques for learning science and social studies lead children to create plans and proposed sets of operations that often result in the creation of sets of abstract relations.

Creativity can exist in the total program. But teaching music, movement, and art cannot be understood only in terms of creativity, for in dealing with them, one must deal with concepts of aesthetics as well. The young child needs to be surrounded by beautiful things to begin to appreciate and understand beauty. He also must learn to criticize his own work and that of others constructively to develop criteria of aesthetic appreciation. Such criticism need not be negative or sophisticated. As children experience the creative process themselves and share their expressions with others, and as they mature to the point that they can separate themselves from their products, they can learn to become critics and accept criticism themselves.

Elwyn Richardson (1964) describes how children develop sensitivity to aesthetic components as a result of the criticism of their art work. Such criticism heightened their appreciation of the individuality of others and helped them develop more artistic approaches to materials.

The Creative Process

Gladys Andrews (1954) suggests that the creative process involves three phases: "(1) The child and his creative power, feelings and imagination, (2) the action or interaction of his experience, (3) and his outward form of expression" (p. 21). The experience of putting one's expressions into concrete form through words, paints, musical rhythms, or movement through space is the culmination of a chain of events. Each aspect of the creative process needs to be supported in the classroom. Children's feelings and imagination can be supported indirectly. Children must be given opportunities to freely use their imaginations, with the products of imaginative thought accepted and cherished. Children must feel a degree of acceptance in a climate in which they are viewed as competent individuals, important and worthy.

Children should be provided with a broad range of experiences. The child who can see, hear, taste, smell, and touch a great variety of things has access to the raw material of creative expression. Jeannette F. Lacey (n.d.) suggests training children in visual literacy to enable them to look, see, select, evaluate, record, correct, and restate their experiences. Children can be made aware of the examples of beauty in their natural environment and the world of their personal vision and response. She suggests helping them learn the elements of artistic composition—line, shape, color, value, and texture—in this way. Perhaps this idea could be generalized to other areas of personal sensation as well, to provide a broad basis for children's creative expression.

Sensory perceptions are meaningless, however, when provided in isolation. Giving children a set of color chips, a range of tone blocks, or a board covered with various textured materials may help them become aware of sensory experiences or learn to name and categorize them, but the creative process may be thwarted if these isolated sensory explorations become the sum and substance of their education. Creativeness grows out of experiencing the rich fabric of sensory images woven into the complexities of real life. Children who are taken to the docks of a seaport can not only perceive the visual images of ships, cargo, and machines but also have this experience heightened by the smell of salt water, the feel of damp air on their skin, and the sounds of seagulls. Personally meaningful portions of the experience can then be represented through the art media.

Similarly, the child who is allowed to sit for long periods of time watching the movement of a lonely insect in a field—seeing how it travels from place to place, how it eats and collects its food—has a perception of the natural world far richer than that provided through a book. Experiencing the world in its realistic state is an important part of the creative process.

The opportunity to interact with their environment is just as important for children. This interaction may be physical, as they move out and talk to people or touch things. It can also be intellectual, an internal process that allows them to reflect on experience and abstract significant aspects for further study. They can compare recent experiences with ones remembered from an earlier time, comparing perceptions and interactions with those of other people. The abstraction of personal meaning from the surrounding world provides the raw material from which creative expressions are derived, while the expressive act serves as a way to integrate these meanings into mental structures.

As children develop outward forms of expression, they learn to master media so that expression is deliberate rather than accidental. This means teaching to use the self—body for movement, hands for painting and modeling—to control the media. Paints and brushes become an extension of the person, as do musical instruments, words, and all the raw material out of which we create artistic products.

The quality of the materials and tools we provide in early childhood classes are important. They must be able to extend rather than limit possibilities. A sturdy brush for painting is better than a string or a piece of sponge if it allows greater control of the expression. Modeling clay that is malleable and responsive is more useful than oil-based Plasticine because the child has greater control over it. The attractiveness of the final product is not the criterion for success. The degree to which the product—painting, pot, movement pattern, or song-theme—was a deliberate outgrowth of the child's intent and to which it extended the ability to express oneself determines the success and the worthiness of the activity.

The young child is to some extent stimulus-bound. The use of a medium of expression becomes a significant experience that, in effect, transforms itself. Colors dripping into each other on a painting may elicit new forms and new colors that will stimulate opportunities not even present at first. These explorations should be supported, for it is through the individual exploration of the medium that the child develops control.

DEVELOPMENTAL STAGES IN ART

Improving artistic expression is not merely a matter of teaching children control. The stages of human development influence the child's creations as much as anything else. A substantive difference exists between children and adults that cannot be explained on the basis of experiences alone. Every person goes through a series of metamorphoses in development so that each level is different in kind from the one preceding it and those following it.

Levels of artistic development have been identified as being similar to those of intellectual development. Victor Lowenfeld and W. Lambert Brittain (1982), describe a scheme of stages in the artistic development of children. The levels of development that are roughly approximate to the early childhood period would include the *scribbling* stage (ages two to four), the *preschematic* stage (ages four to seven), and the *schematic* stage (ages seven to nine).

Between the ages of two and four, children in the scribbling stage have a kinesthetic experience through drawing. They move through longitudinal, then circular motions, becoming more coordinated as they mature. Children first experiment with materials, then find likenesses within their drawing to objects in the real world, thus coming up with "names" to give the drawing.

Between the ages of four and seven, children in the preschematic stage discover the relationships between drawing, thinking, and reality. Although a continuous change occurs in the symbols created in drawings, children start out with an idea of the objects they want to represent. They begin to develop representational forms, although these may not be related in the picture as in reality. They are also developing form concepts.

When children move to the schematic stage, between seven and nine, they begin to create realistic representations of people and things. They learn to use color and space realistically, and to depict movement in pictures. The children then move on to more mature stages of artistic development.

Lowenfeld and Brittain's conception of stages in art closely parallels Jean Piaget's stages of intellectual development. It is quite possible that art as an expression of the child, builds upon perceptions and conceptions and levels of muscular control and coordination. It is to some extent a function of general intellectual development.

Geraldine Dimondstein (1974) suggests that the use of stages to explain changes in children's art products has tended to inhibit the teachers' fresh perceptions of the specific qualities of an art product. It has also perpetuated the myth that the teacher should leave children to grow through these stages. These dangers grow from a conception of development as maturation. Given an interactionist view of development, a conception of stages can help a teacher establish tentative expectations for children. It can also help interpret children's products and determine what are the best next steps for them and how they can be helped to take those steps. Thus assessment and future planning for increased learning can be enhanced.

What children do or how they develop does not predetermine how they should be taught or what the content of instruction ought to be. It does, however, establish a framework within which goals can be determined and expectations set. It also *suggests* directions for education, helping them move through present stages to more mature stages. A child in nursery school, for example, should not be expected to create representational paintings and drawings. Nor should a kindergarten child be expected to be able to draw a room with all the objects shown in proper size and place relationship to one another.

The concept of stages taken by itself does not suggest that the teacher ought to wait for the child to mature. The teacher's role is to guide the child to arrive at more mature ways of handling media and creating expressions. A knowledge of stages of development provides a series of benchmarks that the teacher can use in directing the child's learning.

ARTS AND CRAFTS

Arts and crafts activities are often considered less important in the primary grades than in the nursery school and kindergarten. Too often the arts and crafts work is designed solely to insure that a finished product will be presentable and each child will have something to take home. This makes for good public relations, for parents can see that the children are doing *something* in class.

There are times when it is appropriate to have the children make a product for the home such as the Christmas or Mother's Day gift. It is unfortunate, however, when concern for the image of the school takes precedence over learning, for it is not the product that is the important goal of the school, but the child's growing mastery over materials. The completed work of the child has significance only in that it provides the teacher with insights into what has been learned and what difficulties still must be mastered.

The media of art most productive for children in the early years are those that can be used at any age level. Naomi Pile (1973) identifies the basic art materials as paint, clay, and drawing and collage material. These are basically formless in themselves and offer endless possibilities for change, mastery, surprise, and self-reflection. Paints, clay, drawing, and collage, for example, can be used by the three-year-old as well as by the mature artist. One does not limit a medium to a particular age level. Nor does the child's prior experience with the material need to concern the teacher, because in his developing competency, the young child will continue to see fresh possibilities in these media that represent an outgrowth of increased mastery and the more mature stage of artistic development. The materials, however, do need to be introduced in fresh ways through the years.

Two-dimensional Art Work

Much of the art work we provide for children in the early years relates to the use of materials on a flat surface. Paints, crayon, and collage material are concerned with only a single plane, although collage work can have depth as a result of overlaying various materials and textures. The child's concern is primarily with line, shape, and color.

Painting is one of the mainstays of the early childhood program. In many classrooms, an easel is accessible to the children for a good part of the day. The top of a table or a bit of floor space is just as good. The level surface, as a matter of fact, will limit the amount of dripping that occurs during the painting. Teachers should organize the area used so that cleanup is as simple as possible, having children spread papers under the painting and making sponges and paper towels readily available. Keeping paints in containers that can be covered enables art work to continue with a relative degree of administrative simplicity.

Tempera paints may be either powdered or liquid in form. If powdered, they should be mixed thickly enough so that the colors will be rich and the paint opaque. With young children, the primary colors (red, blue, and yellow) along with black and white are adequate; intermediate colors can be added later. Color mixing using a cookie sheet palette can lead to new discoveries.

Children at this stage experiment with form and color, moving their own arms to stimulate the shapes that form on the paper. These experiments often have rhythm, balance, and interest. Many children appear to have an instinctive aesthetic sense and their abstract paintings sometimes resemble works of art.

Although the young child should be encouraged to explore and experiment, simple techniques can be demonstrated: wiping the brush so that it is not overloaded with paint, cleaning brushes before using them for other colors, mixing colors in specific proportions to achieve desired results, and placing the right brush into the right container of paint. However, a color mixture that results from an improperly placed brush or an accidental drip can lead to exciting learnings.

Brushes should be large and rather stiff so they respond easily to movement. Several sizes should be available. Most of the painting in classrooms is done on unprinted newsprint. The standard size used is eighteen-by-twenty-four-inch; paper of a different size, shape, or even texture will stimulate new ways of painting. The classified section of a newspaper or a piece of wrapping paper with a small design might also be used for painting.

Tempera painting is usually considered an individual activity. Even when two children are painting together at the easel, they are seldom interacting, for their work is separated. Children, however, enjoy painting side by side or in groups. A double easel or the floor supports painting as a group activity as does mural painting.

Murals can be painted on large sheets of brown wrapping paper, which many schools keep available. At first, young children's murals will actually be collections of individual paintings. There is usually little group planning, and teachers often find it useful to simply allocate space on different parts of the

FIGURE 9-1
Murals painted by children can be shared with the entire class.

paper to different children. As the children mature and gain experience, they can begin to plan toward a unified product.

The teacher's role in painting is not to have the children copy models but to encourage them to explore the media, to observe their progress and guide it, providing new techniques consistent with their development and needs.

Wax crayons are almost universally found in early childhood classrooms. Their use requires little teacher preparation; they seldom create much of a mess, and they are easily available. Large hexagonal or half-round crayons are available that make bold, controllable strokes and that will not roll off the table. Children may be given their own sets of crayons, or crayons may be kept in a class pool. Large sheets of manila paper are useful for coloring with crayons, but other kinds of paper can be used as well.

As the children learn to use crayons, they can also be encouraged to mix crayoning with other media. The waxy crayon drawing provides a surface to which tempera paint will not adhere, so covering the surface with a single coat of paint allows the crayon drawing to stand out in interesting relief.

Children can use colored or white chalk at a blackboard. Chalk can also be used on paper; wetting the paper with water or buttermilk makes the colors show up more brilliantly, and spraying a fixative on the chalk drawings keeps them from rubbing off the paper.

Cutting, tearing, and pasting paper to create interesting designs has long been a school activity. Papers of adequate stiffness can be folded to create three-dimensional shapes; the Japanese art of origami creates three-dimensional forms by folding a piece of paper. Interesting designs can also be created at the two-dimensional level. For very young children, the teacher could prepare various-shaped pieces of colored paper to be pasted on a background, and as children develop competency in using scissors, they can create their own shapes.

Other kinds of materials can increase the variety of textures, colors, and shapes in collage. Teachers might pick up many scavenged materials in their daily travels rather than order them from a supply house. A variety of these, organized so that teachers and children can select them without too much difficulty, enhances an art program.

Various kinds of special paper and cardboard, pieces of fabric of various sizes, shapes, colors, and textures, bits of rope and yarn, feathers, buttons, colored sawdust, metal foil, and almost any other kind of material can be shaped, cut, pasted, and otherwise included in a creation. Children should be offered a limited variety of these materials at any one time, but can also be encouraged to think of new materials. This may require other ways of attaching them: rubber cement, white glue, staples, and cellophane tape.

Finger paints are often difficult for children to control, but they offer the child release not matched by other media. The child has direct contact with the medium. For finger painting, glossy nonabsorbent paper is available from school supply houses; glazed shelf paper may also be used. Sometimes the painting can be done on the plastic surface of a table. When the child is through a print can be made by carefully placing a paper over the painting, pressing it down firmly all over, and carefully lifting it off.

There are many ways of printing designs. Dipping an interesting textured or shaped object into a shallow dish of tempera paint and pressing it firmly on a sheet of paper works well. Sponges, grainy ends of wooden boards, and vegetables such as carrots or potatoes are among the many materials that can be used. A design can be carved into these materials to enhance the printing. With the youngest children, the teacher can create the designs and let the children print. Using different colors and patterns makes this an interesting medium.

Three-dimensional Constructions

In the early years, the three-dimensional media include woodworking, cardboard box constructions, clay modeling, and the creation of mobiles and stabiles.

Children get a great deal of pleasure out of working with wood—the simple activity of hammering and sawing is often enough to satisfy very young children. Unfortunately, teachers in many classes hesitate to include woodworking, usually because they lack experience with carpentry and tools. Hammers, saws, and other tools, if improperly used, can injure children. But young children can develop a respect for tools and skills and learn to use them safely.

A woodworking area should promote positive activities and avoid danger; it requires a certain amount of isolation from other activities. Tools and supplies should be stored so they are readily accessible, and be in good order and in proper repair, with saws sharp and hammer handles firmly embedded in the heads. A good supply of soft wood such as common pine is necessary. Wood can often be collected from the scraps of local lumber yards. A number of accessories can be included as the children mature in their ability to use wood and tools.

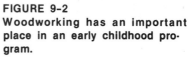

FIGURE 9-2
Woodworking has an important place in an early childhood program.

Lightweight but good quality hammers and short crosscut saws should be provided. Sandpaper, block planes, rasps, and wood files help children smooth their woodwork. A brace and drill bits and hand drill are useful. Screwdrivers can be added as children learn to use screws as well as nails for fastening boards together. A woodworking vise, workbench or saw horses, and "C" clamps are useful, too.

Children usually begin by building simple constructions. These can often be put together with nails and glue. As the projects are elaborated, teachers can add dowels, empty paper rolls, spools, and just about anything they and the children find useful. Woodworking projects can be painted with tempera and then covered with shellac or lacquer so the color will not run; enamel paint is harder to work with and to clean up.

Clay modeling has been a mainstay in early education for many years. Potter's clay is soft and malleable, and can be used over and over. If it has dried out, water can be added to it; if it is too wet, it can be left to dry.

Very young children enjoy manipulating clay. They knead it, pound it, roll it into balls or snakes, flatten it, break it up, and push it all together again. Playing with the clay often takes precedence over creating something. Later, children learn to make pinch pots, pulling the clay into shapes and tearing off pieces. They create figures, adding pieces of clay—heads, arms, and legs—to a rolled body to create people and animals. After a while, they can even learn to build pots, using the coil or slab method.

After the children are through working with clay, they are often content to put it back into the crock. When they wish to save what they have made, however, the clay can be dried slowly and then painted. If a kiln is available in the school, it is exciting to watch the clay transformed by the heat. Care should be taken, however, that work to be fired in a kiln is sturdy and will not explode or come apart. If the children have worked over the clay for a while, it may not need to be wedged. The pieces should not be too thick and the appendages should be securely attached. The teacher might even wish to glaze some of the children's work.

In some classrooms, other modeling material such as Plasticine, an oil-based clay, is sometimes substituted for clay. Although Plasticine is not as responsive to modeling, and the children's work cannot be preserved, it can be used again and again and will not dry out. Some teachers also use modeling dough. It can be purchased commercially or made out of simple household ingredients—salt, flour, and water.

Simple constructions—houses, cash registers, rocket ships, or model automobiles—can be made out of cardboard boxes and cartons that are cut up, pasted together, elaborated with paper, and painted and colored. The skills the children have developed in two-dimensional work can be elaborated and used in endless constructions.

Mobiles and stabiles are three-dimensional designs. Mobiles are designed to move; stabiles remain stationary. They are created by combining a variety of material in interesting fashions—dowels, tongue depressors, wire coat hangers, pipe cleaners, metal foil, yarn, balls, sponges, rubber bands, and so on. Bases for stabiles can be easily fashioned out of clay or styrofoam; mobiles are designed to hang, and do not need a base.

Young children can weave on simple looms early in their school careers. "Loopers," using cotton loops and simple metal looms, are a beginning. Teachers can also make simple looms out of squares of corrugated cardboard. Half-inch-deep slots in two opposite ends allow the child to thread the loom; the yarn can then be woven back and forth until a square is completed. Simple looms can also be made by driving nails into the edges of wooden boxes or frames.

Children can begin to sew designs onto pieces of burlap with tapestry needles. In time, these can be combined with sewn pieces of felt or a similar fabric to create interesting pictures.

The classroom should be a place where children can explore material. Accomplishment can be acknowledged and criticism provided, but only in the spirit of guidance and to move children to further accomplishments. This work is the children's way of expressing themselves and becomes personally important.

MUSIC

As in art, children may go through stages in music. Frances Aronoff (1979) uses Jerome Bruner's conception of three modes of learning—*enactive, iconic,* and *symbolic*—in her framework of music education: "(1) the *enactive* through action and manipulation; (2) the *iconic* through perceptual organization and inquiry—aural, kinesthetic and visual; and (3) the *symbolic* through words and symbols" (p. 7). She suggests that the enactive and iconic modes are the ways in which young children know music. They respond readily to the elements of music through movement and play. Without the use of symbols they are able to organize their perceptions of and responses to music, forming mental structures that become the basis of understanding, remembering, and creating music. This use of a Brunerian framework also suggests the development of concepts in music as a function of general intellectual development. Aronoff defines the discipline of music as including concepts of music, concepts about music, a repertoire of songs and patterns and qualities of sound, and musical skills. Skills include listening, singing, playing, moving, and reading and writing music. A music program in early childhood education, therefore, should provide children with opportunities to listen to music, learn to understand its elements, reproduce these through singing and playing instruments, and relate bodily movement to musical expression. Creation of musical compositions or movements should also be included. The music program must relate to other parts of the curriculum, especially the language arts and social studies, to help children learn about the uses of music in any culture. Such a program provides opportunities for them to deal critically with music, to learn to reproduce it, and to learn to express themselves through it.

Creative music and movement are noisy activities—a teacher cannot allow a child to experiment with the sounds of a drum while a reading lesson is in progress. Specific times should be set aside, and musical noise and movement controlled so that real learning can occur.

Many music and movement sessions are organized as large group activities; children also need times to work alone or in small groups. During the activity period, a portion of the room can be set aside for movement. Musical instruments can be furnished for use by a few children; others can listen to a tape recorder or phonograph, possibly using headphones. The music that children create in their ongoing activities can be recorded or transcribed by the teacher. A multipurpose room, the play yard, an auditorium, or a gymnasium are often available for a portion of the day for such activities.

Music programs for the early years of school generally consist of singing, playing simple instruments, listening, and creative movement. Often creative movement involves children in mime and creative dramatics. Even when musical activities are the responsibility of a music teacher, the classroom teacher has some obligation. There are many opportunities in a school day that support music education and many ways to integrate music into children's learning.

Singing

Almost all children enjoy singing. They sing loudly, often with more energy than skill. Young children pick up songs they hear and repeat them to the best of their ability, sometimes repeating a phrase over and over, often mispronouncing or not completely learning the words. At times the pitch is off, but this seldom deters a young child in his continued singing. A teacher should capitalize on this enthusiasm. Greater adherence to melody and verse comes with experience and repetition.

Robert Smith (1970) has designed a singing program to develop and improve children's vocal accuracy, range, and quality. Songs chosen to help this development, according to Smith, should continue to appeal to children after many repetitions; there should be melodic phrase repetition, repeated word phrases, and the appropriate range for the child's particular stage of vocal development.

The piano and other instruments such as the autoharp, guitar, or ukelele can be played to accompany the children's singing. However, some music educators feel that instrumental accompaniment is unnecessary for singing, even with young children. The Kodaly method suggests that human voices be used to accompany other human voices, leading to a program of unaccompanied singing and simple two-part singing for primary children. The Kodaly method offers a sequential system of sight singing leading to an understanding of musical notation.

Carl Orff has developed an approach to music education beginning with young children. The program's basic premise is that feeling precedes intellectual understanding. The early focus is on rhythm—through the rhythm of speech and movement, children are encouraged to explore music. Some educators have suggested the integration and adaptation of Orff and Kodaly methods as an approach to music education for children (Wheeler & Raebeck, 1972).

A focus on rhythm and movement is certainly a possible approach to teaching music in the early years and is one that has been suggested by early childhood educators in the past. Teachers who want to adopt and adapt Orff and Kodaly approaches, however, might need specific training in music theory, performance, and music education. All teachers can help children develop rhythmic awareness. Listening to natural speech, poetry, rhymes, and jingles, children can learn to identify rhythmic patterns. They can clap out the rhythms they hear and improvise movement patterns to follow them. Musical instruments might also prove helpful.

Teachers who need help beyond these simple techniques can find resources. A number of music textbooks and books of children's songs are available on the market. Some of these are listed at the end of this section. Teachers who cannot read music may be able to learn children's songs from records; some music textbooks have accompanying records.

Sources of children's songs are varied. Many, of course, are written especially for children. Popular songs should also be welcome in class. The folk tradition is rich in children's songs, which include the nursery rhymes. Many folk songs are simple, contain much repetition of musical phrases and words, and are easy for children to learn. Children should have opportunities to explore many kinds of music. Much contemporary music is rich in line, harmony, and meanings. Jazz, folk, and rock should also be included in both singing and listening activities.

Many of the ethnic traditions composing American culture provide musical resources as well; for example, the music of black Americans, Spanish-speaking people, Native Americans and people of various European heritages should be included in the repertoire of the class. Teachers should select songs they like, that also meet Smith's criteria, stated earlier. Songs can be selected to fit a particular area of study in the program, such as African songs as related to a black studies program, or holiday songs at appropriate times of the year.

Although most portions of the singing program are concerned with the recreation of musical experiences, singing has creative aspects as well. Children can compose their own verses to familiar songs and can write new songs. Teachers can write these songs in musical notation, reading them back to the children, or use tape recorders to capture their creations.

Playing Musical Instruments

Early childhood classes should provide opportunities for children to play many musical instruments. Group playing is desirable at some times, but children also need to explore the use of musical instruments independently. They should not be required to beat out a particular rhythm, but should be given the freedom to experiment. Drums, tambourines, rhythm sticks, maracas, and tone blocks are all instruments simple enough for young children to use.

Some commercially made instruments should be provided, because many homemade instruments do not achieve a high quality of tone. Children can create their own instruments as well. These can be as simple as shakers made out of milk containers or plastic boxes holding beans or sand; different objects in the box give different tones to the shaker. Sandpaper attached to wooden blocks and rubbed together makes a suitable instrument. Many objects found around the house or salvaged from the trash heap can also be fashioned into instruments—pot covers and automobile brake drums make percussion instruments, for example. All instruments, whether purchased or homemade, should be treated with respect.

Simple tonal instruments should be included along with rhythm instruments, although teachers should avoid those that must be placed in the mouth to be played. Tone blocks in small sets, xylophones, marimbas, and tuned bells can be provided for the children. These instruments encourage exploration of tonal as well as rhythmic relationships, and the children often begin to play simple tunes by themselves.

Musical instruments can be used to accompany the children's singing or

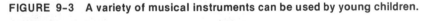

FIGURE 9-3 A variety of musical instruments can be used by young children.

movement, to reproduce rhythmic or melodic patterns, or to create original compositions. They also provide an avenue for free musical exploration. Sometimes merely leaving an instrument on a table is enough to stimulate children to "mess about" with sound. A teacher can direct this type of activity by helping them extend from simple explorations. Sometimes children can abstract patterns from the world around them: the sound of running, the noise of the mimeograph machine, and activities in the streets. The pattern of names, objects, or words in a story can also be reproduced on a percussion instrument.

Children can also listen to songs, abstracting the meter or the accented beat and reproducing it. Changes in tempo should be felt and produced by the child. Individual explorations lead to group playing, with children playing in unison or even against one another as in a dialogue.

As children play instruments, they should attend to the range of sounds that can be made with each instrument. A drum when struck with the hand sounds different from when struck with a stick. Struck in the center it emits a different tone from when struck at the edge. Children can learn to create different effects using the same instrument.

As children move into the primary grades, they can begin to learn aspects of musical notation. They can clap out different note values, or run, walk, and skip to different rhythms. They can even learn to follow the melody line of a song as the music rises and falls in tone. The teacher, moving a hand up and down, or marking the blackboard, illustrates changes in tone.

Children should not be forced into a rigid pattern of music production. Activities with instruments need to be a function of the children's interest and willingness to try out new ideas in sound. In the early years, the teacher should help the children explore and discover the rich area of music through the use of instruments.

Listening to Music

Listening is the basic music skill. Children, listening to the world around them, abstract the sounds as a way of knowing about the world. They can also listen for elements of music such as pitch, intensity, and rhythm, as well as for patterns and themes. Attentive listening helps characterize music and determine its mood. In addition, listening is needed for singing or developing creative movement.

As children listen to music they soon become aware of various qualities. Some music is loud, some is soft; some is fast in tempo, some is slow; musical pitch rises and falls. Teachers can help children become aware of and characterize the elements, design, and texture of music.

Children can also learn to distinguish the various musical instruments and identify their sounds. Differences between families of instruments—brass, woodwinds, strings, and percussion—can be noted first, and later, differences among the instruments in each family. Records of musical pieces highlighting the various instruments are useful, as are pictures and charts of them. The teacher might also be able to bring live musicians to class to play for the children.

Children often listen to music actively in the early years, responding to rhythm and melody with bodily movement or through the use of musical instruments or voice. Active listening can extend into creative expression. At other times children are expected to listen to music more passively, attending to it the way they would attend to a story.

Teachers can develop discussions that enhance attentive listening and lead to critical listening. Children can talk about the feelings generated by music and the kinds of activities that might be evoked. They can also talk about the *uses* of music: for relaxation, to accompany dancing, to facilitate work, to set a mood, or accompany a story. The teacher should help children explore their music preferences and help them discover which elements appeal to them most.

Almost every aspect of the music program is built on the development of listening skills. If children are to learn to sing properly, they must accurately reproduce the pitch and rhythmic pattern of a song; this requires that they attend to it and recall it. Creative movement activities in which children respond to music require that they listen.

Although music recorded for children is plentiful, they should have opportunities to hear live musicians as well. Sometimes a teacher is talented enough to play for her class. Parents or older children might be found who are willing and able to perform. In some communities, local orchestras or ensembles perform in schools. Sometimes young children are considered too immature to be included in the audience, but they can profit from this experience. The one problem that may be encountered is that young children sometimes do not manifest "proper" audience behavior. Audience behavior can be taught: although children naturally move in response to music, they can learn that there are times when it is appropriate to sit quietly.

SONG BOOKS FOR YOUNG CHILDREN

Dietz, B. W., and T. C. Parks. *Folk Songs of China, Japan, and Korea.* New York: Harper & Row, Pub., 1964.

Fowke, Edith. *Sally Go Round the Sun.* New York: Doubleday, 1969.

Glazer, Tom. *Eye Winker Tom Tinker Chin Chopper: Fifty Musical Fingerplays.* New York: Doubleday, 1973.

Jenkins, Ella. *The Ella Jenkins Song Book for Children.* New York: Oak Publications, 1969.

Landeck, Beatrice. *Songs to Grow On.* New York: Morrow, 1950.

_____ . *More Songs to Grow On.* New York: Morrow, 1954.

Langstaff, Nancy, and John Langstaff. *Jim Along, Josie.* New York: Harcourt Brace Jovanovich, 1970.

Palmer, H. *The Hap Palmer Songbook.* Baldwin, N.Y.: Educational Activities, 1971.

Seeger, Ruth Crawford. *American Folk Songs for Children.* New York: Doubleday, 1948.

_____ . *Animal Folk Songs for Children.* New York: Doubleday, 1950.

Sendak, Maurice. *Maurice Sendak's Really Rosie: Starring the Nutshell Kids.* New York: Harper & Row, Pub., 1975.

Winn, Marie. *The Fireside Book of Children's Songs.* New York: Simon & Schuster, 1966.

_____ . *What Shall We Do and Allee Galloo!* New York: Harper & Row, Pub., 1970.

MOVEMENT

Movement education is concerned with helping children gain an understanding of the structure of movement and improve their bodily skills and coordination. They learn to adapt movements to factors of space, different tempos and speeds, different levels, various numbers of people, variations of force and intensity, and different shapes of small and large objects. The activities of dance, gymnastics, and games are introduced in the early years to achieve these goals (Schurr, 1980). Conceptions of basic movement are used to integrate learnings within these three areas.

Basic movement is best seen in a developmental framework. David L. Gallahue (1982) has described the motor development of children as moving through a series of phases, each divided into two or three stages. These parallel stages are described by other developmentalists. The first, *reflexive movement phase,* begins in utero and extends through approximately the first year of life. The first part of this phase consists of the information encoding stage. During this stage the infant gains information, nourishment, and protection through reflexive action. In the second, information decoding stage, the infant develops voluntary control of skeletal movement and processes information gained from sensory stimuli.

The second phase, labeled the *rudimentary movement phase,* overlaps the first and extends from birth through the second year. It, too, is divided into two stages. In the first, the reflex inhibition stage, reflexes are replaced by voluntary behavior in the child's movement repertoire. Though purposeful, these movements appear uncontrolled and unrefined. At about one year, the precontrol stage begins. At this point children show greater precision and control of their movements. They learn to maintain their equilibrium, manipulate objects, and locomote throughout their environment.

The third, or *fundamental movement phase,* extends from about age two through age seven, approximately the age span covered by educational programs discussed in this text. This phase is divided into three stages. During the first of these, the initial stage, children explore and experiment with their own movement capacities involving locomotor, stability, and manipulative movements. The integration of movement patterns is poor at this stage. Greater control and better coordination develops in the elementary stage. The third stage of this phase, the mature stage, is characterized by more mechanically efficient, controlled and coordinated performance.

The fourth phase of movement development, the *sports-related phase,* lasts from age seven through age fourteen and beyond. This phase also consists of three stages: the general or transition stage, the specific stage, and the specialized stage. In this final phase of development, basic locomotor, manipulation and stability skills are refined, combined and elaborated. They are also applied to games, sports, dance, and other recreational activities.

The initial stages of motor development are primarily influenced by maturation. However, Gallahue views development as especially influenced by opportunity, motivation, and instruction in the latter two phases.

Movement education programs generally emphasize developing and refining fundamental movement patterns. Gallahue (1982) views the movement curriculum at the preschool-primary level as focusing on three categories of movement: stability, locomotion, and manipulation. Within the area of stability, the program should help children develop axial movements, as well as static and dynamic balance. In the area of locomotion the program should focus on such activities as walking, running, jumping, sliding, and climbing. The manipulation area would include activities related to such skills as catching, trapping, throwing, and kicking.

Victor P. Dauer (1972) suggests that preschool movement programs focus on (1) gross motor experiences which allow children to manage their bodies efficiently; (2) learning manipulative skills through handling such play objects as balls and beanbags; and (3) using floor apparatus such as boxes, boards, ladders, and planks that allow children to slide down, jump down, go through openings, and bounce. At the kindergarten-primary level Dauer feels the program should focus heavily on movement experiences and body mechanics and on rhythmic activities, with increasing emphasis given to apparatus, stunts, tumbling, and simple games as children move through the grades, with fitness routines and sports skills introduced in the late primary grades.

FIGURE 9-4   Climbing helps young children develop locomotor skills.

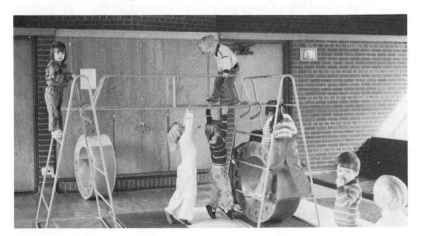

These two approaches basically reflect a physical-education orientation. Other educators emphasize a more creative, dance-oriented approach to movement education in the early years. This latter approach has been heavily influenced by the work of Rudolph Laban (1948), who analyzed and described basic body movements and developed an approach to movement education in England.

Bonnie Gilliom (1970), using the work of Laban and his followers, analyzed the structure of movement education. Through movement education, she states, children should experientially learn about

1. time, space, force, and flow as elements of movement;
2. the physical laws of motion and the principles of human movement which govern the human body's movement; and
3. the vast variety of creative and efficient movements which the human body is capable of producing through the manipulation of movement variables. (p. 6)

Gilliom has developed a series of units that focus on problems of movement. The teacher sets up problems and helps guide children to develop creative ways of solving them. Much of the teaching is indirect, but verbal instructions and demonstrations are also used.

A variety of activities can be created by the classroom teacher to enable children to explore their bodies and their abilities to move through space, using time, rhythm, force, and flow to create movement sequences.

Movement education is a worthy curriculum area in its own right. It has also been considered in relation to its contributions to other program areas.

Lydia Gerhardt (1973) reports how the young child orients himself in space and uses movement to understand concepts of space, time, length, shape, and direction. She also offers suggestions for enhancing the early childhood curriculum through movement. Concepts of topological geometry, geography, and the measurement of time, space, and weight can all be encountered through movement exploration. Such a use of movement suggests systematic ways in which motor patterns generated by children can be integrated into cognitive schema. Betty Rowen's book on movement education (1982) contains examples of strategies for using movement as an aid to learning about language, science, social learnings, and number concepts.

Movement also helps children explore the structure of music. The Eurythmics of Emile Jaques Dalcroze provided the basis for the music program developed by Aronoff, mentioned earlier. Although most teachers lack the specialized training of a Dalcroze teacher or a dance instructor, they have many ways to encourage children to explore movement.

Movement activities should include developmental exercises, stunts, tumbling, and performing on small and large apparatus. At the nursery-kindergarten level, these activities are generally provided informally. Adequate space is needed both indoors and outdoors for running, jumping, walking, and crawling and for other large-muscle activities. Equipment should be available for jumping, grasping, and climbing with stairs, ladders, and ropes. Balancing beams, hoops, rings, ropes, bicycles, scooters, and wagons all contribute to these skills at this level. As children move into primary grades more formal activities might be introduced. An exploratory approach to gymnastics is wise in the primary grades.

Games must be played flexibly in the nursery school since children are generally not able to stay with game rules or goals for any length of time. In kindergarten and the primary grades, rudimentary games can be introduced. The use of games in early childhood education is discussed in relation to all play activities in the next chapter.

Teachers can help children use movement to express ideas and feelings. Joan Russell (1965) has grouped the dimensions of movement thus used under four main headings: the body, the instrument of expression; effort, how the body moves; space and shape, where the body moves; and relationship, relationship of body parts to each other, of dancers to each other, and of groups to each other. Russell has built upon the work of Rudolf Laban to develop a program of creative dance aimed at helping children develop competency in movement through a series of basic themes.

Simply playing music on a phonograph or piano often stimulates them to move, and varying the pitch, intensity, and rhythm leads them to move in different ways. Sometimes just a drum beat stimulates them. It is also possible to encourage movement without any musical accompaniment by using descriptive phrases, or asking them to show a soft movement, a hard movement, high steps, or a close-to-the-ground movement—all allowing them freedom of expression within a framework established by the teacher.

FIGURE 9–5   Young children express ideas and feelings through movement.

Such experiences are often enhanced with simple props. Hoops or fine silk scarves affect children's motion, often enabling them to make more flowing movements. Asking them to move in ways that represent specific things can also extend their movements. A child can be a jet, a slithery snake, a boat, or a flower growing. Each object calls forth certain associations for the child, which he should be able to interpret in his own way. Having the children all move in the same stereotyped way stifles rather than supports creative expression. Indeed, individual interpretation is essential in these rhythmic activities. The teacher's role in the early years is to elicit movement and to encourage new ways of using one's body rather than to teach specific forms and techniques.

However, there should be opportunities for other kinds of dance activities as well. Rhythmic games coupled with songs or chants are enjoyable and can be learned by young children. Such games as "Looby-Loo" or "Bluebird, Fly Through My Window" are simple to direct and so full of repetition that they can master them with ease. Many of these activities grow out of folk tradition, and the teacher sometimes finds that children know versions somewhat different from the one she is teaching. This may occur when she introduces a folk song. These differences are interesting to study, for they represent a portion of the folk tradition in American society. It may be easier, however, for the teacher to learn the local version than to teach a foreign version.

Play party activities can give way to folk dancing, of both American and European derivation. Children can learn the simple basic steps of folk or square dances and then do the patterns as called by the teacher. Records and books are available that provide music and directions for the simple dances. More formal dances should probably be postponed until later in the child's school career.

Children's exploration of the body's uses, and the extension of the child's ability to express feelings and ideas through the body and through instruments and media, are the goals of this portion of the program. Children in the early years are not being prepared to become musicians or artists any more than they are being prepared to become scientists and mathematicians. Learning to express themselves and to appreciate the expressions of others, and to find beauty in themselves and in their surroundings, are discoveries that can last throughout their lives.

REFERENCES

ANDREWS, G. *Creative rhythmic movement for children.* Englewood Cliffs, N.J.: Prentice-Hall, 1954.
ARONOFF, F. W. *Music and young children* (expanded ed.). New York: Turning Wheel Press, 1979.
CLEMENTS, R. B. A case for art education, *Art Education,* 1975, *28*(3), 2-7.
DAUER, V. P. *Essentials of movement experiences for preschool and primary children.* Minneapolis: Burgess, 1972.
DIMONDSTEIN, G. *Exploring the arts with children.* New York: Macmillan, 1974.

GALLAHUE, D. L. *Understanding motor development in children.* New York: John Wiley, 1982.

GERHARDT, L. A. *Moving and knowing: The young child orients himself in space.* Englewood Cliffs, N.J.: Prentice-Hall, 1973.

GILLIOM, B. C. *Basic movement for children.* Reading, Mass.: Addison-Wesley, 1970.

LABAN, R. *Modern educational dance.* London: McDonald and Evans, 1948.

LACY, J. F. *Young art: Nature and seeing.* New York: Van Nostrand Reinhold, n.d.

LOWENFELD, V., and BRITTAIN, W. L. *Creative and mental growth* (7th ed.). New York: Macmillan, 1982.

MARKSBERRY, M. L. *Foundation of creativity.* New York: Harper & Row Pub., 1963.

PILE, N. F. *Art experiences for young children.* New York: Macmillan, 1973.

RICHARDSON, E. S. *In the early world.* Wellington, New Zealand: Council of Educational Research, 1964.

ROWEN, B. *Learning through movement* (2nd ed.). New York: Teachers College Press, 1982.

RUSSELL, J. *Creative dance in the primary school.* London: Macdonald and Evans, 1965.

SCHURR, E. L. *Movement experiences for children* (2nd ed.). Englewood Cliffs, N.J.: Prentice-Hall, 1980.

SMITH, N. R. *Experience and art: Teaching children to paint.* New York: Teachers College Press, 1983.

SMITH, R. B. *Music in the child's education.* New York: Ronald Press, 1970.

WHEELER, L., and RAEBECK, L. *Orff and Kodaly adapted for the elementary school.* Dubuque, Iowa: William C. Brown, 1972.

SUGGESTED READING

ANDRESS, B. *Music experiences in early childhood.* New York: Holt, Rinehart & Winston, 1980.

ARONOFF, F. W. *Music and young children* (Expanded ed.). New York: Turning Wheel Press, 1979.

DIMONDSTEIN, G. *Exploring the arts with children.* New York: Macmillan, 1974.

GERHARDT, L. A. *Moving and knowing: The young child orients himself in space.* Englewood Cliffs, N.J.: Prentice-Hall, 1973.

LASKY, L., and MUKERJI, R. *Art: Basic for young children.* Washington, D.C.: National Association for the Education of Young Children, 1980.

LOWENFELD, V., and BRITTAIN, W. L. *Creative and mental growth* (7th ed.). New York: Macmillan, 1982.

MacDONALD, D. T. *Music in our lives: The early years.* Washington, D.C.: National Association for the Education of Young Children, 1979.

PILE, N. F. *Art experiences for young children.* New York: Macmillan, 1973.

SHEEHY, E. D. *Children discover music and dance.* New York: Teachers College Press, 1968.

SMITH, N. R. *Experience and art: Teaching children to paint.* New York: Teachers College Press, 1983.

SULLIVAN, M. *Feeling strong, feeling free: Movement exploration for young children.* Washington, D.C.: National Association for the Education of Young Children, 1982.

10

Child's Play
as Education

Play activities or their derivatives have always been part of early childhood educational programs. The original Froebelian kindergarten included the manipulation of *Gifts,* the use of craft activities or *Occupations,* and the involvement of children in the *Mother's Plays and Songs,* described in an earlier chapter. Although the children did not engage in freely expressive forms of play, the activities were manipulative and derived from the free play of children. The source of kindergarten activity was the natural play of German peasant children. The essential elements of the play, as identified by Friedrich Froebel, was abstracted and systematized to insure that they would be given to all children.

Maria Montessori, in the development of her educational method, similarly abstracted the essential elements from the natural play activities of ch:"dren, reconstructed them, and systematized them as an instructional method. Activities in these two instances were meant to achieve different instructional goals. Froebel wanted children to gain the spiritual meanings symbolized by the materials and the activities. Montessori, however, wanted them to gain a greater understanding of the properties of the objects themselves as well as specific skills through manipulating them. In both instances, the elements of the activity considered educationally productive were abstracted and many of the qualities of play were eliminated from the educational method.

It was only with the advent of the reform kindergarten movement and the modern nursery-school movement in the first quarter of the twentieth century that the organic play of children became accepted as a vehicle for learning. No attempt was made in these educational systems to abstract distinct separate elements from the play. Instead, the children's natural play activities were supported and nurtured as being educationally significant in their own right. However, in neither of these newer educational institutions was play considered the only way for children to learn.

In these new early childhood education programs, equipment and materials were designed to foster play in classrooms, intended to be used by teachers to stimulate and elaborate the play activities. Even a cursory glance into a nursery school or kindergarten classroom reveals many of these objects. Almost all classrooms at the preprimary level have some sort of doll corner or housekeeping area. In these areas miniature representations of kitchen equipment—play pots, pans, and dishes—household furniture, dolls, cleaning equipment, plastic food, and other similar items are available to the children to help them act out their representations of home life. The block area is another place having equipment designed to foster children's play. In addition to the equipment in these areas, one might also find dress-up clothes, steering wheels, toy cars and trucks, and innumerable other devices for supporting play activities.

With increased concerns about the educational consequences of early childhood programs, alternative approaches to educating young children have developed, and there have been numerous studies of the consequences of varying approaches, including the outcomes of young children's play. A review of the definitions of play and of the theories of play, along with an analysis of the ways that teachers can use play to further educational objectives, should prove useful.

DEFINITIONS OF PLAY

There have been innumerable attempts to define play, each one solving some of the definitional problems but not all of those problems associated with distinguishing play from nonplay activities. While intuitively most of us know play when we see it, it is difficult to specify what it is that helps us separate play from nonplay. We do not have clearly definable, observable, mutually agreed upon criteria. An activity might be considered play in some settings at some times but be considered nonplay in other settings or at other times. One method students of play have used to define play is to state what it is *not*. Helen B. Schwartzman (1978) suggests, "Play is not *work;* play is not *real;* play is not *serious;* play is not *productive;* and so forth . . . (Yet) work can be playful while play can sometimes be experienced as work; and likewise, that players create worlds that are often more real, serious and productive than so-called real life" (pp. 4-5).

Eva Neumann (1971) attempted to create a unified definition of play by identifying those elements that many definitions have in common. These elements were organized into *criteria* for play—characteristics that differentiate play from nonplay; the *processes* of play—their form and method; and the *ob-*

FIGURE 10-1   Sometimes the boundaries between work and play seem blurred.

jectives of play—the elements toward which play is directed. Neumann suggests that there are no clear-cut lines that separate work, or nonplay, from play. Activities are more work or more play to the extent that they are characterized by the absence or presence of play elements identified by these three criteria.

J. Nina Leiberman (1977) has identified a quality of *playfulness* that characterizes play. This includes physical, social, and cognitive spontaneity; manifest joy; and a sense of humor. These have been identified by Leiberman as related to divergent thinking and creativity. While these characteristics are often manifest in play activities, they are also manifest in nonplay activity. Thus, they lack the ability to discriminate play and nonplay.

In a recent review of child development research related to play, Kenneth H. Rubin, Greta G. Fein, and Brian Vandenberg (1983) have suggested that most definitions of play identify it in relation to dispositional factors. Play can be distinguished by its motivational sources and according to the organism's orientation to goals, physical stimuli, rules, and nonplay behavior.

Features of play behaviors identified include

1. Play is intrinsically motivated and not governed either by appetitive drives or by compliance with social demands.
2. Play is characterized by attention to means rather than attainment of specific goals. Goals are self-imposed, and behavior is spontaneous.
3. Play occurs when objects are familiar. It follows exploration of unfamiliar objects. Children impose their own meanings on the activity and internally control it.
4. Play is related to instrumental behavior and thus can be nonliteral.
5. Play is free from externally imposed rules, and the rules of play that do exist are not ironclad.
6. Play requires that its participants be actively engaged in an activity.

While such a set of criteria may not incorporate every belief about play and may not be conceptually pure, it is probably as good a definition as we need. Play, in a sense, defines itself. The need for clear-cut rules of definition may be more important to researchers studying play than to educators, using play for a range of purposes.

THEORIES OF PLAY

Elmer Mitchell and Bernard S. Mason (1948) have identified six classes of theories of play. These include the surplus energy theory, relaxation theory, pre-exercise theory, recapitulation theory, cathartic theory, and self-expression theory. J. Barnard Gilmore (1965), building upon this taxonomy, has divided the theories into two groups: the classical theories and the dynamic theories. The dynamic theories have been further elaborated by Michael J. Ellis (1973) and Greta G. Fein (1979). While the classical theories attempt to explain why children play, the dynamic theories concern themselves with the content of the play.

The Classical Theories

Surplus energy theory.　This postulates that a quantity of energy is available to the organism and that the organism tends to expend that energy either through goal-directed activity (work) or through goalless activity (play). Play occurs at any time the organism has more energy available than it needs to expend for work. In this theory, the content of the play activity is not important and one form of play could easily be substituted for another.

Relaxation theory.　This postulates that play is used to replenish expended energy. After a period of fatiguing activity (work), the organism needs an opportunity to be involved in a relaxing activity (play). According to this theory, play occurs when the organism has little energy left rather than when it has too much energy. Again, one kind of play activity could be substituted for another as a replenishing device.

Pre-exercise theory.　According to the pre-exercise theory, play is instinctive behavior. The child instinctively involves himself in play activities that are, in essence, a form of some more mature behavior he will later have to assume. The content of play is therefore determined by the content of mature future adult activity. Play may be conceived of as preparation for future work.

Recapitulation theory.　From this position, play must be understood, not in terms of the future activities of the individual organism, but in relation to past activities of the race. Play becomes an instinctive way of ridding the organism of the primitive and unnecessary instinctual skills that have been carried over through heredity. The stages of play correspond to the stages of development of the human race, going from the most primitive to the relatively sophisticated. By allowing the person to rid himself of primitive activities, play prepares him for modern work activities.

The first two of the classical theories of play, while not grounded in research, have a commonsense ring of truth to them. Teachers often feel that a classroom full of children is less capable of serious learning on a Friday afternoon or on the day prior to the start of a vacation. They will postpone lessons until the children return with greater stores of energy amassed during the play times of weekends and vacations. Similarly, after a period of inclement weather, when outdoor play has been denied children, teachers will look for ways to help them work off their surplus energy.

It is also interesting to note how the same activity—play—can be understood through a series of opposing theories. Play represents either surplus energy or an energy deficit. Play can be either a form of pre-exercise for sophisticated action or the purging of primitive action forms found within the organism. Either alternative offers a legitimate and testable possibility.

The Dynamic Theories

The dynamic theories of play do not attempt to understand why children play; they simply accept the fact. They focus on attempting to explain the *content* of play. Included in the dynamic theories of children's play are those of Sigmund Freud and Jean Piaget.

Piagetian theory. Piaget believes the development of the human intellect involves two related processes: *assimilation* and *accommodation.* In the process of assimilation, the individual continually abstracts information from the outside world and fits it into the organized schemes representing what he already knows. He also modifies these organizational schemes when they do not fit adequately with his developing knowledge. The latter process is called accommodation. According to Piaget, play is a way of taking the outside world and manipulating it so that it fits a person's present organizational schemes. As such, play serves a vital function in the child's developing intellect and remains, to some extent, always present in human behavior.

Piaget has defined three distinct stages in the development of play. The first is the sensorimotor stage of infancy based upon existing patterns of physical behavior. The second is a level of symbolic play, representing the stage of dramatic play that we find in young children. The third is the stage of playing games that have rules, representing the play behavior of older children.

Freudian theory. Freud considered play a cathartic activity, allowing children to master difficult situations. The child can use the fantasy play situation to act out adult roles, gaining a feeling of mastery that allows him to cope with reality situations. Through play the child can act out personally painful occurrences and master the pain by coming to grips with it in the fantasy of the play situation. This same mastery in fantasy can help children cope with the affective elements of more positive life situations as well. Lois Murphy, in her book *The Widening World of Childhood* (1962), presents vivid descriptions of young children using play activities to cope with problems of living.

Michael J. Ellis (1973) characterizes as modern theories those that view play as a function of competence motivation and those that view play as an arousal-seeking device. Traditionally, psychological theories conceive of man as passive in his natural state. Thus human activity needs to be explained usually in terms of external rewards and punishments or internal drives. Robert White's (1959) theory of competence motivation suggests that people receive satisfaction from developing competencies, independent of whether external rewards are gained in the process. From this point of view, human activity can take place without external reinforcement. Play is one way that children act on their environment, becoming more effective in their actions and receiving more personal satisfactions. The activity of playing is self-rewarding.

The arousal-seeking theory suggests that human beings normally need to be continually involved in information-processing activities; hence their normal state is active. The absence of stimuli in one's environment leads to discomfort that causes him to increase the amount of perceptual information available. This can be done by seeking additional stimulation externally or by creating it internally, possibly by daydreaming. Too much stimulation leads the individual to attend less to his environment. Play is seen as a vehicle by which the child can seek and mediate the amount of external and internal stimulation available to create an optimal balance.

Studying play from a cognitive-affective framework, Jerome Singer (1973) considers the imaginative play of children an effort to organize their experiences while utilizing their motor and cognitive capacities. The child shows interest, alertness, and positive emotional reactions as he interacts with novel play materials, and shows the positive emotions of joy and laughter as he becomes familiar with and masters materials. The play of children is seen by Singer as a vehicle for exploration, the achievement of competence, and the development of creativity.

Greta G. Fein (1979) has used Vygotsky's theory of language and cognitive development to understand the play of young children. According to Vygotsky, mental structures are formed through the use of tools and signs. Play, the creation of imaginary situations, grows out of the tension between the individual child and society. It liberates the child from the constraints of immediate reality and allows the child to control the existing situation. In play, meanings are freed from their related objects and actions. This allows the child to engage in higher-order thought processes. As such, pretend play serves a central role in the acquisition of language and problem-solving abilities in children.

The dynamic theories of play suggest that play activities have significant consequences for children's development. These consequences are consistent with the basic goals of early childhood education. This suggests that play activities can serve a significant educational purpose. Our concern as teachers needs to be with the content of play and how to move it in desired directions. From Freud we learn that the content of play has a strong affective tone; from Piaget we learn that it has a strong cognitive tone. Learning can be supported in both these domains. Play can also have an important socializing role, a third significant domain.

According to George Herbert Mead (1934), children use play as a way of developing their concept of *self*—what they are. They learn this by actually trying on the roles of those about them in dramatic play. The concept of the "generalized other," upon which mature socialization is built, develops in the next stage as children play games. The games are based upon rules and require, for the child to perform them properly, that he internalize the role behavior of others as well as his own in the games.

EDUCATIONAL USES OF PLAY

The theories of play discussed here are descriptive theories. They attempt to explain play as it exists. An understanding of these theories can allow us to extrapolate guides for action appropriate to use in teaching situations.

A productive distinction might be made between *educational* play and *noneducational* play. The difference is not in the activities or the degree of enjoyment that a child may receive, but rather in the purposes ascribed to the play by those persons responsible for the child's activities. Educational play has as its prime purpose the child's learning. Such play is still fun for children, for without providing personal satisfaction, the activity stops being play. Educational play activities, however, serve an educational purpose while being personally satisfying. Thus a child in the housekeeping area of a classroom is receiving personal satisfactions from playing out the particular role he has ascribed to himself interacting with persons in other roles, and using various play properties in innovative ways. The value of this play is that it helps the child explore and understand role dimensions and interaction patterns, thereby supporting his further understanding of the social world and helping him to build a realistic sense of *self*.

Educational play may take many forms. The key role of the teacher here is in modifying the natural spontaneous play of children so that it has educational value while maintaining its qualities as play. Teachers also create less spontaneous educational play activities. Such play is evaluated not only by the child's degree of involvement but by its effectiveness in achieving educational aims.

In most nursery school and kindergarten classrooms one can usually find four kinds of educational play: manipulative, physical, and dramatic play, and games. In manipulative play the child handles relatively small pieces of equipment such as puzzles, Cuisenaire rods, or peg sets. The actions are relatively self-contained; that is, there is no necessary interaction between the manipulative activity and other kinds of activities, nor is there a dramatic element to the play. The goals of manipulative play activities are achievable directly through the child's handling of the material. The use of Montessori apparatus, although defined as "work" by Montessorians, provides a good example of educational manipulative play. A child may be given a series of wooden cylinders and a case into which they fit. By comparing cylinders and attempting to fit them in the case, he begins to learn to make size comparisons and to seriate. Manipulative play activities generally have fairly narrowly defined educational goals.

Physical play involves children's large actions, such as running, jumping, or riding a tricycle. These activities help children increase their physical skills or learn to use them in new situations. Physical play can have a dramatic component to it and teachers can elaborate the play either by making the physical activities more challenging or by providing social content to the play.

Dramatic play requires that the child pretend to act out a role, often in relationship to other children playing their roles in informal dramatic situations that may represent true life experiences. The housekeeping area (or doll corner) is the most readily observable setting for play. Here children act out the roles of family members in actions representing home situations. The teacher may set up other dramatic play situations to enable the children to play many roles.

Often children manipulate smaller things that represent objects or characters. Informal puppet play allows children to act out roles through puppets. Building with unit blocks can also involve miniature dramatizations. In this, the teacher must provide adequate accessories, enough time for children to go beyond manipulative building, and ideas as sources for dramatic themes.

Games are a different kind of play activity. They are highly structured and include specific rules to be followed. Children at the four- and five-year-old levels are beginning to move into a stage where game playing is possible. Simple games or musical activity containing elements of games are quite appropriate. Children need to be taught the strategies of game playing. Teachers need to guide the games, for they may be the only one mature enough to maintain its rules and to help the children understand rule-appropriate behavior.

Many educators accept play as a part of nursery school or kindergarten classroom activities. Play has equally valid uses with primary children as with children at lower educational levels. The "messing about" of the science program is a form of play, as are many of the newer materials-oriented programs in mathematics. Dramatic play is often a useful avenue of social studies education and a support for language learning. Appropriate play activities can be integrated in almost all areas of learning in the primary school.

The distinctions made here between different types of play are useful. However, they are not absolute. There can be manipulative qualities to dramatic play, for example, and dramatic qualities to physical play. The distinctions are useful in identifying the predominant qualities of play activities and in suggesting ways of supporting play in school.

Manipulative Play

A manipulative play center is desirable in the nursery or kindergarten class. In the primary grades, manipulative materials are generally organized along subject-matter lines. A manipulative play center may have materials placed on open shelves, so they are readily accessible. A set of tables and chairs can also be included, but many of the materials can be just as easily used on the floor, preferably with a rug. The shelves can hold the following materials:

Puzzles.   A wide range of children's jigsaw puzzles is presently available, from puzzles that have just three or four pieces, each representing a single item, to rather complex puzzles made of two or three dozen pieces. Sturdy puzzles made out of wood or masonite will stand much use. It is a good idea to have a number of puzzles ranging in difficulty. If a puzzle rack is used for storage, the children can learn to carefully take out and replace puzzles, limiting the number of puzzle pieces that get lost. Marking the backs of each puzzle's pieces with a common symbol also helps children locate missing pieces. When losses do occur, teachers can shape substitutes out of wood putty, painting them to match the rest of the puzzle.

The teacher should organize the puzzles according to their difficulty and check the children periodically to see how they have progressed in their ability to complete puzzles. Although most children have had some experience in working with puzzles prior to school, some have not learned the appropriate skills. Teachers should not take skills for granted, and a session or two at the beginning of the year explicitly teaching children the procedures of puzzle completion may be useful.

Parquetry blocks and pegboards.   Parquetry blocks with wooden pieces of varying shapes and colors, and pegboard sets with pegs of different colors, are useful for teaching form and color discrimination and retention. Many of the skills gained lead to formal reading and mathematics instruction. Although children need opportunities to manipulate these materials freely, teachers can make model cards for the children to replicate with their manipulative materials. These cards can be presented to children in order of difficulty to support mastery. Pegboard sets can also be equipped with elastic bands with which the children can create various shapes.

Constructive materials.   Small sets of constructive materials such as *Lego* or *Lincoln Logs* are useful. Children can make fanciful creations or construct small buildings with these. A large variety of construction materials is available from manufacturers for this purpose.

FIGURE 10-2   Construction materials allow children to make their own creations.

Science materials.   Plastic boxes containing sets of science materials can be included in the manipulative materials center. A battery, bulb, and a couple of lengths of wire could constitute one set. A magnet with some small bits of material, some magnetic and some not, could constitute another set. A plastic jar covered with a rubber membrane, half-filled with water, and containing a medicine dropper; a small basin of water and materials that float and some that sink; and a box of variously textured materials, are examples of the range of materials that can be included for science exploration.

Mathematics materials.   Cuisenaire rods, counting frames, simple measuring devices such as a balance, primary ruler, measuring cups and spoons, and materials to be measured or counted can all be incorporated into the manipulative materials center.

Montessori materials.   Many of the Montessori didactic materials are ideally suited for the manipulative play center. They can be used independently by the children and are self-correcting in nature. These need not be used according to orthodox Montessori prescription.

Other manipulative materials.   A quick glance through an educational supply catalogue can provide further ideas for this center. Teachers might rummage through their own homes or through hardware stores and see materials that can be included in the classroom. Often some of the most stimulating and exciting materials for educational purposes result from the teacher's ingenuity.

Manipulative play with natural materials.   While generally not included in a manipulative materials center, natural materials such as sand and water are

FIGURE 10-3
A galvanized tub provides for water play in class.

important adjuncts to play. While specially designed sand and water tables are available commercially, a galvanized tub or a plastic wash basin can also be used. Children need freedom in using these materials, but must also learn how to care for them and know the limitations on their use. A number of accessories including containers, spoons, and shovels should go with the water and sand. Wet sand can be molded in many shapes; dry sand can be sieved and run through funnels. Equipment for cleanup such as sponges, a floor brush, and dustpan should be readily available for children to use.

Physical Play

Physical play generally requires much more space than manipulative play. Much of children's outdoor play in early childhood classes falls in this category.

Outdoor play. The content of outdoor play depends as much upon the climate and weather conditions as upon space and other considerations. In some schools, outdoor play consists mainly of sledding and building with snow during the bulk of the school year. In other areas, there are possibilities for free exploration and a wide use of materials, because the weather remains temperate during the school year. Teachers should vary outdoor play with the possibilities created by local conditions.

Outdoor space—both soft-surfaced and hard-surfaced areas—should be available and easily accessible to the classroom. Teachers should provide outdoor storage space for equipment; but they can also bring classroom materials outdoors.

Outdoor play activities and equipment should allow opportunities for climbing, running, jumping, riding on large pieces of equipment, and digging. Recent concern about playgrounds for young children has brought about the design of more complex pieces of equipment to support creative physical activities and social interaction in outdoor play. Some of these may be permanently installed and require little maintenance. In addition to permanent structures, other equipment should also be available, including

Sand pit for children's digging
Play houses and platforms
Wheel toys, including tricycles, wagons, wheel barrows, and boxes on casters
Movable equipment for climbing, such as saw horses, walking boards, barrels, packing crates, and ladders
Balls and jump ropes to be used for games

Indoor play. Many of the same physical play activities that are offered to children outdoors can be provided indoors as well. Sometimes they must be scaled down to the space available. In some schools a multipurpose room is available for more vigorous play. In other situations, classes are limited to their own rooms. In any event, some physical play can take place indoors.

Teachers can often include some climbing apparatus in their classrooms. Boards, sawhorses, and ladders can be combined into rather elaborate exciting edifices that require relatively little storage space and are fun for the children. Wheel toys can also be provided indoors for younger children, but these should be smaller than the ones used outdoors—sturdy wooden trucks or variplay boxes rather than tricycles and wagons. In many cases schools have built playhouses with elevated platforms, ladders, staircases, slides, and other artifacts into small spaces in a classroom.

Dramatic Play

In dramatic play or sociodramatic play children assume various adult roles, which unfold with a great deal of spontaneity. While children are generally acting out roles as they perceive and understand them, elements of fantasy may move the play far from reality. Children also use objects to stand for

FIGURE 10–4
Dress-up clothes help extend children's dramatic play.

something other than what they really are, so that a doll may stand for a baby, a stick for a horse, or a piece of hose for a gas pump.

In setting up an attractive dramatic play area, the classroom teacher stimulates role playing. If the materials reflect the home life of a family and little else, the play will generally remain in the realm of family play. However, the total adult world is the legitimate scope of school play situations, including work as well as family living.

For a play situation to be educationally useful it should be guided by the teacher. This guidance requires the teacher's awareness of and sensitivity to children's play activities, a sense of the goals of play, and an ability to move into the play on occasion, make suggestions, and even become a player.

Most important, the teacher's responsibility is to provide the information that will move the play ahead; reading books or showing films and filmstrips often provides this information. Discussions, resource persons, and trips are all legitimate sources of new information for children in their play, allowing the activity to shuttle between fantasy and reality in a wholesome way.

Block play.   Falling somewhere between the categories of physical play and dramatic play is block play. Two basic kinds of blocks are used in early childhood education: the smaller unit blocks, which allow the child to miniaturize his world, and the larger hollow blocks, or comparable variations on the Patty Hill blocks, which allow him to build large structures suitable as stages for dramatic play.

Caroline Pratt and Jessie Stanton (1926) describe children going out into the neighborhood of the school and returning to symbolize their perceptions of it in block structures. Lucy Sprague Mitchell (1934, 1971) and Helen Robison and Bernard Spodek (1965), provide examples of blocks being used to further the young children's geographic understanding. Blocks can also be used in rela-

FIGURE 10-5   Constructing with unit blocks furthers children's learning.

tion to science and mathematics learning. As children mature in their use of blocks they move through various stages of block building. An awareness of the stages, as originally identified by Harriet Johnson (Hirsch, 1974) or as modified by others—beginning with just carrying blocks around and advancing to simple constructions and to building elaborate structures that suggest dramatic content—is useful for teachers as an aid in guiding children's block building.

If blocks are to be used effectively, teachers must provide them in large numbers as well as adequate space for block-building. In addition, it is helpful if children can work on a block structure for longer than a single period or a single day, to further elaborate it.

Games

A wide range of games can be used in early childhood classes. Some games are oriented only toward physical movement; others require little movement but a great deal of attention to problem solving. Different games can be used for different purposes.

In the nursery school and kindergarten years, games should be rather simple, with uncomplicated rules. Games at this level can include activities accompanied by singing and simple physical games in which children must follow a few directions. Lotto and other table games also have a place at this level. As the children move into the primary grades, more complicated physical activities requiring strict adherence to rules, and many of the traditional games of childhood, can be incorporated into the school day. In the classroom, teachers can use games to provide practice opportunities in the academic areas. Games such as these are often suggested in the teacher's manuals of textbook series and in teacher-oriented magazines such as *Instructor* or *Early Years*. Board games can also be used. Those requiring evolving strategies and planning before making moves, such as checkers, can help children develop thinking skills.

In their book, *Group Games in Early Education* (1980), Rheta DeVries and Constance Kamii state that educationally useful games should

1. suggest something interesting and challenging for children to figure out how to do
2. make it possible for children themselves to judge their success
3. permit all players to participate actively throughout the game (p. 3)

They argue that group games can help children achieve the aims of early childhood education, including becoming more autonomous, developing children's ability to decenter and coordinate different points of view, coming up with interesting ideas, problems, and questions, and putting things into relationships. Among the games these authors suggest are aiming games such as *Dodge Ball;* races; chasing games; hiding games; guessing games; card games like *Old Maid* and *Animal Rummy;* and board games such as *Candyland, Chutes and Ladders,* and *Lotto.* In teaching these games teachers should modify the games to be in harmony with the way the children think, and they should reduce adult power as much as possible while encouraging cooperation among children.

Although some games require specific equipment or sets of materials, many require little besides direct instructions from the teacher and her supervision. Often a piece of chalk or a ball is all that is needed to keep children involved in playing a game for a long period of time.

GUIDING EDUCATIONAL PLAY

If play is to be educational, teachers have a prime role in setting the stage for play, in guiding its direction, and in modifying it. Sponseller's review of research on play and early education (1982) suggests that

1. The physical factors of the play space affect social play, sex role learning, and activity level and quality.
2. A child's interaction with parents affects the ability to play.
3. A child's interaction with peers influences social play, sex-role learning, and play level and quality, and assists with the decentering process.
4. A teacher's direct or indirect facilitation of play affects the type, quantity, and quality of play. It signals the appropriateness or inappropriateness of play in the school.
5. Training or experience in certain types of play can affect play behavior in the classroom and it may improve the learning of academic skills, especially ones requiring higher cognitive processes. (p. 233)

Thus, while some of the influences on play are beyond the abilities of teachers to effect them, there are others that they control. In order to ensure the quality of play in a classroom which leads to positive educational consequences, preparation for educational play, careful planning, and guidance are necessary.

Planning for Educational Play

Although extremely satisfying play can erupt spontaneously in almost any class, adequate preparation greatly increases the chances of productive play activities occurring. Teachers must be aware of topics for play that are of interest to the children and have the possibility for rich educational experience. Play activities revolving around various social roles can help children explore the functions of these roles and their limitations. Store play can help children understand economic principles. Block play can help them become aware of geographic relationships in their community. Play at being a builder gives them practice in measurement skills.

In planning for play, the teacher should assess the learning potential of the play activity, then search for resources to help children gain information about it. Informational books, films, filmstrips, picture files and recordings on the topic can be helpful. A search of the community might produce field trip possibilities or resource persons who can be brought into the classroom. Museums or educational resource centers may loan dioramas or other resource materials.

The teacher may not use all the resources identified in the classroom, or introduce everything to the children at one time. But a careful search will allow a choice of materials to provide enough information to stimulate the play and to carry it forward. In planning, the teacher should also identify the play materials that will be used: articles of clothing for dramatic play, manipulative materials, and raw materials to allow the children to create their own props. Many of these things can be used from year to year; teachers often develop extensive collections of play materials over time.

The materials teachers bring into class affect children's play activities. Singer (1973) suggests that there is probably a curvilinear relationship between the degree of realism of a toy and its usefulness in stimulating a child's imaginative behavior. Toys without definite structure, such as building blocks, because they are relatively nonspecific and flexible, may lend themselves best to long-term use and can be mixed with more specific playthings to stimulate make-believe play.

The teacher should also think through the strategies to be used for stimulating play, and the goals to be achieved. An understanding of these goals can provide her with guidelines for the constant evaluation and guidance of the play activities.

Initiating Play Activities

Simply setting out new materials in the classroom is often enough to start the children's play. If new materials are introduced into a situation in which children are offered choices, the teacher might initiate new play activities in two areas at the same time. This will keep the whole class from focusing on just one exciting area and allow small group play to develop without undue coercion.

The introduction of new materials and equipment frequently requires a certain amount of direction. Teachers may talk with their students about how the materials are used and their limitations. A short meeting prior to the introduction of the materials can prevent problems from occurring later.

In generating play activities, the teacher can look for ways to stimulate the children's imagination. Dramatic play activities are often initiated through a field trip, the showing of a film, or the reading of a book related to the topic of play. This initial infusion of information gives the children ideas for the use of materials provided and will also suggest themes for play.

Guiding the Play of Children

Teachers should be aware of the processes of play that unfold and use the cues they get from their observations as the basis for supporting or modifying the play. Techniques that are useful in guiding children's play can be identified by observing effective teachers and parents. Burton White (1973) describes the role of the more effective mothers in his study of the influences of the environment on the development of competency in very young children:

> What they seem to do, often without knowing exactly why, is to perform excellently the functions of designer and consultant. By that I mean they design a physical world, mainly in the home, that is beautifully suited to nurturing the burgeoning curiosity of the one-to-three year old. It is full of small, manipulable, visually detailed objects, some of which were originally designed for young children (toys), others normally used for other purposes (plastic refrigerator containers, bottle caps, baby-food jars and covers, shoes, magazines, television and radio knobs, etc.). It contains things to climb, such as chairs, benches, sofas and stairs. It has available materials to nurture more mature motor interests, such as tricycles, scooters, and structures with which to practice elementary gymnastics. It includes a rich variety of interesting things to look at, such as television, people, and the aforementioned types of physical objects. (p. 243)

Teachers are also designers and consultants, creating a world in which children can learn through play, and modifying play opportunities to increase their educational value. Teachers, however, will play a somewhat more active role in guiding educational play than did the mothers described in White's study.

Teachers should guide play by modifying situations. In dramatic play this might mean either adding new materials or withdrawing some when their use no longer seems productive; in manipulative play, terminating one form of play and suggesting another. The teacher may also modify the situation by suggesting important roles for them, or modifying the play situation to include them. Children who are disruptive might be eased out of the situation. At times teachers might want to determine the membership in play groups to support specific social learnings. They might also use play tutoring—working with children to help them learn *to* play or learn *through* play.

Observing the play of children sometimes shows the teacher that they lack some necessary information or are operating under certain misconceptions. Providing information by telling, or by having children read information books or look things up in resource books, can clear these up. Sometimes a field trip or the visit of a resource person also provides significant information that will modify the play.

There are occasions when teachers become active players for varying periods of time. This can allow teachers to modify the direction of the play by introducing new elements. It can also limit disruptive behavior. It also provides a role model for the play of the children by asking clarifying questions that allow them to better understand the content of play and the meanings of certain behaviors. In becoming active players, teachers should not distort children's play, otherwise the involvement becomes a disruption and the play activities may terminate.

Sylvia Krown (1974) presents a report of a program for Israeli children that includes delightful descriptions of how their play changed over time. In the beginning the activities were highly stereotyped. Two years later, the children had modified and enriched their play. Four basic strategies were used to stimulate children's play:

1. The teachers spent time "startling children out of vagueness into purposeful activity," sometimes inviting themselves into the play activities for a period of time, then withdrawing (as in play tutoring).
2. The teachers added new materials to the play situation as needed to move the activities on.
3. The teachers asked questions to stimulate more detailed observations to be used in play and to help children recall and associate past experiences.
4. Some teachers developed discussions to stimulate more detailed observations and play. They provided additional information to children through books, trips, and the like.

Thus the teachers influenced the play of children while still allowing them to maintain control over the play situation.

These strategies can be used by all teachers. The "startling of children" into purposeful activities can be accomplished by interacting with the children in the context of the play while asking questions about the play plot. This can cause cognitive dissonance to extend both the play activities and the children's thinking about those activities. New materials, like new ideas, stimulate new play activities. Teachers' questioning techniques can help the children become more aware of what they already know and of how they can use that knowledge, comparing play situations to real situations and applying previously acquired knowledge to new situations. Finally, teachers can find many ways to provide children with additional information that feed into current play structures and extend them.

The decision of when to intervene or how far to go in extending children's play can only be made situationally. The judgment must be based upon knowledge of children in general and of the particular children involved. The potential of a play situation for learning must also be assessed. Too much intervention can stop play or distort it; the absence of intervention can keep a play situation from realizing its potential. The teacher must continually strive to achieve an appropriate balance. This sensitive, provocative balance, and design, consultation, and intervention, can help generate educational children's play. Learning can thus occur in the context of playfulness. The essence of good teaching lies in the ability to plan learning goals for children, to respond, to intervene without unnecessary interference and distortion, and to change direction when appropriate. Perhaps this requires an adult who brings a quality of playfulness as well as a respect for children to the classroom.

REFERENCES

DeVRIES, R., and KAMII, C.   *Group games in early education: Implications of Piaget's theory*. Washington, D.C.: National Association for the Education of Young Children, 1980.
ELLIS, M. J.   *Why people play*. Englewood Cliffs, N.J.: Prentice-Hall, 1973.
FEIN, G. G.   Play and the acquisition of symbols. In L. G. Katz (Ed.). *Current topics in early childhood education* (Vol. II). Norwood, N.J.: Ablex, 1979.
GILMORE, J. B.   Play: A special behavior. In R. N. Huber (Ed.). *Current research in motivation*. New York: Holt, Rinehart & Winston, 1965.
HIRSCH, E. S.   (Ed.). *The block book*. Washington, D.C.: National Association for the Education of Young Children, 1974.
KROWN, S.   *Threes and fours go to school*. Englewood Cliffs, N.J.: Prentice-Hall, 1974.
LEIBERMAN, J. N.   *Playfulness: Its relationships to imagination and creativity*. New York: Academic Press, 1977.
MEAD, G. H.   *Mind, self and society*. Chicago: University of Chicago Press, 1934.
MITCHELL, E., and MASON, B. S.   *The theory of play* (Rev. ed.). Cranbury, N.J.: A. S. Barnes, 1948.
MITCHELL, L. S.   *Young geographers*. New York: Bank Street College of Education, 1971. (Originally published, 1934.)
MURPHY, L.   *The widening world of childhood*. New York: Basic Books, 1962.
NEUMANN, E. A.   *The elements of play*. New York: MSS Modular Publications, Inc., 1971.
PRATT, C., and STANTON, J.   *Before books*. New York: Adelphi Co., 1926.
ROBISON, H. F., and SPODEK, B.   *New directions in the kindergarten*. New York: Teachers College Press, 1965.
RUBIN, K. H., FEIN, G. G., and VANDENBERG, B.   Play. In E. M. Heatherington (Ed.). *Carmichael's manual of child psychology: Social development*. New York: John Wiley, 1983.
SCHWARTZMAN, H. B.   *Transformations: The anthropology of play*. New York: Plenum, 1978.
SINGER, J. L.   *The child's world of make-believe*. New York: Academic Press, 1973.
SPONSELLER, D.   Play and early education. In B. Spodek (Ed.). *Handbook of research in early childhood education*. New York: Free Press, 1982.
WHITE, B. L., WATTS, J. C., et al.   *Experience and environment: Major influences on the development of the young child* (Vol. 1). Englewood Cliffs, N.J.: Prentice-Hall, 1973.
WHITE, R. F.   Motivation reconsidered: The concept of competence. *Psychological Review*, 1959, *66*, 297-333.

SUGGESTED READING

BIBER, B.   *Play as a growth process*. New York: Bank Street College of Education, 1959.
BRUNER, J. S., JOLLY, A., and SYLVA, K.   (Eds.). *Play—Its role in development and evolution*. New York: Basic Books, 1976.
CHERRY, C.   *Creative play for the developing child*. Belmont, Calif.: Fearon, 1976.
FROST, J. L., and KLEIN, B. L.   *Children's play and playgrounds*. Boston: Allyn & Bacon, 1979.
GARVEY, C.   *Play*. Cambridge, Mass.: Harvard University Press, 1977.

HILL, D. M. *Mud, sand and water.* Washington, D.C.: National Association for the Education of Young Children, 1977.

HIRSCH, E. S. (Ed.). *The block book.* Washington, D.C.: National Association for the Education of Young Children, 1974.

RUBIN, K. H. (Ed.). *Children's play.* San Francisco: Jossey-Bass, 1980.

SCHWARTZMAN, H. B. *Transformations: The anthropology of play.* New York: Plenum, 1978.

SUTTON-SMITH, B. (Ed.). *Play and learning.* New York: Gardner Press, 1979.

TIZARD, B., and HARVEY, D. (Eds.). *Biology of play.* London: Heinemann, 1977.

11

Young Children with Special Educational Needs

Over the last two decades we have seen a major expansion of educational opportunities for all children. Most dramatic, however, has been the expansion of services for young handicapped children. We have moved from a situation where many handicapped children were excluded from school because of their handicaps to the point where schools are reaching out to identify and serve handicapped children even before the normal school-entrance age. In addition, there has been a shift from serving handicapped children in predominantly segregated settings to educating handicapped children in the least restrictive educational environment. This has meant that many mildly and moderately handicapped children are being integrated with their nonhandicapped peers in regular classes. Thus all teachers, whether identified as teachers of handicapped children or not, are potentially teachers of some handicapped children. This is true in all public-school programs. It is also true in Head Start programs and in many nursery schools and day care centers. In many cases this has led to a requirement in programs preparing teachers of all children that attention be given to teaching handicapped children. This chapter provides a review of issues related to mainstreaming, concerns for identifying and diagnosing handicapping conditions in children, planning for handicapped children in the regular classrooms, and modifying programs and settings to better serve handicapped children.

MAINSTREAMING

The integration of handicapped and nonhandicapped children in common educational settings has a sound rationale. Legal decisions have supported the move to mainstream the handicapped, identifying the right of handicapped children to a free public education, their right to be educated in the least restrictive educational setting, and the right of their parents to review educational decisions related to them. Educational research has also supported the move to mainstream those children who can benefit from instruction in the normal classroom. Evidence has been gathered to show that often there is no academic advantage to placing mildly and moderately handicapped children in segregated educational settings. Added to that is the fact that the social behavior of handicapped children more closely approximates those of their nonhandicapped peers when they are integrated. In addition, nonhandicapped children may benefit from such a placement by developing increased understanding and sensitivity to individual differences without any loss in academic achievement (Spodek, Saracho, & Lee, 1983).

Most important to the public schools has been the passage at the federal level of Public Law 94-142, the Education for All Handicapped Children Act. This law requires that public schools educate all handicapped children between the ages of three and twenty-one. However, if normal children between the ages of three and five and eighteen and twenty-one are not educated by the state, then the state has no responsibility to educate handicapped children of similar ages. Unfortunately, this has meant that young handicapped children continue to be denied public educational services in some states and are provided with these services in segregated settings in others, since there are no nonhandicapped children of comparable age in the public schools with which to promote integration. Thus, young handicapped children are denied the opportunity to be educated in the least restrictive educational setting within the public schools in these places. However, Head Start programs have reserved at least 10 percent of their placements for handicapped children, and other programs for normal children also enroll some handicapped children. Thus, the opportunity for integrating handicapped and nonhandicapped children does exist below the kindergarten level to a limited extent.

LEAST RESTRICTIVE EDUCATIONAL SETTING

The term *mainstreaming* is defined as the integration of handicapped children in a regular classroom containing primarily nonhandicapped children. Not all handicapped children, however, are best served in such a regular classroom and even those placed in regular classes may need help beyond what is offered to nonhandicapped children. The criterion for placing handicapped children relates to the least restrictive educational setting that will provide the type and level of services necessary for a handicapped child. For some children this suggests placement in a regular classroom. Other children, however, may need to be placed in much more segregated settings. A hierarchy of possible placements

ranging from maximum integration to maximum segregation has been identified by Evelyn Deno (1970). In essence it is as follows:

1. Regular classroom assignment, possibly with classroom modification and supportive services provided
2. Regular classroom assignment plus supplementary instructional services (a
   resource room or itinerant teacher might provide these)
3. Part-time special classes with the remainder of the day spent in a regular class or
   resource room
4. Full-time special class with the child segregated into a separate class in a conventional school
5. Special day school
6. Homebound instruction
7. Institutional or residential assignment

Each succeeding level of placement provides a more segregated and less
normal educational environment for the child. It is suggested that most exceptional children can be educated in normal settings with the classroom teacher
providing help directly, or receiving special outside help. Fewer and fewer
children need the more restrictive settings that are lower on the list.

Whatever the educational setting prescribed for a handicapped child,
there should be an effort made to provide that child with as normal an educational experience as is possible.

One of the purposes of education for exceptional children is to help them
cope as well as possible with everyday circumstances, interact as well as possible
with a range of people, and live as normal lives as possible. Given these goals,
the school is expected to design educational experiences to enable the child to
develop coping skills. Contact with a range of children becomes important; but
even in circumstances in which the child is educationally segregated, the
educator is expected to make that learning situation as close to normal as possible.

IDENTIFYING HANDICAPPED CHILDREN

One of the first tasks required in working with handicapped children is to find
out who they are, and oftentimes where they are, as well as to determine the
nature of their handicapping conditions. Often the process of identification is
the responsibility of someone other than a classroom teacher—a psychologist, a
social worker, or the coordinator of special services. Nevertheless, it is important for teachers to be aware of the process and to become involved to whatever
extent possible.

Since most of the children below kindergarten age are not in school, one
of the main problems in identifying handicapped children of this age is finding

them. Some children, particularly those with obvious handicapping conditions, will be referred to the school for educational services by a pediatrician or by a social service agency that deals with children and families. The majority, and especially those with less-obvious handicaps, will need to be identified through a voluntary preschool screening program.

In order to make the public aware of the availability of a preschool screening program, schools will often announce such programs through local newspapers, and radio and television stations. Posters placed on bulletin boards in supermarkets, community centers, and other places where parents are likely to see them are also useful. Schools may also send notices home with their students, in the hope that parents with preschool-age children will respond. Community surveys and house-to-house canvasses for young children are also useful, but they are time consuming and expensive. No matter what method is used to inform the public about a preschool screening program, these programs are voluntary. A parent must choose to bring a child for screening; there can be no coercion.

A centrally located site needs to be selected to house the screening program so that it is easily accessible by families who will use it. The site also needs to have enough space and facilities to allow for a number of children to go through the process at the same time. The screening team, composed of professionals, paraprofessionals, and volunteers, will set up the facilities and be responsible for implementing the various screening procedures.

The purpose of the preschool screening is to identify, in a quick, simple, and inexpensive way, the potential handicapping conditions among the children who are screened. Screening should encompass all the major developmental areas, including speech and language development, intellectual development, social development, fine-motor and gross-motor development, and the development of self-help skills. The instruments used should provide information about possible problems in the specific areas of development for which they were designed. They should be simple to administer and not require too much time or too great a level of sophistication. If the procedures used identify what is potentially a handicapping condition, then a more extensive and elaborate diagnostic procedure is used.

Preschool screening is important. However, because of its voluntary nature, these screenings can never identify all the potential handicapping conditions among the young children of any community. Often the first time a child is identified as possibly having a handicapping condition is when that child first arrives at school, whether at a preschool, a kindergarten, or first grade. The teacher can view each child in relation to the many children in class of similar age; thus a child's problem may stand out more clearly. In addition, as the child responds to common tasks, problems that exist will become more evident. The child's family may consciously or unconsciously have adapted their demands to existing capabilities and problems.

In addition, teachers are trained to observe young children systematically, and they see each child in a variety of situations. Much of the screening that takes place in school is of an informal nature, with the teacher observing children and noting their social behavior, language behavior, or motor skills in situations requiring that those skills be used. Often, however, informal observations are not enough, and teachers need to become more systematic in their observations by using anecdotal records, checklists, rating scales, time samples, and event samples such as those described in chapter 15.

In addition, eye charts might be used by the teacher to test for visual acuity, or an audiologist may pull several children at a time from the class to test their hearing. School nurses, speech and language specialists, and others might also be involved in the systematic screening of children to identify handicapping conditions that might otherwise be overlooked.

These procedures are also relatively simple ones to identify problems in children that might require further study. If further diagnosis is required, parental permission is usually needed, and other resource persons may have to be brought in. The result of the diagnosis will lead to the specific identification of handicapping conditions that exist in the child. These can be of many kinds. Typically they fall into the categories of learning disabilities, mental retardation, behavior disabilities, sensory problems, communication disorders, and physical or motor problems.

Learning-disabled Children

Learning-disabled children are a varied group. Many definitions of this category have been proposed, each complicated and inadequate in defining the attributes of the group thus labeled and in separating this group from other categories of exceptionality. This group includes children with both neurological impairments and functional impairments. Children suffering from hyperactivity; perceptual-motor impairment; emotional liability; impulsivity; specific learning disabilities in reading, spelling, arithmetic, or writing; disorders of speech and hearing; and neurological problems have all been included in this category.

In general, the approaches to teaching children with learning disabilities use a clinical model of teaching, one that includes several steps. It begins with (1) the diagnosis of the specific learning problem, then (2) the establishment of goals often stated in behavioral terms to ameliorate the learning problem, (3) the development of a program specifically aimed at the learning problem, and finally (4) an assessment of the changes in the original problem to determine if the program has succeeded. The curriculum strategy is one of simplifying the program and teaching directly to the area of weakness. Task analysis becomes important in generating learning activities, for if the failure is in a complicated area of performance, the teacher is expected to break down that performance into its simpler components, which can then each be taught separately and, hopefully, be reintegrated.

Some educators suggest that rather than focus on the difficulties of these children, we should try to capitalize on their strengths. Such a strategy might increase the child's sense of success, which could be generalized to other areas of accomplishment. Still other educators suggest a broadly based program. They argue that the educational goals for these children should be no different from goals of normal children and that unnecessary narrowing of curriculum, either toward a child's strengths or toward a child's weaknesses, is essentially wrong. What might be varied, however, is the pacing of instruction, allowing these children more time for learning when it seems desirable.

Mentally Retarded Children

The assumption underlying the label of mentally retarded is that the individual lacks the capacity to learn what a normal child can learn. The assumption underlying the label of learning disabled is that there is a discrepancy between the individual's capacity and that individual's actual learning achievement. Although the judgment of capacity might be made accurately for severely and profoundly retarded children, the accuracy of such judgments for mildly and moderately retarded children has been open to question.

Achievement is assessed by some observation of what a person actually has done. But how can we assess what an individual is capable of doing, unless we rely on what the individual has already done? Thus, no judgment of capacity can presently be made that does not rely heavily on observed achievement. The intelligence test uses achievement to judge capacity. Such a judgment is based upon the assumption that every child has had an equal opportunity to achieve the learnings sampled on the test; hence any difference found must be a difference in capacity. This basic assumption has been seriously questioned by a number of psychologists and educators. While we can determine what a child has or has not learned, we have difficulty determining why the learning has or has not occurred.

Severely and profoundly retarded children are often identified early in life, through either physical abnormalities or the failure to develop normally. These children may not walk or talk when expected as a result of general developmental retardation. More mildly retarded children are often detected only when they begin school. Their failure to learn to read or to respond to other academic requirements can lead to a referral to a psychologist and subsequent diagnosis of retardation.

Mentally retarded young children are generally grouped into one of three categories: educable mentally retarded, trainable mentally retarded, and severely and profoundly mentally retarded. The vast majority of retarded children generally score between 50 and 80 on tests of intelligence, suggesting a rate of intellectual development about one-half to three-fourths that of the normal child. These children usually have interests similar to normal children of the same mental age. It is generally believed that most mild forms of retardation can be ameliorated, especially if an intervention program is begun early in life.

Behaviorally Disabled Children

A number of emotional disturbances, behavioral disorders, and socio-emotional problems can be identified in young children. These range from some of the most severe, such as infant autism, through more moderate problems of conflict with the environment. A variety of explanations as well as classifications characterize this area of exceptionality. Included are children who withdraw totally from reality, such as the schizophrenic or autistic child, or who withdraw less excessively, such as the child who daydreams or lives in a world of fantasy. There are those who manifest anxiety through developmental regression or phobias, and those who manifest antisocial aggression through acting-out behavior or delinquency, the latter being a legal rather than a psychological or educational construct. The causes for the various emotional problems in children are not definitely known. Some theories suggest that the causes are primarily neurological or physiological; others that they are basically a function of family relations or problems of upbringing; still others that they are situationally determined.

The suggestions for treatment are equally varied: drug therapy, family counseling, psychotherapy for the child and/or the family, behavior modification techniques, and other forms of developmental or psychoeducational treatments. For the teacher, the suggestion of psychotherapy or family counseling is not helpful, for although a school might refer a child and his parents to some outside agency for help, the teacher must still respond to the child's behavior in the classroom. Suggestions for the teacher need to be related to helping the child adjust to the school setting or to modifying the setting to be more responsive to the child's needs. Different theories suggest different teaching strategies.

A teacher adhering to one theoretical viewpoint, for example, might welcome a show of aversive behavior and allow children to act out their conflicts in class as a form of therapeutic catharsis. A teacher with a different viewpoint might wish to change the child's behavior so that incidents of acting out are lessened and more desirable social behaviors manifested in the class.

In recent years, advocacy of behavior modification techniques—using operant conditioning to change children's behavior—has increased. The child might be removed from class and put into a special environment that is more manageable in order to decrease the manifestations of negative behavior. The child may then be eased back into the classroom, where the teacher can learn to develop behavior management techniques to sustain the change. If the teacher is not careful to modify those elements in the classroom that set off the negative behavior in the first place, the child may revert to his original condition.

Often the child stays in class and help is provided to the teacher directly in the classroom. The teacher learns to understand the child and the causes of behavior and to increase the ability to work successfully with that child. The teacher might analyze and change the classroom environment to support the more positive aspects of the child's behavior. A crisis-intervention teacher or resource-room teacher could be made available to provide additional help on a long-term basis when the need arises.

Children with Sensory Problems

A number of children are considered exceptional because they are handicapped in normal sensory channels. These include children who are deaf or hard of hearing, and blind or partially sighted. Either condition can exist from birth or occur at any point in the child's life due to accident or illness. The educational consequences of these problems differ, depending on when they began. The ability to hear, both himself and others, is important in the child's development of language. Deafness does not limit the language development of those children who become deaf after the establishment of basic language patterns. Although children blind from birth may be unaware of certain basic concepts, such as color, this disability does not seem to have the same profound effects on development as deafness.

Visually impaired children are usually categorized as either blind or partially sighted. A blind child cannot have vision corrected to better than 20/200; a partially sighted child has the best correction between 20/200 and 20/70. Blind children are generally identified in infancy, but the partially sighted may not be identified until much later. The greater the degree to which the child can respond to visual stimuli, the higher the probability that the problem will not be detected until entrance to school.

In dealing with blind or partially sighted children, the teacher needs to help them use the sensory channels available to gain the maximum information possible from the environment. Much sensory data that can be gained through hearing or touch, less important to the fully sighted child because of its redundancy, becomes of major importance to visually impaired children. Shapes can be learned by touch, and distance and direction can be determined by sound. A child can use existing senses to a much greater extent than is normally expected to compensate for a difficulty in one sensory modality. Thinking skills can still be exercised by mentally operating on available sense experiences. Many of the standard materials of the nursery and kindergarten—such as blocks, puzzles, and manipulative materials—are well suited for the visually impaired child. The teacher needs to help him use materials optimally, and she should acquire and develop other appropriate materials as needed.

Visually impaired children have difficulty moving about independently and caring for themselves. Adults are often overprotective and limit their movement learning opportunities for fear of injury. Children can be helped to become independent in self-care skills and to move about their environment. They can learn to use climbing apparatus, ride tricycles and wagons, dig in sand, and move about the classroom and the outdoor play area. Some assistance will be needed, especially in the beginning. The teacher should be careful to orient the child to the physical environment, and not to make changes in the organization of the room without reorienting him. Rails and ropes might be set up in appropriate places to help mobility. Self-help training might have to be provided in each situation.

As visually impaired children move into the primary grades they will, of course, have difficulty in reading. If the impairment is not great, large-print books and magnifiers can enable the child to read normally. If the problem is more profound, Braille reading and writing should be taught. A blind child can continue in a regular classroom for part of the day if Braille instruction is provided by an itinerant teacher or a resource-room teacher. The classroom teacher could probably cope with arithmetic instruction with some modification of the normal program, but reading and writing instruction will require a special teacher.

The educational problems of hearing impaired children can be profound. They may not only have problems communicating, so important from both a social and educational point of view, but their competence in many language-based activities may be limited. If the children have some residual hearing, they should be fitted with a hearing aid. Even though such a device may distort the quality of sound, it will widen the child's sensory contact with the external world. Care should be taken that they learn how to use the hearing aid, and that the teacher is able to help if a problem arises (e.g., changing the battery).

The teacher needs to modify the room to limit the child's difficulties with it. Care can be taken to diminish unnecessary and confusing noises by covering the floor of the block building area with indoor-outdoor carpeting, for example. In addition, the teacher should speak face-to-face with hearing impaired children, allow them to sit close by when stories are read, and support their production of speech even when there are difficulties.

It is important that the deaf child develop some communicating skills. Speechreading or lipreading is advocated by some educators of the deaf; the use of sign language or the manual alphabet is advocated by others. Still others prefer a combination of the two approaches. Whatever the approach used in the school, it will probably require the availability of a resource or consultant teacher in addition to the classroom teacher.

As important as developing language skills is for the hearing impaired child, developing skills in communicating with nonimpaired children and adults is also important. For this reason, even part-time placement in a regular class should be considered as a way of providing the child with skills to live as normal a life as possible.

Children with Communication Disorders

A survey of the literature suggests that there is considerable incidence of communication disorders in young children. How serious the disorders may be is questionable, however. Among those identified are articulation problems, voice problems, stuttering, and language disorders. The majority of young children's communication problems are related to articulation: sound substitution, sound omission, and sound distortion (including lisping and baby talk). The question of seriousness is related to the prevalence of articulation disorders and the fact that many of them are not evident at later ages. It seems reasonable that many of these are problems of delayed development, which clear themselves up in time. However, some of these disorders will require additional help, and it is difficult to separate the two sets of problems.

Voice problems include excessive nasality or inadequate nasal emission during speech as well as problems of pitch, intensity, and flexibility, leading to monotone or stereotyped speech. Stuttering, or hesitations in speech patterns, may appear in early childhood. Just how serious most stuttering problems are with young children is also questionable. One of the more serious speech problems is delayed speech or aphasia, the partial or total failure of speech to develop. Some speech disorders are the result of other developmental problems, such as cleft palate or cerebral palsy.

While speech and language problems are handled primarily by speech and language specialists in schools, the classroom teacher can do a number of things to help the child with them. One of the important roles of early childhood education is to enhance language development in children. Activities with this aim provided to children with language disorders can have an equal or greater impact than on normal children. Some of these activities are suggested in chapter 4. The child needs to be allowed the time to produce speech communications and to be rewarded in his efforts, even though his achievements may not seem great. The teacher should keep him from becoming too self-conscious or too defeatist in his attempts to communicate with others. As far as the aphasic child is concerned, there is probably little that a classroom teacher can do in helping him with his problem. The teacher should recommend the help of physicians and speech clinicians.

Children with Physical or Motor Problems

Young children can have many different physical or motor problems. While many of these problems do not create learning difficulties, they often create problems for the child in working within the expectations of the school. Those children with more severe problems are dealt with at home or in hospitals. However, the ambulatory child can often be accommodated in schools, fitting well into regular classes if appropriate accommodations are made.

Included in this category of children with special needs are those with cerebral palsy, who suffer from a complex neuromuscular condition due to brain injury prior to or at birth, epileptics, children with other chronic illnesses such as rheumatic fever, congenital heart defects, or cystic fibrosis, and children with congenital malformations of the heart, hip, or spinal column.

Although children with these physical problems represent a small minority of the child population, their numbers are increasing. This is due partly to advances in medical practice and technology, which are saving infants that might formerly have died at birth or shortly thereafter. It is probably also due to the increases in toxic substances in our environment and in drug-related problems among pregnant women.

The key to working with this group of children is to analyze the classroom and modify it as needed to allow them to function as competently and independently as possible. The teacher might also have to design learning experiences and movement activities so that they are within the capabilities of these children.

Each of the exceptionalities discussed in this chapter was presented separately, but they do not always occur in isolation from one another. Often, as noted, physical disabilities are related to speech problems or other problems. Many times teachers are faced with multiply handicapped children. Combined handicaps often complicate diagnosis and create problems in remediation, as well. The fact that children can suffer from a range of exceptionalities underlines the basic problems of classification in the field. For the classroom teacher, a label for a child is less important than a descriptive statement of his educational strengths and weaknesses and of the disabling or strengthening aspects of his development that must be considered in designing an individual program. The major disadvantage of labels is that they can lead to stereotypes, thus preventing the child from being regarded as a child rather than a ''hyphenated child.'' Stigmas are also associated with certain exceptionalities. Parents may be concerned that once the child is labeled, a low learning expectation will be created that will become a self-fulfilling prophecy. Once a child is placed on an educational track, no matter how informal, it is very hard to switch him to a different track.

Some special educators have tried to take a more functional approach to dealing with exceptional children, moving away from the traditional categories and attempting instead to identify those attributes that have implications for educational programming. Ira Iscoe and Sherry Payne (1972) suggest that children differ in several dimensions of basic importance: physical, adjustment, and educational dimensions. Each of these dimensions can be further broken down. The broad categories include

PHYSICAL STATUS

Visibility of physical deviation
Locomotion capabilities and limitations
Communication capabilities and problems

ADJUSTMENT STATUS

Peer acceptance
Family interaction
Self-esteem

EDUCATIONAL STATUS

Motivation
Academic achievement
Educational potential (p. 10)

These categories are useful in identifying information about children that can help in making educational decisions. Information on physical status, for example, can help educators assess to what extent a child can be accommodated in a class, what kinds of modifications might need to be made, and what kinds of learning difficulties might be encountered. Similar judgments can be made on the basis of information on adjustment status and educational status.

Once the handicapped child is identified, the degree of the handicapping condition and the extent to which educational programs will need to be modified in relation to that condition must be determined. An in-depth evaluation, including reports from a psychologist, physical therapist, audiologist, occupational therapist, speech and language therapist, health professional, or special educator should become the basis for a specific educational program designed for each handicapped child. Such a plan is called an *Individualized Educational Program* (IEP).

DEVELOPING AN IEP

An IEP is a written statement of the objectives, content, implementation procedures, and evaluation of a child's educational program. It is required by law to show that a handicapped child is provided with an appropriate education. IEPs are developed by multidisciplinary teams composed of specialists who inform the process from their own particular expertise, the classroom teacher who has a sense of the child's educational performance, and a coordinator. It also includes the child's parent(s) or guardian(s). Even if the child's parents cannot attend an IEP meeting, they must be informed of the process and agree to all actions recommended for the child. If parents do not agree with the team's recommendations, then due-process appeal procedures must be available.

Included in the IEP should be a statement of the child's present level of performance and statements of annual goals and the short-term objectives that are expected to lead to the achievement of the annual goals. Also included should be a statement of special education and related services that will be provided for the child, with descriptions of how often and where these services will be provided, along with a statement of the extent to which the child will participate in the regular classroom program. The criteria by which progress toward the goals will be evaluated should be noted; and finally, a justification for the child's educational program should be included.

In many cases where handicapped children are mainstreamed, the primary responsibility for the education of the handicapped child will rest with the classroom teacher. When this happens, there are usually support services for teachers, often through a resource consultant teacher. Even when this occurs, others may be involved periodically in providing special services to the handicapped child. These can include special education teachers, speech and language specialists and physical therapists. The child may be removed from the class for these services or they might be provided in the classroom, depending on the nature of the services. The organization of the services to be provided, as well as a description of the services and the person to provide the services, may also be noted in the child's IEP.

Teachers are often concerned about stating the long-term goals for handicapped children that are included in the IEP. Making long-range predictions about achievement for any child is a complex process and becomes even more difficult when a child does not make progress in a normal manner. The long-range goals included in an IEP serve as a guide to planning. At best they are rough estimates of what might be accomplished. They should be reviewed periodically and revised if appropriate. Schools and teachers are seldom held accountable for the achievement of these long-range goals.

ORGANIZING FOR AN INTEGRATED CLASS

In working with any group of children a great deal of attention must be given to the organization of resources in the classroom. When handicapped children are integrated into a classroom, this organization may need to be modified. Traffic patterns should be analyzed to ensure free movement for all children. Care should be taken that no unnecessary obstacles are present. Storage arrangements may need to be modified and the classroom environment arranged so that visual, auditory, and physical clutter is as limited as possible. Sometimes new furniture, such as a table high enough for a child in a wheelchair to use, or a tape recorder to be used primarily by a handicapped child, must be provided. The environment should be safe for all children.

The room environment may need to be simplified and safety rules established and enforced. Sometimes simple things, like putting crutch tips on the tables to keep them from sliding, or making sure that blocks are kept out of traffic areas, can significantly improve the safety of the class.

Once the room arrangement is established, it is often best to make as few changes as possible in that arrangement. Change can upset a behaviorally disordered child or make movement more difficult for a visually handicapped child.

If the room is organized to allow for a wide range of individual differences among children, then there will not be too much difficulty in integrating a handicapped child into the program. Different children will be able to function at different levels within the classroom, and what one child does will be less likely to interfere with what others are doing. Activity centers such as those described in chapter 12 help support individualization of instruction and allow for a variety of activities to take place in a classroom at the same time.

In addition to modifying the resources available in the classroom, additional instructional material needs to be procured. In selecting materials, teachers need to ensure that they are both compatible with the program goals of the classroom and appropriate to the child's age, interests, and abilities. Cautions about safety, cost-effectiveness, and freedom from stereotyping that are considered in evaluating all materials should also be considered in relation to special education materials.

MODIFYING THE INSTRUCTIONAL PROGRAM

Many instructional strategies used with normal children are just as effective when used with handicapped children. In numerous cases, for example with orthopedically handicapped children, the handicapping condition does not affect the child's ability to engage in academic learning. There will be problems in movement education for these children, however, as well as in using many of the resources of the school. Other handicapping conditions, such as learning disabilities and mental retardation, may directly affect the learning process or, as with behaviorally disordered children, the ability to function under normal conditions in the social setting of the classroom. Teachers need to meet with special-education resource persons to plan jointly for each handicapped child's learning experiences both inside and outside the classroom.

From the beginning of the identification process, the classroom teacher must become a part of an instructional team which should include a number of persons with different competencies who pool their knowledge and skills to find the most appropriate educational experiences for handicapped children. In public schools such teams usually include resource-room teachers. These may be individuals who work with only a single disability group, such as behaviorally disabled children or cerebral-palsied children, all of whom have the same instructional needs. In other schools resource-room teachers may work with children with a range of disabilities but of a particular age group. There may be similar specialists available from preschools, from the local school district, from the special education district, or from the public health district. These specialists may come to the preschool periodically to serve the handicapped children enrolled there and to act as resource consultants to the teacher. Together with the classroom teacher, these individuals can plan a well-rounded set of educational experiences for the handicapped child, tailored to the specific needs and abilities of the individual.

On many occasions the regular classroom program will have to be modified to meet the needs of the handicapped child. Often the approach used in making such modifications is to plan prescriptively (Laycock, 1980). This approach requires that information be gathered initially in relation to the skills and content that the handicapped child has or has not mastered in each learning area. Such an assesssment might include using many of the procedures discussed earlier in this chapter in relation to the initial diagnosis. Based on this assessment, a series of instructional objectives might be specified for each area of school learning. If the learning needs are complex, the teacher might use task analysis to break down some of the more complex objectives into objectives that are more easily achieved, which can be integrated later. A set of instructional or lesson plans would then be developed aimed at achieving these objectives.

Among the instructional techniques that could be used in these lessons are *verbal instructions,* to tell children in as simple a way as possible what they must do, or *modeling,* whereby the teacher or some other person demonstrates a skill and then has the child imitate the demonstration. *Manual guidance* might also be used, whereby the teacher physically helps the child to move through the tasks to be learned. A set of *prompts* or *cues* that elicit particular actions on the part of the child might also serve instructional purposes, although in time these prompts should be lessened or faded.

Whatever skills are taught to children, there should be ample opportunities for children to practice them to increase their proficiency. While some of this practice might be in isolation, ultimately the child should be given the opportunity to practice the skills learned in situations similar to those in which those skills will have to be used.

Because of the particular needs of handicapped children, it is not always possible for them to learn things informally. Many times more formal and more systematic approaches will need to be used. The degree of formality, and just how systematic the learning will need to be, depends on the nature of the handicapping condition as well as on the nature of the task to be learned. One of the guiding principles of mainstreaming is that the learning activities provided to children should be as close as possible to those offered normal children and should be provided in a way that allows for the maximum integration of handicapped and nonhandicapped children.

TEACHING THE EXCEPTIONAL CHILD

The preparation of teachers of exceptional children is a highly specialized separate field. Programs are specifically designed to train teachers of deaf children, gifted children, emotionally disturbed children, and children with other specific exceptionalities. Each program prepares teachers with special knowledge and skills. The regular classroom teacher is bound to have to deal with children in many of these categories of exceptionality, but could hardly be expected to complete all these programs.

How, then, can teachers learn to cope with the many problems that face them? Perhaps it is unfair to ask teachers to be prepared to work with a range of children with exceptionalities while maintaining a full classroom as before. Special help needs to be provided to classroom teachers as exceptional children are integrated into their classes. Resource personnel, crisis intervention teachers, and consultants have been recommended to help classroom teachers better understand and educate the exceptional child, as well as to provide specific techniques as required. The child may also be taken out of the classroom for periods of time for those aspects of the program which are beyond the capability of the regular teacher or beyond the range of regular classroom activities. Additional supplies and equipment might also have to be supplied. Consideration must also be given to reducing the number of children in a classroom when exceptional children are introduced.

In addition, there are some things a regular classroom teacher must learn. A general understanding of the nature of exceptionalities in children as well as a knowledge of the growth and development of normal children is a desirable, even necessary requirement. In addition, the teacher should know some of the basic techniques of education for exceptional children. This should create no problem, for these basic instructional strategies are little different from the strategies suggested for normal children. There are differences in specific content and methods, however. Here the teacher must learn to rely on outside experts, consultants, resource-room teachers, and clinicians who will join in designing and implementing programs for these children.

In addition, certain personal characteristics are helpful. The teacher needs concern and caring for children without unnecessary sympathy and pity; flexibility in dealing with educational goals and methods; willingness to try new techniques and remain tentative in her approval of tried and true techniques; willingness to communicate problems and to share concerns with others; ability to function in a cooperating relationship; undying optimism and faith in the utility of education; and ability to accept some degree of failure as well as success. Somehow the requirements for teaching these children are the same as those for teaching all children . . . only more.

REFERENCES

DENO, E.   Special education as developmental capital. *Exceptional Children,* 1970, *37,* 229-237.

ISCOE, I., and PAYNE, S.   Development of a revised scale for the functional classification of exceptional children. In E. P. Trapp and P. Himelstein (Eds.). *Readings on the exceptional child.* New York: Appleton-Century-Crofts, 1972.

LAYCOCK, V. K.   Prescriptive programming in the mainstream. In J. W. Schifarie, R. M. Anderson, and S. J. Odle (Eds.), *Implementing learning in the least restrictive environment; Handicapped children in the mainstream.* Baltimore, Md.: University Park Press, 1980.

SPODEK, B., SARACHO, O. N., and LEE, R. C.   Mainstreaming handicapped children in the preschool. In S. Kilmer (Ed.), *Advances in early education and day care* (Vol. 3). Greenwich, Conn.: JAI Press, 1983.

SUGGESTED READING

ALLEN, K. E.   *Mainstreaming in early childhood education.* Albany, N.Y.: Delmar, 1980.

CARTWRIGHT, C. P., CARTWRIGHT, C. A., and WARD, M. E.   *Educating special learners.* Belmont, Calif.: Wadsworth, 1981.

FALLEN, N., and McGOVERN, J.   (Eds.). *Young children with special needs.* Columbus, Ohio: Chas. E. Merrill, 1978.

HEWETT, F. A., and FORNESS, S. R.   *Education of exceptional learners* (2nd ed.). Boston: Allyn & Bacon, 1977.

JORDAN, J. B., HAYDEN, A. H., KARNES, M. B., and WOOD, M. M.   *Early childhood education for exceptional children.* Reston, Va.: Council for Exceptional Children, 1977.

LERNER, J., MARDELL-CZUDNOWSKI, C., and GOLDENBERG, D.   *Special education for the early childhood years.* Englewood Cliffs, N.J.: Prentice-Hall, 1981.

RADCLIFFE, D.   *Developmental disabilities in the preschool child.* New York: SP Medical & Scientific Books, 1981.

SMITH, R. M., NEISWORTH, J. T., and HUNT, F. M.   *The exceptional child: A functional approach* (2nd ed.). New York: McGraw-Hill, 1983.

SOUWEINE, J., GRIMMINS, S., and MAZEL, C.   *Mainstreaming: Ideas for teaching young children.* Washington, D.C.: National Association for the Education of Young Children, 1982.

SPODEK, B., SARACHO, O. N., and LEE, R. C.   *Mainstreaming young children.* Belmont, Calif.: Wadsworth, 1984.

12

Organizing
for Instruction

Once teachers consider the goals and content of the program they design for their children, they must then plan and organize the environment. Building on children's interests, capacities, limitations, and aspirations, they go on to establish the concrete reality of what will happen in the classroom. As a result of planning, teachers organize the day into some form of activity schedule, deploy the children into manageable groups, and organize the room so that children can make the best use of space, materials, and equipment.

In the early years, children's autonomy is a goal rather than an established fact. We wish them to become independent, knowing full well that they will continue to be dependent upon adults well beyond the primary grades. The development of autonomy is important, and is nurtured by teaching children to assume responsibility while providing them with the security and needed guidance of a knowledgeable adult.

PLANNING

Long-range planning helps the teacher organize classroom activities so they build on one another. Short-range planning is required to anticipate the many details of day-to-day teaching. Short term objectives relate to outcomes of specific instruction. Some are defined in terms of observable behavior; others are framed in more general terms.

Planning begins before the children enter school. Teachers gather supplies, materials, and equipment, ordering some well in advance of their use.

Activities and lessons are designed to provide children with opportunities to grow. The teacher should know what specific learning opportunities each child is ready for, and help each one learn to use resources for learning. Finally, every child must be helped to become a responsible member of the class, learning to use the group and respond to it without having personal wishes submerged by it. To do so, children must develop greater self-control and ways of dealing appropriately with their needs and feelings.

Long-Range Planning

Long-range plans attempt to identify threads that will tie the various elements of the program together throughout the year. These can be based on conceptual schemes or sets of specific skills. Teachers must decide the degree to which they expect each child to achieve these goals.

Long-range plans help give a program flexibility. As the children move through the program, teachers must modify their plans to insure that the program is continually appropriate. Without prior thought and preparation, day-to-day learning activities are necessarily limited.

Long-range curriculum planning is often conceived as a linear process. Teachers begin by defining each long-range goal, then the prerequisites needed to achieve that goal; the prerequisites again become a set of more approachable goals. In this way a series of curriculum steps are identified. The assumption is that if a child adheres to these steps without any serious deviation, the ultimate goal will be achieved. Progress toward that goal is readily assessable in this design.

An example of this form of curriculum planning is found in the design of the *Science—A Process Approach* program (see chapter 6). While such planning helps the teacher see the relationship between current and future activities and between immediate and long-range goals, it has disadvantages. The program's linearity creates rigidity. The only form of individual difference that can be accounted for is the pace of learning—differences in learning styles or children's interests are disregarded.

Rebecca Corwin, George Hein, and Diane Levin (1976) have suggested *curriculum webs* as a form of nonlinear curriculum construction. A single interest, experience, or activity may take the child's learning in many different directions, leading to a range of activities in science, mathematics, and the arts as the program moves from the original experience. In a curriculum web various curriculum areas—language arts, math, science, social studies, and art— are woven into the study through the range of activities that the children engage in over a period of weeks.

Using the idea of the web, a teacher can design learning approaches that integrate various curriculum areas in special ways for each group of children. Children will often be able to cope with advanced learning in this fashion without ever having achieved the necessary prerequisites. Teachers who are sure of program goals can be flexible in planning and in responding to children's interests and concerns, straying from the path when it seems appropriate. A digression may lead to a new set of goals or may end up as a short-cut to a set of previously established goals. Dallying or retracing old steps may serve the teacher's and the children's purposes well and still provide a reasonable pace of achievement.

No matter what the design of the program, it is the teacher's responsibility to modify it to be responsive to the needs and interests of the children. No textbook author or curriculum development specialist has personal knowledge of the clients for whom the program is developed. Only the teacher, knowing the children—their strengths and weaknesses, their backgrounds, and the school environment—can modify the program to fit them.

Identifying plans for the year allows the teacher to think through the program in advance and gather the necessary resources to carry it through. Films, filmstrips, new books, and supplies may have to be ordered in advance. Trips need advance planning. It is always easier to cancel a trip, postpone a visit, or decide not to use a film than to want to carry out an activity and find schedules filled or materials not available.

Short-Range Planning

Teachers must also organize for classroom work on a daily, weekly, or periodic basis. This planning helps determine what will need to be gathered. It is necessary to think ahead so that the tape recorder is available when needed, so that enough copies of a worksheet are available, or so that a particular parent can visit the class to speak about a hobby at the proper moment.

The program's daily balance and the relationships that can be established among diverse subject areas should be considered in short term planning. Children can write sentence stories that correspond to number facts or that tell about measuring experiences, thus integrating mathematics with language activities. Stories read in a book can be acted out in pantomime or with puppets. Science experiences often require quantification. The possible ways of relating learning areas to one another are endless. Each allows the teacher to extend the child's experience beyond the obvious.

Some educators suggest that each detail in an instructional program should be worked out in advance. Unfortunately this can limit activities. If the activities are varied enough and if children can differentiate their own roles in each activity, they will find areas of the program that are related to their needs and that will help them grow. Self-selection within carefully prepared alternatives is an important part of education. Adequate planning can insure the availability of legitimate learning activities. The goals of the program need to be different for each child and cannot always be identified far in advance.

Developing Activities

The unit of instruction in nursery school and kindergarten is the *activity*. Unlike the *lesson,* the unit of instruction in elementary school, the activity need not have a formal beginning, middle, and end. Activities are often open-ended, coming to no neatly packaged conclusion, but possibly resurfacing at some later time. The activity is not teacher-dominated. The teacher may plan the activity, make materials available, provide time, and even influence its direction, but it is the children who carry the activity forward and, in the final analysis, determine its content. Each activity may be conceived as a solitary unit having no relationship to any other activity, or, more often, be part of a series of inter-related activities. The teacher can relate block construction, music, and story activities to a single theme on the same day, or have a series of activities that continue from day to day with each an elaboration of the previous one. Activities may be organized into units or planned so that basic concepts and ideas recur in some cyclical fashion.

The teacher should plan a program so that children are involved in different areas of the curriculum. The room must be organized so that each activity has the necessary space, materials, and equipment available when needed, and so that several activities can take place simultaneously without interfering with one another.

ARRANGING THE ROOM

Schools for young children are housed in many kinds of facilities. Some buildings were designed to serve educational purposes, but others were never designed for a school. Church buildings, community centers, homes, or stores may become schools for young children. Sometimes a dual arrangement develops with a school using space for one part of the day or week and another activity housed there at another time. Each arrangement creates different problems for the classroom teacher.

Yet teachers have been able to modify the physical space in which they teach. Suspended ceilings can be installed at reasonable expense if the ceiling is too high, improving lighting and acoustical qualities. A low or high platform can be built to allow for dramatic play or provide some private space. Even painting the wall a brighter shade, hanging curtains on the windows, or developing attractive wall displays changes the nature of the physical space.

What a teacher does with a room or outdoor area needs to be the result of careful thinking about how it can help the program along. If all children are expected to be involved in the same activity at the same time, there should be less concern about room arrangements than if individual and small group activities are to be nurtured in the classroom. In an individualized program, for example, the room should be arranged so that the children can work without constant teacher supervision and not interfere with each other's activities.

Organizing Physical Space

Space requirements for classroom use are often prescribed by law. Many states require a minimum of thirty-five square feet per child of classroom space in a nursery school. The same minimum figure is sometimes suggested for space in a primary classroom. Many experts, however, recommend that as much as one hundred square feet per child be available. In addition, from fifty to two hundred square feet per child of outdoor space should be provided for the program. The indoor space should be well lighted, well ventilated, and well heated. Ideally there should be easy access from the classroom to the outdoor play area and to toilet facilities. If the classroom has a door leading directly to a play yard or terrace, the program can flow easily between indoors and outdoors.

Teachers need to check the physical arrangements of their rooms to ensure that they are safe. Furniture and equipment should have no sharp edges or protrusions that could harm children. Traffic patterns should be designed to avoid collisions. Climbing equipment should be installed over soft surfaces. Sometimes when handicapped children are present in a class, additional modifications need to be made in the physical environment. Furniture might have to be rearranged or crutch tips placed on the legs of tables so they will not slip. In addition, teachers and children should establish and enforce safety rules for functioning in the classroom.

Arranging the Primary Classroom

Most primary classrooms provide more informal seating arrangements, with chairs and desks or tables grouped together in horizontal rows, or in a semicircle. Chairs may be grouped in a corner for reading instruction and an easel or a table for art work placed in the back of the room. There may also be shelves and closets for storage of books and materials, and a display area for science or nature study.

This type of room arrangement supports a classroom in which the basic mode of instruction is verbal, and in which children are expected to function as a total-class learning situation or in small groups under the teacher's supervision. Constructions for social studies and children's experiments require other

FIGURE 12-1   Classroom arrangements facilitate good teaching.

kinds of space and other materials. A teacher who wishes to individualize instruction and provide for self-pacing will also find such an arrangement restrictive. Just as schedules reflect the kind of program a teacher wishes to develop, so does the arrangement of the room.

An activity-oriented primary classroom in which individuals and small groups engage in different activities simultaneously would benefit from a room arrangement closely resembling that of a nursery school or kindergarten. A library center is a critical resource in the primary classroom. In addition, centers for activities in mathematics, science, social studies, language arts and other activities could be developed.

. Because there is so much variation among school facilities and groups of children, it is difficult to suggest an ideal room arrangement. However, there are criteria that teachers can use to judge the balance provided in the room and the degree to which the physical design supports the educational design. Adequate separation between activities is important so that children's work won't be interfered with—both physical and visual boundaries work. Also, noisy and quiet, and messy and neat activities should be separated.

Elizabeth Jones (n.d.) has identified five dimensions that can be used to analyze a physical setting. They can be used in planning the physical facility, and selecting equipment and furniture. The dimensions are

Soft—hard
Open—closed
Simple—complex
Intrusion—seclusion
High mobility—low mobility

Soft areas are places where children can relax to read, listen, talk, or play quietly. Softness can be created by providing a small area rug, some pillows, a stuffed animal, an upholstered or a rocking chair—even curtains. Other areas in the room are characterized by hardness. Hard floor and table surfaces facilitate the cleanup of messy materials and can take the punishment of children's work. Out-of-doors grassy areas are soft—paved surfaces are hard.

The room should allow for easy access to materials through open-shelf arrangements, although teachers will store things in closed areas away from children. A balance of open-ended and closed-ended instructional materials for the children is important as well. Closed materials have constrained goals and modes of relationship (picture puzzles); open materials provide unlimited alternatives in their goals and modes of relations (clay). In addition, both simple and complex learning materials should be provided. Simple units have one obvious use and no subparts; complex units allow for manipulation and improvisation, with many subparts.

Some areas of the room should be secluded to allow for cozy spaces as well as for activities that need to be separated from the group bustle. Other areas should encourage the intrusion of teacher and children. As activities in the classroom encourage both high and low degrees of movement, the arrangement should support high and low mobility. Traffic patterns and the mobility required by different activities need to be analyzed for this purpose.

Ideally, the indoor space should be designed to support flexible educational programs. Surfaces should be treated with acoustical materials wherever possible. Floors can be carpeted or covered with resilient tiles. Walls should be pleasantly but unobtrusively colored and there should be adequate display space, including bulletin boards and possibly a small chalkboard on the walls. Shades or blinds that both reduce glare and darken the room completely can be provided for windows. A drinking fountain and a sink for activity and cleaning purposes limit the number of trips the children make down the hallway. Bathrooms should be adjacent or close to the classroom.

A classroom should also have enough storage and locker facilities for children's coats, boots, extra clothing, and personal belongings, and for the teacher's needs. In addition, considerable and varied storage space should be provided for materials and equipment. Large wheel toys, paper, and art supplies all need different kinds of storage facilities.

ACTIVITY CENTERS

Many early childhood classrooms are organized into activity centers, each of which supports some portion of the program. Though the centers can expand or contract with the needs of the program, most are available throughout the activity period. Activity centers allow rooms to become child centered rather than teacher centered. They help programs become more individualized and allow children's classroom participation to become more active and more independent (Blake, 1977). In the nursery-kindergarten, these centers can include

Arts and crafts center
Dramatic play center
Blockbuilding center
Manipulative materials center
Library center
Music center
Display center

Activity centers in the primary grades are often designed according to subject matter, for example, a mathematics center, a language arts center, a social studies center, and a science center.

At all levels, centers can be organized around specific themes that provide a focus for activities that might otherwise be supported by different centers. An environmental studies center, a transportation center, in fact, a center that focuses on any topic could be created in a classroom. Materials and activities would be organized in that center for as long as the theme holds the children's interest.

A center should include materials related to its purpose for individual and small group activity, with boundaries clearly defined for the use of those materials. Centers should be designed to be easily supervised, and their contents should support independent study and activity. Activity cards such as those described in chapter 7 can provide direction to children without the teacher continually being present. Sometimes activities can evolve out of planning conferences.

A science activity center, for example, should be a place that has reasonable access to water. It could have a display area for plants and animals and shelves that hold magnifying glasses, magnets, containers of various sizes, and a range of measuring devices. These might be grouped and placed in shallow trays for continued orderly arrangement. The materials in the center would be changed from time to time as different areas of science are investigated. Seasonal changes might suggest material changes. Open-ended questions can title displays, such as: "Which materials sink and which float?"

A reading center would have books with titles clearly visible on shelves or racks and comfortable places to read. A rug, some pillows, a soft chair, and straight chairs and a table might complement the library shelves. The books would be of different levels of difficulty, about different topics, and include both fiction and nonfiction. Such a center could be augmented by a listening station, a cassette recorder or phonograph equipped with headsets, and a filmstrip or slide viewer.

A dramatic play center includes the traditional housekeeping equipment or has other areas for dramatic play as suggested in chapter 10. A thematic approach focuses play on various aspects of adult and community life. Judith Bender (1971) suggests collecting materials for play themes in "prop boxes," each supporting one theme. A prop box for automobile repair play would contain discarded, cleaned auto parts, tools, and other materials. The teacher can create a camping box, a beautician's box, or various other boxes.

Outdoor Area

Outdoor play spaces should have both paved surfaces and grassy areas if possible. The pavement allows children to use tricycles or other wheel toys. In addition, blockbuilding is more satisfying on a flat surface. A covered terrace or patio is desirable as part of the outdoors area so that children can be outdoors even when it rains. Some shade is necessary under any circumstances. There ought to be an area for digging; a dirt area will suffice, but a sand box or pit large enough for a group of children to play in is desirable. Such a sand pit can be built right into the ground, with provisions for drainage and a cover to keep the sand clean and usable. A garden should be set aside for the children's use.

Provisions should be made for large-muscle activities and for dramatic play. Permanently installed equipment of wood, steel, concrete, and fiberglass, as well as portable equipment such as packing crates, boards, and ladders are useful. Very young children may be offered simple equipment, then, as they become more competent, more sophisticated and challenging equipment. Adequate storage space in the outdoor area, such as a shed in the play yard or a locker at the door leading to the play area, should be available.

The prevailing climate will determine what kinds of activities will be offered children outdoors, and, in turn, how the outdoor play area should be designed. Other considerations include the problems of vandalism and the uses that will be made of the area when school is not in session. The outdoor area should be considered an extension of the classroom, providing opportunity for exciting learning experiences.

Frost and Klein (1979) suggest that children's playgrounds should be carefully planned, even before schools are planned, to preserve the natural terrain. Permanent equipment such as fences, storage facilities, waterlines, water fountains, hard-surfaced areas, and shade structures should be installed. The playground should then be zoned to provide the range and arrangement of equipment, taking into account such factors as (1) the need for complex multi-function structure, (2) the provision of varied equipment to allow a range of children's play forms, (3) the arrangement of equipment to allow cross-structured play, (4) the creation of zones that can be integrated, and (5) the creation of zones that allow for movement across zones. Spaces should also be provided for creative arts and natural activities. In addition, safety, maintenance, and supervision must be considered.

EQUIPMENT AND SUPPLIES

While educational supply houses have much of the equipment needed in activity centers, some can be purchased locally in hardware stores, supermarkets, and discount stores. This is often less expensive, since there is no cost for packaging and shipping. Teachers who buy locally should be aware of school policy regarding purchases and the possibility of not paying a local sales tax. However, local purchases do take time and the teacher must judge whether the hours spent offset the money saved. Many schools maintain a petty cash fund to help the teacher make small purchases, such as buying cake mixes for a cooking experience or nails for the woodwork area.

Instructional kits for early childhood education contain complete sets of materials and teacher manuals packaged for classroom use. Kits are available for teaching mathematics, reading, language skills, cognitive skills, human relations skills, as well as many other areas of learning. The entire program of a class could be taught through kits.

Some kits can be useful to teachers. They make available materials that would be difficult to assemble, and insure proper instruction through the structure of activities and directions to teachers. They are often well conceived and well designed; some are even field-tested to determine their effectiveness. Other kits, however, lack imagination, contain closed-ended activities, and are often overpriced for the materials provided, can be stereotyped, and provide little evidence that they will teach what they promise.

In fact there are good kits and poor ones, closed-ended and open-ended ones, kits that nurture the children's learning and those that exploit children and provide too narrow a range of activities. The teacher needs to assess each kit as she would assess each set of materials provided in the classroom. Unfortunately, the necessary information for judging kits is often not available.

Some schools have expensive pieces of equipment, such as easels, lockers, climbing apparatus, or storage facilities, contributed or built by parents or members of the community. Power tools needed for their construction may be borrowed or rented locally. Local sewing centers will often lend sewing machines to allow parents to make doll clothes, sheets for resting cots, or curtains. Bringing the parents together for project work has other advantages, for as they meet and work together, they will be knit into a group. They will also have an investment in the school. Care must be taken that parents do not feel exploited by such work sessions, however.

Many useful learning materials do not have to be bought. The teacher can salvage material that would otherwise be thrown away or even involve children and their parents in this process. Beans or pebbles can be used for counting as easily as can carefully designed mathematics material. Cast-off clothes make excellent additions to a dramatic play area. The chassis of a discarded radio, a broken alarm clock, castoffs from repair shops, buttons, egg cartons, and numerous other materials are useful in an early childhood classroom.

Criteria for Selecting Equipment and Supplies

In selecting equipment and supplies, teachers may use a number of criteria.

Cost. The amount of money spent for an object is an important consideration. Price alone, however, is often a false yardstick. Some less expensive items are not as satisfactory for their intended purpose as would more expensive items. Often the more expensive item will last longer and in the final analysis cost less. In any event, the cost of an item has to be balanced with the benefits provided.

Relationship to the school program. Educational equipment illustrated in catalogues may be more fascinating to the adult than to the child. Items may be interesting but unrelated to the program. Teachers should select materials and equipment that will be interesting to children and help further their educational goals.

Appropriateness for the children.   Learning materials need to be selected that are matched to the interests, ages, and learning abilities of a particular group of children. The specific strengths and needs of individual children need to be considered in selecting material.

Quality and Durability.   There are many elements to consider in judging the quality of a piece of equipment. Equipment adequate for home use is often inappropriate for school. While design is important, the way it is executed is equally important. Judgments about the kind and quality of materials used— the care with which the equipment is fabricated, the way pieces are joined, the type of finish applied—go into determining quality.

Safety.   Because of the vulnerability of young children, this criterion is of special concern. School equipment should not have sharp edges or protrusions. Finishes should be nontoxic as well as durable. For very young children, materials should be large enough to prevent swallowing. If the equipment is for climbing, it must be strong enough to take the children's weight without collapsing, and have steps close enough together so that they can be managed easily. While most equipment and materials designed for young children meet safety requirements, this is not universally true. Caution is important.

Flexibility of Use.   Since both budget and space are often limited, teachers should consider equipment that can be used in a variety of ways and situations. Such equipment will be stored less often and used in more ways. In the dramatic play area, equipment that has few details can often be used most flexibly, for the child's imagination turns a simple box into a rocket ship or a covered wagon. Of course, equipment designed for specific purposes should not be overlooked.

Many educational supply houses throughout the United States manufacture and/or sell equipment and supplies for early childhood education. These firms often have regional offices. Their catalogues or displays at conferences can help a teacher select proper equipment and materials for her classroom. Some of the traditional textbook publishers have also developed kits containing materials in addition to books.

Most teachers have difficulty in selecting appropriate materials and equipment and deciding which manufacturer offers the highest quality at the most moderate price. Unfortunately, there are no *Consumer Reports* for this kind of equipment. It is helpful to ask the advice of teachers who have had some experience using specific equipment.

The criteria developed by the Educational Products Information Exchange (EPIE) Institute for evaluating educational materials for all levels are useful at the early childhood level as well. These criteria suggest that information be collected on the producer of the materials, the administrative requirements of the school, the pedagogical and curriculum requirements of the class, and the evaluations made of the effectiveness of the material. (EPIE, 1973).

A number of guides for the selection of equipment for early childhood education are available. These include lists in textbooks and pamphlets. Some useful lists are found in the following material:

> Association for Childhood Education International, *Selecting Educational Equipment for School and Home.* Washington, D.C.: The Association for Childhood Education International, 1976.
>
> Evans, Anne Marie, "How to Equip and Supply Your Prekindergarten Classrooms," in *Early Childhood Education Rediscovered,* ed. Joe L. Frost. New York: Holt, Rinehart & Winston, 1968, pp. 567–76.
>
> Foster, and Headley. *Education in the Kindergarten,* 3rd ed. New York: American Book, 1969, chapter 7.
>
> Heffernan, and Todd, *The Kindergarten Teacher.* Boston: Heath, 1960, pp. 59–65.

Although all classrooms present differing needs for materials and equipment, it is helpful to know what generally fits into classrooms.

Furniture

Furniture for an early childhood classroom should be movable and durable, scaled to the children's size. Tables and chairs should be of varying heights since children in any age group vary in size. Tables of different shapes might also be included for many purposes. The same tables can be used for both art work and eating. Special tables might be designated for use in the doll corner, the housekeeping area, the library area, and for display purposes. Trapezoidal tables are quite flexible in that they can be grouped and arranged to create many different shapes. If chairs and tables are stackable, they can be stored in a corner of the room when not in use.

A teacher might wish to have some furniture for personal use: a desk, a couple of chairs, and a file cabinet. If work space is provided adjacent to the classroom, precious classroom space will not need to be used. Or, an unobtrusive portion of the room can be set aside for planning materials, records, personal supplies, and a first-aid kit.

If young children stay in school a full day, they need cots for rest. Lightweight cots that stack for easy storage can be purchased. These are not necessary for children in a half-day program. In kindergarten an informal quiet activity is advantageous.

SCHEDULING

A schedule allocates time for each day's activities. Children learn to anticipate future events through the regularity of daily occurrences. In the nursery school and kindergarten, time allotments are made for activities. Primary grade learning may be organized into time periods by subject.

Activities are organized in large blocks of time. The range of alternatives available for the children during the activity periods supports a degree of individuality and allows a variety of outcomes to be planned for different children.

Flexibility is necessary in any schedule. On one day conversations with children may stretch to forty-five minutes, although only twenty have been scheduled; on other days, five minutes may seem too long. A teacher might wish to devote a whole day to a craft project and simply not include a story or music activity. Balance over a long time needs to be considered. Children do not have to be involved in every area of the school curriculum on every day.

An alternative to scheduling time into periods would use some variation of the *integrated day*. Teachers concerned with individualizing instruction and developing autonomy in the children can plan many program strands to operate at the same time so that children can move from one curriculum area to another at their own pace. Such an organization limits the amount of waiting children do in class, because they make optimal use of their school time in individual learning opportunities. Such organization could also be an aid to integrating school subject matter, for artificial time barriers could be lessened considerably or done away with entirely.

Much of the success of open scheduling rests on preparing the children to function autonomously. Some teachers may prefer to retain a structured portion of the day in addition to providing some time for independent activity. Such a period might include opportunities for independent reading, project work, craft activities, and individual research, as well as opportunities to complete elective assignments in various interest areas. Teachers should work with children in joint planning before the activities begin and in evaluation sessions afterward.

TRANSITIONS

While teachers generally plan carefully for the content of activity periods, the problems that arise in a classroom often occur between these periods. The demands that children clean up, line up, move from one area to another, or wait can create difficulties. Some children finish their cleanup well ahead of others, and some are naturally less patient than others. Often, scheduling must rely on the movement of other classes, which may be late.

Elizabeth Hirsch (n.d.) suggests that a number of factors contribute to difficulties around transition time including boredom, the insistence on conformity, the absence of a future orientation in some children, the absence of clearly defined tasks, and a possible fear of failure. Anticipating the problems of transition periods and planning for them can ease potential difficulties. The teacher can quickly learn which children will have problems during transitions and support them particularly. Making a game of cleanup makes it seem less overwhelming. Giving children specific directions, and seeing that the require-

FIGURE 12-2 Transitions can flow more smoothly when children are involved in cleanup.

ments of the transition are not beyond their capabilities, also help. A store of short games, stories, poems, and finger-plays fills unanticipated periods of waiting. Most important, the teacher's sense of calm and order will help the children overcome problems that do arise.

ORGANIZING PEOPLE

Placing fifteen, twenty, or more children of like age into a single room for many hours each day creates conflict between the needs of the individual and the group. We expect young children to give up the natural rhythm of their daily activity when they enter school. We demand that they all come to the school at the same time, sit in place for the same period of time, take care of bodily functions at prescribed periods, eat and play together at specific periods, and learn at the same pace. We expect all children to "behave properly" irrespective of their earlier patterns of behavior or the particular expectations of the outside world. Some degree of conformity is necessary for a child to get on in the world and is a form of acculturation, but how *much* conformity is really necessary is an open question.

Many educators have looked for ways to lessen the inherent conflict between the individual and the group in school. Some children learn faster than others and are more competent in certain areas. Children have different styles, different interests, and need different kinds of learning supports.

Many techniques have been used to cope with this conflict. One way is to provide a broad range of activities for children to choose among. A portion of the day may be assigned to an indoor or outdoor activity period during which children may select from structured or unstructured tasks and may change tasks. Only during short periods of the day are they required to be with the group—for "routine" activities, such as snacks, or rest, or for large group activities like music, storytelling, or discussion times.

Grouping

Traditionally, the criterion for assigning children to classes has been academic achievement or reading performance. Although this might be comfortable for teachers who work with the total class, it presents certain problems for children. Narrowing the range of differences in one area of behavior may have no effect on the range of differences in other areas. In addition, the placement of a child in a homogeneously grouped classroom creates an expectation of performance that may become a self-fulfilling prophecy. A child assigned to a slow class often performs according to what is expected of that group.

While homogeneous grouping is advocated by some teachers and parents, there is no evidence that it increases children's learning in any appreciable way. With the mainstreaming of children with special needs into regular classes, a broader range of educational abilities in each class has become the norm.

Instructional Grouping

One way of dealing with individual differences used at the primary level is grouping children for instruction. Organizing a classroom into three reading groups, each representing a limited range of performance levels, is typical. The teacher can work with one group at a time, listening to children read, holding phonics lessons, or engaging them in other tasks while other children are engaged in seatwork activity. Using a team approach or individualizing instruction may limit the seatwork needed, since more than one instructional group can be dealt with at one time.

Individualized Instruction

Individualized instruction tasks keep the goals of education constant but allow children to move through the same tasks at different paces. Work is broken down into small steps and children are given individual instructional tasks based on diagnostic tests. They complete work sheets, are tested, and upon evidence of successful attainment, move on to the next set of tasks. All children move through the same series of tasks, but at their own pace. Opportunities are provided for children to skip sets of tasks if they evidence competence in the area.

Within such an approach only the pace is individualized. An activity-oriented class individualizes other aspects of instruction. The classroom can become a workshop, allowing children to pursue different enterprises. Both the means and goals are different for each child to achieve them. Children can also be given greater opportunities to feed their interests into the classroom situation, thus modifying the program.

Multi-Age Grouping

Another way of dealing with individual differences in the classroom is to do away with the age-grade organization of the school. By increasing the differences in any one classroom, the teacher cannot have the same expectations for all children. In addition, less formal methods of instruction are possible and greater individualization may result. Children can help and teach one another, age-grade expectations are lessened, and the children's own performance capabilities become the basis for judgments about programs.

William Schrankler (1976) has identified several advantages of family grouping, as multi-aged grouping is sometimes called. The multi-aged class represents a microsociety that provides an enriched intellectual community for young children. It eliminates age-grade lines and thus allows for cross-age tutoring. It also lengthens the time period for teacher-parent and teacher-child interactions beyond a single term or year. In studying children in multi-aged and unit-aged classes, Schrankler found that a positive relationship existed between multi-age grouping and affective factors, including the child's self-esteem and his positive attitude toward school. There were no differences in academic achievement between children in the two types of classes.

Multi-age grouping, like any organizational scheme, presents the possibility for increasing the individualization. What teachers do with this potential becomes the crucial factor in supporting children's learning. Unfortunately, in some cases, nongrading has meant replacing one criterion for grouping (age) with another (possibly reading achievement), with no change in classroom practice. In the nongraded approach, the individual differences in the classroom are viewed as an asset. If children are considered learning resources, then increasing the range of children in a school unit can increase the range of learning resources available.

Methods of dealing with individual differences can be combined in any number of ways to improve the match of instruction to children. Each arrangement requires a different way of thinking through the classroom organization. The layout of the physical facilities can enhance or thwart small group activities. The availability of materials and equipment is also a concern. The teacher does not need a full set of textbooks in an individualized program. On the other hand, a greater *variety* of materials and equipment must be available that the children can use independently.

Organizing Adults

Adults play many roles in the education of young children. School principals and center directors assume primarily administrative responsibilities, although they may do some teaching. Head teachers, teacher-directors, and classroom teachers assume primary responsibility for classroom planning and teaching. Teacher aides, assistants, and volunteers may also be involved in teaching as well as supportive activities. Volunteers might be resource persons who are invited into the classroom briefly or part of the ongoing teaching staff, as in many cooperative nursery schools. In addition, new roles are being defined for persons in early childhood education, such as the Early Childhood Educator (Almy, 1975).

Others in the school community also contribute to the education of young children; each leaves an imprint. The cook, custodian, bus driver, and others all influence the education of children. While teachers cannot be responsible for or supervise all the encounters the child has with school personnel, they need to be aware of them, utilizing them to integrate learnings from many sources. Teachers must coordinate the use of volunteers, spend some time training them and providing an orientation to the school.

Parents participating in a nursery school must be made aware of the school's philosophy, routines, techniques of teaching, and methods of control. Their particular roles and responsibilities must be delineated. The reasons for the classroom's organization should be explained, and practice sessions for parents might help to create consistent performance.

Some educators advocate differentiated staffing patterns as a way of using and rewarding teachers with different skills and expertise. Such a pattern, according to Clinton Boutwell, Dean Berry, and Robert Lungren (1973), has five characteristics: a formal system of shared decision making, formal provisions for self-renewal, performance-based organizational roles, formal provisions for professional self-regulation, and a flexible use of human and physical resources. Teams created this way lessen teachers' isolation and lead to flexible teaching arrangements.

Nursery classes that use a head and assistant teacher in each classroom represent one type of team. Teaching aides in kindergarten or primary classroom allow two individuals to work together and facilitate splitting the classroom in various ways, so that adults can attend to several individuals or groups at all times.

More extensive teams can be created by merging classes of children into larger instructional units. Some activities require little teacher supervision and a teacher might have responsibility for more children than would normally be found in a self-contained classroom during these activities. Other learning situations might be better organized as small group activities, independent activities, or as conferences. Members of a teaching team have greater opportunities to work with individuals and small groups and to specialize.

All teachers do not have to be equivalent in competency or responsibility. A master teacher and a fledgling teacher can learn from each other. Part-time teachers can be incorporated into the team, adding additional skills. Team teaching eliminates the problem of teacher isolation, for each teacher constantly interacts with others.

In creating a large instructional unit, care must be taken that it does not become so large as to overwhelm the child. There is the danger of creating a mass in which strong relational bonds between adult and child and between child and child are submerged. Large groups also tend to be handled in a more bureaucratic fashion than small ones. Although there are no reliable rules about the optimal size of a group, some school systems and licensing agencies have established guidelines. These judgments should be made in relation to educational goals, facilities available, teacher competency, and basic conceptions of education, in addition to the absolute number and ages of children involved (Spodek, 1972).

A teacher who wishes to support independent learning must provide a classroom that allows children to behave freely and reasonably. In a physical setting with interest centers, children can move into areas that support a particular activity rather than being constrained at a single desk for most of the day. The test of a good room arrangement is the degree to which it helps children achieve the goals of the program. Teachers should experiment with room settings and modify them regularly so they fit supportively into a dynamic learning situation.

REFERENCES

ALMY, M.   *The early childhood educator at work*. New York: McGraw-Hill, 1975.

BENDER, J.   Have you ever thought of a propbox? *Young Children,* 1971, *26,* 164–169.

BLAKE, H. E.   *Creating a learning-centered classroom*. New York: Hart, 1977.

BOUTWELL, C. E., BERRY, D. R., and LUNGREN, R. E.   Differentiated staffing: Problems and prospects. In M. Scoby, and A. J. Fiorino (Eds.). *Differentiated staffing*. Washington, D.C.: Association for Supervision and Curriculum Development, 1973.

CORWIN, R., HEIN, G. E., and LEVIN, D.   Weaving curriculum webs: The structure of nonlinear curriculum. *Childhood Education,* 1976, *52,* 248–251.

EDUCATIONAL PRODUCTS INFORMATION EXCHANGE.   *Report 54, Improving materials selection procedures: A basic "how to" handbook*. New York: EPIE, 1973.

FROST, J. L., and KLEIN, B. L.   *Children's play and playgrounds*. Boston: Allyn & Bacon, 1979.

HIRSCH, E. S.   *Transition periods: Stumbling blocks of education*. New York: Early Childhood Education Council of New York City, n.d.

JONES, E.   *Dimensions of teaching-learning environments*. Pasadena, Calif.: Pacific Oaks College, n.d.

SCHRANKLER, W.   Family grouping and the affective domain. *Elementary School Journal,* 1976, *76,* 432–439.

SPODEK, B.   Staffing patterns in early childhood education. In I. J. Gordon (Ed.). *Early Childhood Education*. 71st yearbook of the National Society for the Study of Education. Chicago: University of Chicago Press, 1972.

SUGGESTED READING

BAKER, K.   *Ideas that work with children*. Washington, D.C.: National Association for the Education of Young Children, 1972.

Bits and pieces.   Washington, D.C.: Association for Childhood Education, 1967.

Criteria for selecting play equipment for early childhood education. Rifton, N.Y.: Community Playthings, 1981.

JONES, E. *Dimensions of teaching-learning environments.* Pasadena, Calif.: Pacific Oaks College, n.d.

KRITCHEVSKY, S., and PRESCOTT, E., with WALLING, L. *Planning environments for young children: Physical space.* Washington, D.C.: National Association for the Education of Young Children, 1977.

MATTERSON, E. M., *Play and playthings for the preschool child.* New York: Penguin, 1967.

SCOBY, M., and FIORINO, A. J. (Eds.). *Differentiated staffing.* Washington, D.C.: Association for Supervision and Curriculum Development, 1973.

13

Working
with Children

For many children, entrance into the kindergarten or primary grades is just one of many school beginnings. For others, the first school day may be the first experience away from home and the teacher may represent the first authority figure other than parents to whom the child has had to relate. In any event, the beginning of school is always fraught with some fear, for the child may not yet know exactly what to expect. School beginnings, therefore, require special consideration.

BEGINNING SCHOOL:
NURSERY-KINDERGARTEN LEVEL

The child's introduction to school often begins months prior to the first school day. Many schools provide a spring visit for children who will enter that fall. New children may be brought into the classroom individually or in small groups, either when the class is in session or after school. They view the physical layout and explore the materials and equipment, most of which will be there when they return in fall. Most of all, they have a chance to meet the staff. The teacher in charge of the class visited will probably be their teacher.

This orientation also provides parents a chance to find out about the school's expectations and routines, allowing them to prepare their child for entrance to school.

Teachers like to gather information about their new children's backgrounds and needs. Conferences with parents are helpful but cannot always be arranged. A student information form (see Figure 13-1), filled out by parents

Name of child _____ Sex _____

Name used at home _____ Date of birth _____

Does your child have any health problems that need special attention in school? _____

_____

Does your child suffer from allergies? (please list) _____

_____

Is your child toilet trained?	Yes _____	No _____
Likely to have accidents?	Yes _____	No _____
Does your child need help in toileting?	Yes _____	No _____
Need help in dressing?	Yes _____	No _____

Does your child have any need of which the teacher should be aware? (please specify) _____

_____

_____

Has your child previously attended nursery school? _____

Has he had experience away from parents? _____

Have there been separation problems? (describe) _____

_____

Does your child have any favorite activities? (describe) _____

_____

Are there discipline problems at home? (describe) _____

_____

What methods of behavior control are used at home? _____

_____

FIGURE 13-1   Student Information Form

and returned before or when school begins, provides much information. Different schools, however, need to know different things about their students.

Most children enter school in the fall. Having the children come to class at the same time creates several problems. All are ignorant of the resources available and the procedures they are to follow. In addition, they all have highly individual reactions to this new experience. Some find the new school setting stimulating and exhilarating and, rising to the challenge, immediately plunge into exploration. Other children find the newness of the situation frightening and withdraw from contact with people or things.

In addition to being aware of the children's reactions to the new school situation, the teacher must be sensitive to parents' reactions. Some parents wish to leave the child immediately, thus freeing themselves for independent pursuits. Some feel guilt at the sense of freedom and relief they may be experiencing. Others react hesitantly to "giving up" their children. At times, children's attendance in school is also a sign of the parents' aging, a hard realization to face for many in our society.

If the child has recently moved to the community, adjustment problems may be compounded, as the child deals with additional uncertainty. And the child who is bused from his or her own neighborhood to a strange, possibly hostile one, has other problems.

This is the situation with which teachers must deal in their first days. New teachers find the first day more anxiety-provoking than do experienced teachers who are firmly entrenched in a familiar situation. But to all teachers, the sense of novelty and uncertainty about a new set of children and a new class continues to produce anxiety, possibly generating feelings in the teacher that closely parallel those of the children.

Many teachers find that the transition is eased for them as well as the children if the school term begins with some form of staggered enrollment, with only a part of the group at school for the first week. Teachers may have only one-third of the class attend each day. The three groups may alternate attendance during the first few days, or the children may come cumulatively. The former plan creates a situation in which no one child attends any more days than another child. But children who come to school on the first day and then are kept out for the next two may feel strange when they return.

Starting the school year with a small group each day allows the teacher to give each child additional attention. It also lessens the child's need to work each day within a large group of unfamiliar children.

Problems of induction are lessened in a nongraded setting. With only a few children in the class beginning school each year, most are already familiar with the teacher, room, and total school situation and do not require a formal induction. The more experienced children can help in orienting the younger and newer ones, thus simplifying matters for the teacher.

Children do not naturally know how to behave in school nor do they enter school aware of the rules and regulations. The teacher must make a conscious effort to acquaint them with unfamiliar routines and procedures, and teach them appropriate behavior. Going through a typical schedule, perhaps in simplified form, helps during these first days. At each transition and before each set of new routines, the teacher can talk to the group and tell them what to anticipate next, demonstrating such routines as cleaning up after a work period or getting ready for dismissal. These demonstrations may need to be repeated before the children master routines and feel comfortable. Keeping a degree of constancy in the schedule helps them learn a routine and adds a degree of predictability to the school day. Once established, routine is a base from which to operate rather than a system to be slavishly followed.

Teachers should not forget the parents in these early days. In some schools, the parents are expected to leave their children outside the door on the first day and immediately depart. In many schools parents bring the new children to school the first day and stay with them if possible. The child need not feel abandoned or that school is entirely separate from home, for parents can provide a transition. The teacher may begin separation by having a parent leave for a short period for a cup of coffee. Usually children can be weaned from their parents relatively quickly.

BEGINNING SCHOOL: THE PRIMARY GRADES

The primary grade teacher may not have to deal with problems of separation. Generally, primary children have been to school before and have some idea of what to expect; there are many similar concerns, however. As early as possible teachers should establish classroom routines and organize school life, posting a daily schedule and adhering to it as much as possible. They should also introduce the procedures of group life. Ways of getting teachers' attention, using materials in the classroom, gaining access to the bathroom, and moving to the outdoor area, lunchroom, or other places in the school need to be presented, explained, discussed, and practiced. In addition, children need to learn what resources are available and how they can be used. Even though they may have had similar experiences in earlier years, each teacher has some different routines. If operating procedures are clearly communicated to the children, there is a greater chance that they will be followed.

In addition to acquainting children with school procedure, teachers must get to know them and establish positive relations with each one. They should also become familiar with the children's records, which describe academic progress and other aspects of school experiences. The meaning of entries in this vital record must be interpreted, for not all teachers have the same expectations of children or the same interpretations of their behavior. Being aware of the expectations of the child's former teacher can allow better use of records.

Academic work can be assessed in a variety of ways. The teacher probably should give informal inventories or tests in the area of reading and mathematics. Children may also do some writing in class so that writing skill and ability to communicate may be ascertained. Group discussions and short conferences allow judgments to be made about the children's oral language abilities, and information gathered about social abilities, interests in school, abilities to handle conflict and deal with frustration, and many other important things. A number of formal and informal evaluation techniques are discussed in chapter 15. These should be only tentative judgments, for children change as they become familiar with new people and new surroundings. It would be unfortunate to create expectations based only upon information gathered in the first few days of school.

Just as the teacher is testing the children in the first few days, children also test the teacher. Teachers and children participate in a series of interactions that allow them to establish a balanced relationship that may last for the entire school year. Each child finds his place in the classroom social structure, establishing personal identity and a set of relationships with the other children and the teacher. Although friendships and animosities may be carried over from earlier years, the fact that most children are in a new class with a new teacher means that a fresh set of balances must be created each fall.

ORGANIZING THE CHILDREN

The teacher can organize the classroom to reflect the children's interests and work needs. Children need places to call their own. The nursery-kindergarten child is usually provided with a cubby or locker, ostensibly to keep his wraps, but also a place of refuge since there is no assigned work space. Primary children may only have a hook for clothes. In most classes, each child has a desk at which to spend most of the day and work. In an activity program, individual desks may be eliminated and the child may work in many areas, moving around the room as needed. Though a personal desk becomes unnecessary, every child needs a place for personal treasures: a drawer in a cabinet, part of a shelf, or even a plastic stacking vegetable bin.

Children need to assume responsibility both for their own space, and for the rest of the room, seeing that things are neat and uncluttered. Early in the year, the teacher should try to instill a sense of responsibility in the children. Every time an area or a piece of equipment is used, it must be cleaned up and equipment replaced so that others may find and use it.

Rooms should be properly designed to enable children to operate in this fashion. Equipment and materials should have designated places; shelf areas should be clearly labeled with the names of things. If children cannot read, the teacher can substitute pictures or symbols on these labels. Shelves should be uncluttered and there should not be too much equipment in the room.

Crayons and pencils can be placed in open-topped boxes, paper stacked in neat piles, small jars of paste put on shelves, and small objects like beads or pegs stored in covered containers. There should be racks for drying paintings and a place where clay work can dry undisturbed until it is ready for firing, painting, or taking home.

Finally, the teacher must make sure that the children know how to use and care for the materials. Children may pick up proper habits from the teacher or peers, but unless a conscious effort is made to teach them, they may never learn some of the skills that lead to individual responsibility.

Children can also assume responsibilities for general care of the room. Every child need not be responsible for every part of the cleanup chore—the group can share responsibility. Sharing, they can set tables and clean up after lunch and snacks, prepare a room for rest, clean scraps of paper from the floor, and care for animals, fish, or plants. A teacher may assign these tasks on a rotating basis, possibly by setting up a chart and changing jobs weekly. Children enjoy this kind of work, since it allows them to show their developing competencies.

PREPARING FOR SPECIAL ACTIVITIES

While classroom routines are important, teachers and children should feel free to depart from routines when appropriate. A special visitor, bringing a pet to class, the extension of an activity that takes a long time, or a field trip are all occasions for departing from routines for which teachers can prepare the children. This requires planning that may even involve them.

Most teachers believe in pupil-teacher planning. There are legitimate decisions that young children can make. Whether the arithmetic lesson will be held in the morning or the afternoon is not an important decision, since the consequences are minor, but decisions about the distribution of resources or preparation for special events are important and can be made by children.

The visit of a resource person might be such a special event. Though the teacher might make the arrangements and extend the original invitation, the children can be involved in planning for the visit.

In planning with children, teachers should talk about the purposes of the visit and how they can best use the resources. If the visitor is coming to talk about an occupation, the children may wish to question responsibilities, equipment, and other aspects of the job. Asking appropriate questions requires that children have a basis for judging the value of questions, and this sometimes requires research prior to the visitor's arrival.

If the visitor is to perform, the teacher may help the children plan for appropriate room arrangement. They might also wish to invite pupils from another class to share the experience. It helps to have children begin to anticipate future contingencies and makes use of their ideas in providing adequately for future events. Children cannot always be involved in these plans, and when involved they may not always make major contributions, but the act of planning and thinking about the future is important.

Children can also contribute ideas to planning a field trip. Pupil-teacher planning includes helping children anticipate what will be happening on the trip and what uses will be made of it, for it is not a time-filling excursion, but a means of collecting primary source data to be used in school studies.

If the children are to gain maximum benefit from the trip, they should be helped in focusing on significant things. Prior knowledge about what will be seen is helpful, as is more general knowledge about the area of concern. They may do research on the topic by themselves or the teacher may present information from books or films and filmstrips. Children can help to formulate questions that the field trip might answer.

What constitutes appropriate behavior on a field trip may vary, for what is appropriate in one setting is not in another. Children walking through a business office or factory where people are working need to behave in quite a different way than in a park or a field. Similarly, traveling on a school bus requires different kinds of behavior than walking through a city street or using public transportation systems. In setting codes of behavior, the teacher should communicate to the children not only the limits of acceptable behavior, but the reason for them. Within these limits, the children should be able to set their own behavior patterns.

DISCIPLINE

Setting rules for appropriate behavior is no different at school than it is at home. The school has to establish appropriate kinds of behavior for children.

Children entering school for the first time are not sure what behavior is considered appropriate. In addition, very young children have often not yet learned to control their desires. If they want a toy they might take it, even though another child is using it. They may also react immediately and physically to hurt or frustration. An occasional tantrum by a nursery-age child is not necessarily a sign of emotional disturbance.

Proper behavior in school settings is learned gradually. It should be a goal to be achieved through extended experience rather than an expectation. Teachers should plan for teaching proper behavior as they teach other things.

The type of individual developed is a result of the form of discipline used. A teacher who continually sets limits and tells a child how to behave without explanation, is teaching that proper behavior is rooted in the commands of authority. On the other hand, a child who is given no limits may learn that inner desires alone should be responded to continually. Ultimately, we wish to develop autonomous individuals who realize there are reasons for order and limits. We want them to become flexible in their behavior, responding to each situation differently. The development of disciplined behavior requires the use of intellectual abilities. The child must use his intellect to understand the social as well as the physical world, and realize that patterns of behavior have regularity and reason that can ultimately be understood.

John Holt (1972) distinguishes among three different types of discipline. According to Holt, a child encounters the discipline of nature—how things work—when he fixes or builds things, learns a skill, or plays a musical instrument. He learns this discipline through feedback from reality. The discipline of society relates to how adults behave within the culture. It is learned through feedback in social settings. The third type of discipline—coercion—is used to protect the child from the consequences of his actions that he cannot anticipate. While some coercive discipline is necessary, coercion for its own sake is improper.

In attempting to develop an approach to discipline based upon reason, the teacher may follow several guidelines:

1.   BEHAVIORS EXPECTED OF CHILDREN SHOULD BE KNOWN TO THEM. Children should be told what is expected of them. Children's improper behavior may be a result of ignorance. Instructions will have to be repeated many times in many contexts before they are understood.
2.   CHILDREN NEED TO BE TOLD WHY RULES ARE IN EFFECT. Even if they cannot fully *understand* them, children need to be given the reasons for rules. Most rules for school behavior are reasonable. Children can begin to see the reason for lining up at a slide or limiting the amount of time a child can ride on a bicycle. They can understand why they should behave differently in a crowded lunchroom than in their own room and why rules are promulgated for behaving certain ways in class, others in the hall, and still others on a school bus.
3.   CHILDREN SHOULD HAVE OPPORTUNITIES TO OBSERVE AND PRACTICE PROPER BEHAVIOR. Children need demonstrations; they learn through modeling. They must also have opportunities to *practice* proper behavior, with feedback from the teacher.
4.   THE BEHAVIOR EXPECTED OF CHILDREN OUGHT TO BE POSSIBLE FOR THEM. Children are not miniature adults and should not be expected to behave like adults. Teachers should develop goals of reasonable child-like behavior.
5.   CHILDREN CANNOT ALWAYS BE EXPECTED TO BEHAVE PROPERLY AT ALL TIMES. Nobody is perfect, including adults. We do not expect adults always to be on their best behavior. The same is true for children. They should not be expected to conform to standards of model behavior at all times any more than adults should.
6.   TEACHERS SHOULD BEHAVE WITH CONSISTENCY. The teacher's behavior communicates a message to the children about what is acceptable and appropriate and what is not. If teachers vacillate or accept certain kinds of behaviors one time and reject or punish the same behavior another time, they confuse children and blur their goals. Though teachers cannot always behave consistently, this is a goal for which they should aim.

IMPROVING CLASSROOM BEHAVIOR

A number of distinct approaches have been suggested by educators and psychologists to improve children's behavior. These include behavior modification techniques, modeling techniques derived from social learning theory, psychodynamic approaches, redirecting children's activities, and an ecological approach. Sometimes a teacher can combine several of these approaches in a classroom.

Behavior Modification

A number of psychologists have suggested systematic ways for modifying the behavior of children, based on the application of behavioral analysis theory. These techniques are proposed for all kinds of behavior problems, including academic as well as discipline problems. The overall strategy is that the teacher first studies the problem empirically, then through the systematic application of reinforcers and punishment tied directly to the valued behavior, works on the problem until it is eliminated.

Charles and Clifford Madsen (1974) have identified four steps in this process: *pinpoint, record, consequate, and evaluate.* To *pinpoint* is to identify the specific problem behavior and to define the goal of the strategy in terms of observable behavior. The teacher should observe the conditions under which the problem behavior is occurring and the frequency of its occurrence, and *record* these observations directly. Next, one should develop a systematic program in which the target behavior comes under control of external reinforcers. To *consequate,* a system of rewards can be offered contingent upon the child's manifesting the target behavior. If the target is to reduce a negative behavior, manifestations of that behavior may be ignored, and alternative behaviors reinforced. Reinforcers can include social rewards, such as statements of approval or a pat on the back, or material rewards, such as food treats or toys. The opportunity to participate in valued activities can also become contingent upon proper behavior. Sometimes tokens, to be exchanged for rewards later, are used as reinforcers. To *evaluate,* the teacher should allow the program to operate for a reasonable time to determine its success. If unsuccessful, a new program should be developed and tried.

An example of such a program is with a child who does not seem to be willing to clean up after activities. The teacher might observe that at each cleanup time the child takes a piece of equipment into a corner of the room and plays with it. The teacher might then decide to help the child clean up, giving an opportunity to play with a special toy on condition that help be given. If the child then does help, the teacher gives him the toy. On occasions when the child does not help, all toys might be withheld. After a while, the teacher tries to get the child to clean up with only an occasional offer of special toys, finally fading the use of the toy completely.

A large number of successful experiences with behavior modification have been reported in laboratory situations, homes, and classrooms. The technique, however, continues to be controversial. Some feel that the focus on behavior leads to a concern for symptoms rather than causes. Others object to the use of rewards, equating this with bribery. Still others feel that this technique places the control of behavior outside the individual and never helps the child deal with the judgment of what is proper behavior, thus limiting autonomy. While advocates of this approach have countered these arguments, the controversy continues to rage.

Modeling

Modeling techniques, based on social learning theory, involve learning by watching someone perform. This concept was discussed briefly in chapter 3. All of us learn some proper behaviors by watching and emulating others. When we are in a strange social situation, we may look to a person who seems socially accepted to get cues to proper behavior, and then emulate this person while trying to abstract rules for the situation.

Modeling is a technique that can be used to learn both positive and negative behavior, depending upon what is modeled. By providing a model of good social behavior a teacher could get the entire class to behave in appropriate ways. The model should be someone who has status in the group so that children wish to emulate his behavior. Some cuing of proper behavior is helpful so that the teacher can point out the behavior that should be modeled. Rewarding the target behavior in children will reinforce it and increase the probability of their maintaining it (Bandura & Walter, 1963).

As with reinforcement theory, the focus of this technique is on the behavior rather than on the reasons for behaving. There is less manipulation of the child in modeling, and since the child ultimately decides whether to model the target behavior, autonomy is increased.

Psychodynamic Approaches

Psychodynamic approaches focus on the causes of behavior. Psychodynamic theorists often view behavior as a manifestation of developmental conflict or needs. Since conflict is seen as a necessary part of growth, neither conflict or aversive behavior is avoided. Instead, teachers need to provide children with the means to work out these conflicts or manifest their feelings in socially acceptable ways. Sometimes catharsis is suggested—children are encouraged to show their feelings, channeling hostile feelings into dramatic play, or pounding clay or a punching bag. Serious problems might be handled by a therapist, but day-to-day conflict can be handled by a teacher at school. Teachers can also deal with these behavior problems or developmental conflicts in indirect ways, anticipating the problems that might arise.

The human development curricula and the affective curricula discussed in chapter 8 are attempts to help children deal with their feelings and become more sensitive in interpersonal relations. In so doing, these programs are designed to improve classroom behavior by indirect means. To varying extents these programs are an application of psychodynamic theories.

The work of Rudolph Dreikurs has attracted its share of advocates in the field of early childhood education. Dreikurs (1968) considers that children misbehave for one of four reasons: to gain attention, to display power, to gain revenge, and to display a deficiency in order to seek special service or be exempted from some expectation. Dreikurs proposes that parents and teachers respond to children's misbehavior using *logical consequences* rather than punishment. These consequences, which are set by the authority, are different from punishment in that logical consequences express the reality of the social order, are intrinsically related to the misbehavior, involve no moral judgment on the part of the implementor, and are concerned only with present occurrences (Dreikurs & Grey, 1968).

A logical consequence could have a child miss a valued activity because of dawdling, or require the child to clean up an area where a mess deliberately was created. The key to these actions in changing behavior is that the teacher realize the reasons for children's misbehavior and, rather than letting them achieve their goal, demonstrate why the behavior is both inappropriate for the situation and ineffective in achieving the desired result. The child is also told, if possible, why the particular consequence has been selected.

The use of logical consequences might seem appropriate to what Holt has called social discipline situations; it is not suggested for dangerous physical situations.

Redirection

One traditional approach to misbehavior, derived from experience rather than theory and used by teachers of young children, is *redirection*. The basic ploy is to take children's attention from situations creating difficulty and focus on situations that provide immediate satisfactions. A child who is fighting with another over a fire truck, for example, might be steered to the woodworking area. For redirection to be possible, the teacher needs to know which activities have high appeal for the children and have alternatives available.

Although redirection may avoid conflict, conflict cannot be completely avoided nor is conflict necessarily bad. There are always some situations that will lead to conflict in any classroom: the opposition of individual needs or the clash of strong personalities. Teachers should help children develop acceptable means of dealing with conflict: compromise, and use of verbal skills to negotiate problems, rather than use of physical coercion in influencing persons. Teachers continually have to step in to resolve conflicts among children. Unfortunately, they may have to use some forms of arbitrary coercion and even physical restraint; however, this should not mean physical punishment. Ultimately, any system of discipline should move from the teacher controlling the child's behavior to the child becoming autonomous. The success of a teacher's discipline can be judged by the degree of autonomy found in the class.

Ecological Approach

An intriguing alternative to these approaches to discipline can be extrapolated from an article by Susan Swap (1974) dealing with emotionally disturbed children. Swap's thesis is that the disturbance does not reside within the child, but in the interaction between the child and his environment. This argument seems related to Lilly's suggestion that we look at exceptional school situations rather than at exceptional children (1970).

Swap says that many emotionally disturbed children misbehave because they are going through the resolution of conflicts associated with early development stages while most of their peers have successfully resolved these same developmental conflicts earlier. The resolution of these conflicts may be aided or thwarted by environmental conditions in the child's educational setting. Often, because the setting was designed for more emotionally mature children, the conflict is irritated by conflict with the environment. By understanding the child's conflict level and modifying the environment to help in conflict resolution, the teacher can effectively limit disturbances in the classroom. Elements in the school environment that can be modified include the physical setting, the educational requirements placed upon the child, and the nature of the teacher-child interaction pattern.

We know that children are rapidly confronted with developmental change in their early years that can produce personal conflict. We also know that children develop unevenly; for instance, a child may be more mature in his language development than in motor development at a particular time. In addition, in any one class there will be children at many developmental levels. The teacher needs to become a careful observer of children's behavior and a skillful judge of developmental levels. Rather than attempting to modify the child to fit the setting, teachers can work to modify the setting to fit the child. By modifying academic requirements, creating varied space in the classroom, and using different kinds of educational materials and degrees of structure in the program they can limit the number of conflicts between the child and the school setting.

Some children require formal structure; others do better in open settings. Some learn mathematics best with manipulative materials, but later their presence may hamper learning. Some children do best in large groups of peers while others prefer seclusion. Some require challenge while others need security. No one program or set of teacher behaviors best fits all children. A flexible teacher in a flexible environment can match the demands and requirements of the setting to the needs of the child, and thus lessen discipline problems.

The acceptance of individual differences in children requires that the teacher become aware of the child's developmental level and the conditions that enhance or thwart learning, whether academic or social. From a behavioral analysis point of view, this means becoming aware of *setting events* that lead to particular behaviors, and of the *natural reinforcers* in the environment.

In addition to being aware of individual differences among children, teachers must be aware of the influences children have on each other's behavior, as well as the sense of control they convey to students. Jacob Kounin's early studies of the "ripple effect" in classrooms demonstrated how teachers' ways of correcting a single child's behavior in class influences the behavior of other children in the room. This seems especially true with young children.

Kounin also found that a teacher's awareness of classroom processes is communicated to children and contributes to the effectiveness of classroom management. Teachers with "eyes in the backs of their heads," those who are able to attend to many activities at once, and those who are aware of the many things happening in a class seem most effective in managing group activities. Similarly, alert teachers manage the flow of classroom activities, pacing them to maintain the momentum and watching for the need for transitions (Kounin, 1970).

By managing the flow of activities and matching environmental conditions to each child's developmental level, the teacher can improve educational conditions for all children. Thus a classroom's organization for instruction, discussed in the previous chapter, is a major tool for improving classroom discipline.

In the final analysis the classroom teacher must realize that "proper behavior" is as much a goal as is learning to read or to express oneself through art. The child is not born with a sense of what is appropriate behavior; he must learn it. In addition, what might be good behavior in one setting is not necessarily good behavior in another. A parent might want his child to act in an assertive manner, telling the child to stand up for his rights. The teacher might consider the same child aggressive or even combative. Such differences might stem from differences in values and goals or from a distortion that could arise when a child attempts to overstress a parent's goal. Another child might be lacking in social skills and find that socially inappropriate behavior is the only means available to gain the attention of other children or adults. Still another child may simply be unaware of the rules for appropriate behavior in school. Each of these situations requires a different response as well as a different approach to teaching appropriate behavior.

All classrooms have some children who do not behave appropriately at all times. Teachers also find that they are not as effective with some children as with others. Too often, teachers feel that their ability to control a class at all times is crucial to their ability to teach, and that any failure in dealing with a child or a group means failure as a teacher. They need to realize that teachers are not infallible, and that they, like all other professionals, need help from others: other teachers, a principal, a school counselor, a psychologist, or a social worker. Appropriate use should be made of all these resources.

REFERENCES

BANDURA, A., and WALTER, R. H.   *Social learning and personality development.* New York: Holt, Rhinehart & Winston, 1963.

DREIKURS, R.   *Psychology in the classroom* (2nd ed.). New York: Harper & Row, Pub., 1968.

DREIKURS, R., and GREY, L.   *Logical consequences: A handbook of discipline.* New York: Meredith Press, 1968.

HOLT, J.   Discipline: The most perplexive subject of all. *Teacher,* 1972, *90*(1), 54-56.

KOUNIN, J. S.   *Discipline and group management in classrooms.* New York: Holt, Rhinehart & Winston, 1970.

LILLY, S. M.   Special education: A tempest in a teapot. *Exceptional Children,* 1970, *37,* 43-45.

MASDEN, C. H., JR., and MASDEN, C. K.   *Teaching/Discipline: A positive approach for educational development* (2nd ed.). Boston: Allyn & Bacon, 1974.

SWAP, S. M.   Disturbing classroom behaviors: A developmental and ecological view. *Exceptional Children,* 1974, *41,* 163-174.

SUGGESTED READING

CHARLES, C. M.   *Building classroom discipline: From models to practice.* New York: Longman, 1981.

DUKE, D. L.   (Ed.). *Helping teachers manage classrooms.* Alexandria, Va.: Association for Supervision and Curriculum Development, 1982.

Discipline and learning: An inquiry into student-teacher relationships. Washington, D.C.: National Education Association, 1975.

GNAGY, W. J.   *Maintaining discipline in classroom instruction.* New York: Macmillan, 1975.

HYMES, J. L.   *The child under six.* Englewood Cliffs, N.J.: Prentice-Hall, 1963.

MADSEN, C. H., JR., and MADSEN, C. K.   *Teaching/Discipline: A positive approach for educational development* (2nd ed.). Boston: Allyn & Bacon, 1974.

14

Working
with Parents

The close relationship between the education of children and parents has been evident throughout the history of early childhood education. This reflects an understanding of the close bond between parent and young child, with parents the prime influencer of the child's learning and development. Because this bond may have a greater impact on the life of the child than any educational programs, educators have learned to use it to extend their programs.

Johann Amos Comenius and Johann Heinrich Pestalozzi, childhood educators who predated the creation of kindergartens and nursery schools, expressed the belief in the importance of the mother's role in the education of the young. Friedrich Froebel, pioneer of the kindergarten, also believed in the importance of educating mothers for child rearing as well as in the significance of the harmonious education of children in school and at home.

As kindergartens were established in the United States, mothers' classes were used to carry out Froebel's philosophy. In some philanthropic kindergartens, the mothers' clubs were concerned with the acculturation of the family, helping to "Americanize" parents as well as teaching about child-rearing practices. Classes for all kindergarten parents were concerned with teaching about child study and about the theory and practice of kindergarten education.

The importance early kindergarten educators placed upon involving mothers significantly affected American education. The National Congress of Mothers grew out of a convocation of women connected with these kindergarten mothers' classes. This group eventually became the National Congress of Parents and Teachers, an organization well-known in school circles today.

Nursery schools were also viewed as an important influence in augmenting and improving parent-child relationships. Margaret and Rachel McMillan's emphasis on placing nursery schools close to children's homes, allowing parents to observe nursery-school practices, and establishing a good working relationship between parent and teacher was meant to support close cooperation between home and school. The hope of the pioneers of nursery education was that the parents themselves would ultimately become responsible for the education of their young children in nursery schools.

As the nursery school was transplanted into the United States, this concern for a close relationship between family and school in the early years continued. One of the first established in the United States was a parent-cooperative nursery school started by a group of twelve faculty wives at the University of Chicago in 1916. These parents wanted to secure "social education for their children, parent education for themselves and a little free time for Red Cross work" (Taylor, 1968, p. 294). Nursery schools are still organized by groups of parents and concerned community members and kindergartens not too long ago were sponsored by parent-teacher associations.

Relationships between schools and parents are as diverse as the kinds of schools that exist and the populations they serve. Day care centers operate quite differently in their relationship to the families than do parent-cooperative nursery schools. Similarly, the primary grades of an elementary public shool support a different relationship between home and school than do private nursery schools.

Recently, concerns about parent programs have shifted from viewing parents as clients of educational institutions to viewing them as policy makers. The concern for community control of schools and the parents' demand to have a voice in educational policy making at all levels must be understood as an extension of their responsibility for the education of their children.

In the education of handicapped children, working with parents takes on added importance. Public Law 94–142, the Education for All Handicapped Children Act, requires that parents give consent prior to the evaluation of their child. They have the right to examine all records regarding the placement of their child as well as the right to participate in the development of their child's individual educational program. In addition, they have the right to a due process hearing in relation to any complaint they may have regarding the education of their handicapped child.

Beyond the law, however, the involvement of parents in the education of their child has educational and moral justifications. As the child is primarily the responsibility of his or her parents, they should be involved in the determination of educational decisions. Parental involvement is critical to the success of any educational program designed for children with special educational needs (Bronfenbrenner, 1974). When parents enter into partnership with the school, work with children can go beyond the classroom. Learning at school and at home can become supportive of each other.

Teachers' views of the role of parents in the education of their children vary widely. Some teachers deny the importance of family background to the education of their children, excluding families from school life. Others view children as totally shaped by their parents, seeing the parents within the child. In between are a range of teachers who believe that information on family backgrounds allows them to communicate with and educate children more effectively (Lightfoot, 1978). Most early childhood teachers believe that an understanding of a child's home background is necessary to understand the child and that some involvement of parents in the child's education is necessary.

WHO OWNS THE CHILD?

Parents in our culture have the right to rear their children in any way they see fit. Actually, however, the parents' right is significantly abridged. No parents have the right to inflict bodily harm on their children. Every parent *must* send his or her child to school for a certain period or provide a reasonable alternative. This requirement grows as much from the cultural need to maintain the social order as from personal needs of children and their parents.

It becomes evident that the "ownership" of children by parents is far from unencumbered by our society. In many schools, however, teachers feel that their right to determine what experiences to provide is inviolable. It is a "right" delegated to them by society by virtue of their special knowledge and preparation. Only recently have the rights of children begun to be recognized. Child-advocacy groups have been established to protect these rights from incursion by parent or social institution.

One of the larger issues confronting education today relates to the extent to which parents' wishes and demands should also constitute a legitimate set of restraints upon teachers' actions. Parents have traditionally been kept out of decision-making roles in school. Parents who came to school to meet with teachers were to be informed, listened to, placated, and counseled. Seldom did the teacher see the parent as a source of decision making about classroom procedure.

Conflict has often characterized the relationships between schools and families and communities, especially in connection with the poor and minorities. This conflict may be viewed as a vehicle of oppression or as an expression of liberation and interaction (Lightfoot, 1978). Whatever the view, schools must look for ways to transcend whatever conflict exists or use it in the best interests of children.

The establishment of policy advisory committees, including many parents in Head Start programs, and the demands for community control of schools, suggest that the relationship between parent and teacher may be changing in many communities. Parents and other community members are becoming more involved in important areas of decision making relating to school policy and classroom practice.

As this change does come about, teachers need to view their roles in relationship to schools and children in a somewhat different light, and need to develop skills in working with parents and alternative perceptions of what constitutes a viable parent-teacher relationship.

Traditionally the boundary of teacher-parent-community power has been determined by the kinds of decisions that need to be made. Parent and/or community agents have been responsible for policy decisions, and teachers and administrators for decisions relating to policy implementation. These lines, however, are often blurred, for implementation can affect policies considerably and policy decisions often require professional knowledge of probable consequences.

DIFFERING ROLES IN WORKING WITH PARENTS

The content of a parent-teacher relationship can vary greatly. Teachers should be sensitive to the needs of parents and provide a range of programming possibilities. Teachers may be concerned with communicating pupil progress to parents, sharing information, jointly solving problems, organizing parent meetings, developing parent education programs, supervising classroom participation, and providing professional consultation to policy-making groups. Each element of a parent program requires different skills and techniques of the teacher. Although teachers are not prepared as parent counselors and often lack the preparation to be parent educators, their position allows them to serve the parent population in a unique way. Within the limitations of skills and roles, teachers should accept the challenge in each area.

Reporting Pupil Progress

One part of evaluation is the report to parents of the child's progress in school. Report cards, letters, and individual conferences are discussed more fully in chapter 15. It is important in reporting to be sure that parents understand the goals of the program and the way their child's progress is being assessed. Avoiding adverse reporting can be dangerous; parents should be informed regularly and frankly.

Sharing Information

Reporting pupil progress is usually one-way communication. Parents and teachers both have information about the child that would be useful to exchange—information not necessarily related to pupil progress. Teachers often elicit useful information about children through the applications that many nursery schools and kindergartens require prior to admission. Data on children's health and developmental background are required in this form, an example of which is presented in chapter 13.

Individual conferences at the beginning or during the school year allow teachers time to collect information about the child and ask specific questions relating to important areas of behavior. What is significant for one child may be irrelevant to the teacher's understanding of another child.

Such a sharing conference is useful particularly if the teacher has problems with a child. The information provided by a parent may help explain a child's change in behavior. Similarly, parents may elicit information from the teacher that will help them deal with the child at home. If the teacher and parent are both concerned primarily with the child's welfare, information-sharing conferences may provide the beginning of a beneficial mutual relationship. Such conferences can easily lead to joint problem-solving sessions.

Joint Problem Solving

In many families, the child may have had few contacts with other children of the same age up to the time of school entrance. Sometimes the parents will have made few demands of him, or not had the opportunity to compare him with other children at a similar developmental stage. If, in addition, the family has had few contacts with a pediatrician, the parents may suddenly see problems or abnormalities that have existed but not been evident to them.

The entrance into school, with its new demands on the child, may suddenly bring forth a series of behavior problems. Hearing losses, poor vision, or other problems may also appear as new pressures are placed upon the child. At times, a change in the family situation—divorce, the arrival of a new baby, or moving to a new community—may also cause problems to occur in class. Sharing information, pooling ideas for dealing with the problems, and developing a consistent way of handling the child both at home and at school may go a long way in providing solutions to difficult problems. The teacher may play a crucical role in helping parents deal with these problems, for quite often the teacher is the only professional with whom they have regular contact.

The teacher is not a psychologist, social worker, or guidance counselor and is a child development specialist in only the broadest sense. Yet teachers must find ways to help the parent become aware of problems and deal with them. Sometimes this requires a friendly conversation over a cup of coffee; at other times it may require a series of conferences leading to referral to an appropriate agency. The teacher must be careful not to overstep the bounds of the educator's role. Often it is best to refer a problem to someone else better qualified. The teacher should become familiar with the agencies that service children and their families in the community and with the procedures used to seek the help of each agency. Many schools have ancillary personnel—guidance workers or family coordinators—that can help the parent and teacher deal with problems.

Although referral is a significant contribution that teachers can make, the importance of the personal support they can provide should not be underestimated.

Home Visits

A home visit has many advantages. A conference in the home may allow parents to talk more freely than at school. In addition, teachers can learn about the home environment, and perhaps understand the child better. Home visits may also be more convenient for parents not able to come to the classroom during school hours; often, fathers as well as mothers can be reached by the teacher through home visits.

If a home visit is to be effective, the parents should feel that they are inviting the teacher into their home. Forcing a visit on an unwilling family may cause hostility. The teacher might propose a number of dates and times so the visit can take place at a mutually convenient time. A teacher who visits the home without warning is acting unfairly. Such an action can be disastrous to the hopes of establishing a working relationship.

The purpose of a home visit is similar to that of a conference: sharing information and working on problems. The teacher should be careful that these purposes are achieved while friendly social relations are established.

Informal Contacts

There are many opportunities for informal contacts with parents. The child's arrival or departure from school, the meetings of the parents' association, and the invitation to a parent to accompany the class on a field trip provide these opportunities. The teacher should convey a feeling of friendliness and mutual concern for the children in these sessions. Holding parents at a distance or talking down to them can destroy the relationship that the rest of the parent program is attempting to build.

These occasions also allow teachers to hold mini-conferences—short informal sessions in which minor problems can be dealt with or information elicited easily. Teachers should encourage them, being careful not to become too involved with the parents when they need to be working with children.

Parent Meetings

There are many occasions when the teacher must deal with parents in groups rather than individually. The teacher may be called upon to plan and direct parent meetings, or looked upon as a resource for meetings planned and executed by the parents themselves.

FIGURE 14-1   Meetings can put parents into contact with early childhood specialists.

The first contacts between parents and teachers is often the orientation meeting that takes place close to the children's entrance to school. This provides an opportunity to communicate about what school will be like for them and for their children. If parents have never had a child in school before, this type of information is important. Such a meeting may also be used to provide parents with information about the school's expectations of them and their children.

The teacher should be careful to communicate the fact that the school is a friendly place that welcomes parents as well as children (assuming that this is true). Teachers should allow time for informal chatter and opportunities for parents to become acquainted with one another. If information is printed in a simple brochure or leaflet, more of the meeting time can be devoted to establishing relationships and less to lecturing. It is a waste of meeting time to read materials to parents that they could easily read themselves.

During the school year, the teacher may want to call other meetings, to talk about the program, show some of the children's work, and answer parents' questions about what their children are doing. Because such meetings deal directly with their children, parents are usually happy to attend them. Care must be taken to schedule meetings at times when there can be maximum attendance. It may be necessary to provide an informal baby-sitting arrangement for the children of invited parents, or to allow the children to come to the meetings in order to insure attendance.

Most schools have a formal parent or parent-teacher association that attempts to organize all the parents in the school. It plans regular meetings and social events throughout the school year. Though the responsibility for such meetings is often in the hands of the parent officers, teachers may be asked to serve on programs or to act as resource persons.

The attendance of teachers at these meetings is important in building close ties with families. A brief word to a parent on such an occasion can frequently do more in establishing good relationships than can a lengthy conference.

Parent Education Programs

Many schools provide formal or informal parent education programs varying from highly organized courses that teach about child growth and development, child-rearing practices, and homemaking skills, to informal club activities whose content is determined by the parents themselves. Still other programs may focus on group process and parent interaction rather than on any substantive content.

Honig (1979) has suggested a set of parents' rights that could provide the basis for parent education programs. These include the right to

> know about child development
> develop observation skills for more effective parenting
> have available alternative strategies for problem prevention and discipline
> know how to use a home to provide children with learning experiences
> have language tools and story-reading skills
> be aware of being important in their children's lives

Many parent-cooperative nursery schools require that parents enroll in a parent education program as a prerequisite for the child's enrollment in the program. Nursery schools in settlement houses, parent-child centers, and Head Start programs often include a strong parent education component in their total service program. Sometimes parents will spend many hours in classes. A parent library can be a strong addition to a program.

Many parent education programs are concerned with teaching specific parental skills that will support children's intellectual and language learning in the school. A program may portray model parental behavior such as including children in discussions, conveying to them the meanings of parental action, reading simple stories aloud, and providing instructional activities and material in the home. The specific techniques needed are often taught directly to parents, who then practice them under supervision. Sometimes kits of materials are lent to parents to use with children at home. Working with babies may be stressed as much as with preschoolers; ultimately all the children in a family will be affected by what the parent learns.

Many parent education programs are becoming home based rather than school based, with parent educators working directly in the homes of their clients. These programs usually make provision for pretraining and orientation of workers as well as orientation of parents. The workers generally provide specific guidance to parents and often demonstrate activities with the child as they observe. Programs for low-income parents rely heavily on paraprofessionals as trainers, while programs for handicapped children use primarily professionals. The parent worker is generally responsible for evaluating the children's progress and parents are often consulted in regard to activities for the children (Levitt & Cohen, 1976). In addition to these common elements, many differences exist among parent education programs that parallel the differences in approach to the education of young children discussed in chapter 3.

Supervising Parent Participation

Parent participation in classroom activities is an integral part of cooperative nursery school and Head Start programs. Parents can be invited into classes to read stories to children, provide tutoring services for needy children, help with instructional groups, help with classroom routines, and serve as resource persons. They can often participate as teaching assistants as well.

Careful supervision should be provided when parents participate in the classroom. Orientation meetings with participating parents can help lessen possible confusion. They need to know about daily schedule of activities and the rules and patterns of behavior expected of children in different areas of the classroom and the school. They also need to be told their specific responsibilities. The development of a parent manual containing this information is helpful if a number of parents are used in the program.

Teachers should supervise parents who participate in the program, keeping track of their behavior and possibly making notes to be used in evaluative conferences later. It is useful for the parents and teachers to periodically review the work that both have done. Praise and support should be amply given, as should careful criticism and advice for improving practice. As parents continue their work with the teacher, their areas of responsibility and amount of freedom can often increase.

FIGURE 14-2
Parents can provide varied resources for the classroom.

Working with Parent Policy Boards

The most difficult part of the teacher's relationship with parents may be in developing educational and administrative policy for schools. Sometimes teachers feel better prepared than parents to make decisions because they have a greater amount of specialized knowledge upon which to base a decision. In addition, teachers have a vested interest in the decisions made about school practices.

Both parents and teachers may come to board meetings with their own particular difficulties. Some parents may view teachers with distrust. Teachers, on the other hand, may have difficulty communicating with persons who do not share their personal and professional vocabulary.

A teacher's effectiveness with a board is based on mutual trust. This grows out of a series of encounters in which the teacher demonstrates trust; it is facilitated by a show of competence and a concern for children. Keeping lines of communication open, listening to parents, and keeping the sources of decisions public also help the teacher gain trust.

Ultimately, the teacher's role is to help parents make decisions. The teacher should educate the parents, seeing that they have appropriate information upon which to base their decisions. Further, the teacher must help them anticipate the consequences of their decisions.

DEVELOPING TECHNIQUES
FOR WORKING WITH PARENTS

Working with parents requires the development of long-range plans, interview and guidance skills, and the ability to work with small and large groups. Teachers must also develop skills in evaluating and recording the results of encounters with parents.

Planning

A teacher must be clear about the purposes of parent contacts, know about resources, and be able to think through the consequences of parent activities. Most important is the need to match the parent activity to the specific purposes of parent work.

If teachers wish to refer a parent for help to a social agency, they must be able to communicate that need without becoming too threatening. They should have available the names and addresses of social agencies and know how to apply to them. If teachers wish to enlist parents in helping with a child's behavior problem in class, they should have observational records of the child's behavior available.

Planning a parent program on a full-year basis allows teachers to create a balance of different kinds of parent contacts. Meetings can be scheduled so they don't interfere with school operations or family traditions. In addition, teachers can anticipate the needs of the parent programs and prepare for them. If conferences are to be held, examples of children's work or behavior records relating to school performance should be gathered.

In planning group meetings, teachers should think through the content of the program, make arrangements for needed speakers or films, and assign responsibility for specific tasks such as hostessing or cleaning up to insure a smooth-running meeting.

Planning requires providing appropriate space. A large meeting may require a school auditorium or multipurpose room. A class mothers' meeting might be held in a classroom after school with some rearrangement of the furniture. A conference with individual parents is best held in a quiet place that is free of interruptions. A parents' work session, using woodwork tools or sewing machines, requires special facilities and adequate space. Just allocating space for a parent bulletin board or a display of books requires the teacher to plan.

Interviewing

Interviewing techniques allow information to be gathered from and offered to parents. Teachers should put parents at ease in a conference, providing coffee or speaking first about general school matters to establish rapport. Too much time should not be spent in preliminaries, however.

Teachers often use an interview outline to make sure they elicit the information they want and cover all points in a conference. Such an outline should be used flexibly to insure that the purposes of the conference are met.

It is vital to learn how to *listen* to parents, being sensitive to their feelings as well as to the information communicated. It is important to listen responsively, reacting to messages when appropriate and helping parents work toward realistic solutions of problems regarding the children.

Although it is sometimes easy to give advice, within a parent-teacher context the counseling must be particularly meaningful and relevant to each specific situation. If a child should be read to at home, the teacher should help the parents find the source of books, or make books available. The teacher should also help them learn some of the reading techniques that will eventually benefit the child.

Working with Groups

Large groups are not as useful as small ones for discussions and interactions. Small-group sessions require the teacher to use group leadership techniques. As leaders, teachers convene groups and chair discussions; being sensitive to the group needs and allowing members to become responsible for its actions. Teachers should not impose their will on a group nor allow the discussion to move too aimlessly for long periods of time. A teacher must become a democratic leader, responsive and flexible, while maintaining authority to best use the group process.

Sometimes a "hands-on" approach is useful for working with parent groups. Engaging parents in workshop activities utilizes nonverbal as well as verbal forms of learning. Teachers can lead parents into activities parallel to the children's to help them understand the learning potential of the activities. "Open science" or "new math" is often not well understood by parents unless they have experienced these forms of learning. Similarly, parents might consider play activities or craft activities useless unless they can realize the outcomes of these activities are valuable learnings. Sylvia Newman (1971) describes a set of workshops and auxiliary activities that she instituted in a school program to help parents understand its content and to develop ways of extending the children's school learning in the home.

Large group meetings are practical for expository purposes—the same speakers or films used for these can be used for small groups as well.

A group convened by a teacher frequently develops its own independent life. Projects undertaken by parents may develop for the education of the group's members or as a service to the school. Changes in the nature of the group sometimes require more time than a teacher can possibly give; in this event, finding another leader may help, either someone from the group or from outside. The teacher may then continue working with the parent group as an advisor. Teachers can feel legitimate pride when groups they have started become autonomous as a result of their leadership.

The group process is a powerful force. Groups can be helpful and supportive, or aggressive and oppressive. It is important to use the group process carefully, ever cautious of any limitations in skills involving working with groups.

USING PUBLIC RELATIONS TECHNIQUES

Most of the ways of working with parents involve face-to-face relations, but other types of relationships with family and community should also be established. A good school should have a strong program of public relations. Because the school belongs to the parents and the community, it must communicate what happens in school.

A good public relations program ensures that parents and others in the community feel welcome in the school. This should go beyond the annual "Open School Week."

Displays help in telling the community what children are doing. Art work, the results of projects, or tapes of children's songs and stories, can be tastefully organized and used to tell about children's school experiences. Local merchants are often helpful in making space available for display and in other kinds of support and local news media can tell the school's story to the public. Field trips, holiday celebrations, and other special events are often considered newsworthy by local media.

Teachers can carry on their own public relations activities through newsletters, notes sent home, and invitations to parents to participate in special events.

While good public relations are important to a school, teachers need to be careful that their parent programs do not become *just* public relations programs. When parents are invited into school, when their opinions and advice about educational matters are solicited, when they are invited to become members of advisory committees and boards, they expect that their ideas will be considered worthy, that their contributions will be respected, and that they will be heard and responded to. At times, however, schools have established parent boards and advisory committees, often in order to meet requirements of state and federal programs, without making use of the products of these groups. Under these circumstances parents may feel that although they are involved in school activities, they are powerless. What seemed a program of parent involvement can easily be distorted. Such programs of public relations, however, can be counterproductive and lead to frustration and even anger on the part of parents.

WORKING WITH PARENTS: A TWO-WAY STREET

Orville Brim (1965) has identified the primary goals of outstanding parent education programs: making the parents more conscious of their role performance, making them more autonomous and creative, improving their independent judgment, and increasing the rationality of their role performance. These goals are appropriate for early childhood education. Just as we wish children to become more autonomous, more creative, more aware, and more rational in their judgments and performance, we wish these things also for parents. The differences in developmental levels of adults and children require that these general goals be manifest in different ways and in relation to different social roles. To support parent autonomy, rationality, creativity, and competence, the teacher must have a helping relationship with the parent, rather than a prescribing one.

Too often teachers feel that a parent program is an opportunity to do something to parents to change them. In a good parent program parents should also have an opportunity to influence teachers and possibly to change the school. A strong parent program can open new avenues of communication. When there is no information there can be little criticism; as parents become more knowledgeable about the school, there will be more—hopefully constructive to a large degree.

Actually, the judgments of parents can be considered another source of information about the effectiveness of the program. Parent reactions should be considered along with other data in making school decisions, and teachers should always be receptive to parents' ideas and criticisms. Changes should not be instituted merely as a way of placating parents, however—teachers should feel strong enough in their professional role to be able to justify their acts in school and to stand by programs they believe to be sound professional practices.

REFERENCES

BRIM, O. G., JR. *Education for child rearing.* New York: Free Press, 1965.

BRONFENBRENNER, U. *A report on longitudinal evaluations of preschool programs: Is early intervention effective?* Washington, D.C.: U.S. Department of Health, Education, and Welfare, 1974.

HONIG, A. S. *Parent involvement in early childhood education* (Rev. ed.). Washington, D.C.: National Association for the Education of Young Children, 1979.

LEVITT, E., AND COHEN, S.   Educating parents of children with special needs— Approaches and issues. *Young Children,* 1976, *31,* 263–272.

LIGHTFOOT, S. L.   *Worlds apart: Relationship between families and schools.* New York: Basic Books, 1978.

NEWMAN, S.   *Guidelines to parent-teacher cooperation in early childhood education.* Brooklyn, N.Y.: Book-Lab, 1971.

TAYLOR, K. W.   *Parents and children learn together.* New York: Teachers College Press, 1968.

SUGGESTED READING

BEYER, E.   *Sharing—A new level in teacher-parent relationship.* Washington, D.C.: National Association for the Education of Young Children, 1968.

CROFT, D.   *Parents and teachers: A resource book for home, school and community relations.* Belmont, Calif.: Wadsworth, 1979.

D'EVELYN, K. E.   *Individual parent-teacher conferences.* New York: Teachers College Press, 1952.

GINOTT, H. G.   *Between parent and child.* New York: Macmillan, 1965.

HEFFERNAN, H., AND TODD, V. E.   *Elementary teacher's guide to working with parents.* West Nyack, N.Y.: Parker Publishing Company, 1969.

HONIG, A. S.   *Parent involvement in early childhood education* (Rev. ed.). Washington, D.C.: National Association for the Education of Young Children, 1979.

HONIG, A. S.   Parent involvement in early childhood education. In B. Spodek (Ed.), *Handbook of research in early childhood education.* New York: Free Press, 1982.

How to involve parents in early childhood education. Provo, Utah: Brigham Young University Press, 1982.

HYMES, J. L.   *Effective home-school relations* (Rev. ed.). Sierra Madre: Southern California Association for the Education of Young Children, 1974.

MORRISON, G. S.   *Parent involvement in home, school, and community.* Columbus, Ohio: Chas. E. Merrill, 1978.

NEDLER, S., and McAFEE, O.   *Working with parents: Guidelines for early childhood and elementary teachers.* Belmont, Calif.: Wadsworth, 1979.

TIZARD, B., MORTIMORE, J., and BURCHELL, B.   *Involving parents in nursery and infant schools: A source book for teachers.* London: Grant McIntyre, 1981.

15

Evaluating Education
in the Early Years

Teachers make decisions about the selection of programs, program elements, program materials. They make judgments about children's ability to profit from educational programs, and the effects of these programs on them. Each decision requires that the teacher be involved in the process of evaluation; that is, collecting information, making judgments based on this information, and developing ways of recording and communicating the results of these evaluations.

The process of evaluation needs to be considered separately from instruction, although the two are interrelated. Evaluation includes both the description and judgment of school programs and children's attainment. Central to this process is a consideration of the goals of education and whether they are achieved.

The achievement of program goals can sometimes only be assessed over a period of years. Studies of long-term outcomes have been done, with children followed through high school to determine the long-term effects of early educational programs (Lazar & Darlington, 1982).

Such long-term evaluation, although complicated and expensive, is necessary, especially as an aid to policy decisions about early childhood programs and in selecting specific programs. Not only should the programs' effectiveness be evaluated in these long-term assessments, but the worthiness of the goals must be evaluated as well. As discussed in chapter 3, early childhood programs have a variety of goals, and not all programs agree about their goals.

Long-term evaluation has limited use for the classroom teacher. The teacher needs to act immediately, using evaluation as the basis for judging immediate past actions in order to plan immediate future actions—short-term goals. Long-term goals are expected to be met if the related short-term goals are continually achieved. Evaluation of short-term goals can be based upon observation of children's actions, analysis of their products, or some form of testing.

Many programs state goals in specific behavioral terms that are immediately identifiable. Indeed, some psychologists feel that behavioral objectives based upon the requirements of later schooling are the only legitimate goals of education in the early years. The ability to make a specific judgment, categorize an object by a visible attribute, or manifest a particular skill such as reading a prescribed set of words, might constitute such a goal. Behavioral goals are attractive because their attainment is easily judged. Often a criterion level attainment is stated, thus defining the judgments even more clearly. Information about attainment can be used to modify the program and improve its effectiveness. The availability of evaluation results is an attractive aspect of the use of behavioral goals.

Behavioral goals become significant because of their relationship to broader goals of education. The relationship between observable goals and the more significant nonbehavioral ones is inferential. A child may get the right answer to a math problem (a behavior), and we assume from this that he understands the mathematical process involved (an inference). The assumption may not be true, however, and unless we seek additional verification, the evaluation can be faulty. The difference between behavioral and nonbehavioral goals may, in the final analysis, be one's conscious use of inference and belief.

Teachers, nevertheless, need to state goals in such a way that information about the effectiveness of their programs can be collected. The goals of a program should be attainable during its duration, whether this be a day or an academic year. Though behavioral objectives may not be appropriate for all areas of the program, some degree of specificity should be in any statement of goals so that the teacher can determine attainment (see, for example, Mager, 1975).

While instructional objectives might be appropriate for evaluating some learning activities, they can be a hindrance in evaluating others. Teachers often engage children in classroom activities, especially in play, music, art, and on field trips, without a clear conception of what each child should learn. Expressive objectives that describe educational encounters might be more appropriate for evaluating these activities. Expressive objectives allow the teacher to examine the quality and relevance of a learning experience for a child without undue concern for its particular outcome (Eisner, 1969).

Much discussion of evaluation centers totally around pupil achievement, but other forms of evaluation should be the teacher's responsibility as well. These include evaluating program models, program materials, and classroom program implementation.

EVALUATING PROGRAMS

Even at the nursery-school level, different programs exist. Some stress academic achievement, some social relations, and others combinations of goals. Judging and selecting a curriculum is a difficult task.

One way to select programs is to determine the program's value base and match it with the value preferences of the teachers who must implement it. EPIE Report 42, discussed in chapter 3, presents a self-analysis checklist of views of human development and related early childhood program preferences that teachers can use to clarify what programs they prefer (EPIE, 1972). After working through the checklist, they can seek to match programs and preferences.

Often teachers' decisions about programs relate to selecting a textbook series in a single subject area. Teachers and curriculum committees may be swayed by book salespersons, special interest groups, or popular articles, adopting programs without comparing alternatives because they are familiar or have been endorsed by someone.

Robert Hillerich (1974) feels that teachers selecting a reading program need first to determine its philosophy and desired emphasis. They must develop guidelines so they know what to look for in a reading program. The entire staff should be involved in a consensus decision rather than a majority vote. Hillerich presents an evaluation form showing what a group could use to evaluate a kindergarten through second-grade reading program (see Figure 15–1).

Arthur Nichols and Anna Ochoa (1971) have presented criteria for selecting social studies textbooks that are relevant to the primary grades. They feel one must evaluate both the knowledge and the intellectual components of these books. In looking at the knowledge component, teachers should judge how social issues are handled, whether information is objectively presented, whether an interdisciplinary conceptual base is used, and whether the most recent scholarly findings are reflected in the material. The intellectual component refers to the development of intellectual skills in the book. Teachers need to determine if the book can serve as a base for inquiry, if higher-order questions are asked, if the book could serve as a basis for decision making, and if the knowledge presented is related to the children's life span.

A system for analyzing social science curricula has been developed by the Social Science Education Consortium (SSEC). This system describes program attributes using the following categories:

1. *Descriptive characteristics*—The "nuts and bolts" of the curriculum
2. *Rationale and objectives*—Why the program was created and what the anticipated outcomes are
3. *Antecedent conditions*—The particular conditions under which the program might be successful

		Name of program			
Evaluating teacher _____ Grade _____					
3=Very good; 2=Good; 1=Poor; 0=Omitted in program					
Teacher edition	Philosophy clear (introduction)				
	Specific direction for skill teaching				
	Ease of use				
	Provision for individual differences				
Content	Interest appeal to children				
	Variety of types of reading				
Format	Physically clear and attractive				
Illustrations	Aesthetic appeal				
ADEQUACY OF SKILL DEVELOPMENT					
Readiness deals with letters and sounds in words, not just with general language development.					
Skills are learned through use, not just through memorizing rules.					
Child is shown how the skill is used in reading.					
Reading includes use of context, emphasis on reading for meaning.					
Suggested questions for discussion cover the inferential and critical as well as literal levels.					
Readiness for comprehension and study skills begins with these skills at the listening level.					
The child is taught a definite system for attacking an unknown word (mark *Yes* or *No* in each column).					
What is the system? (Put a check in proper columns.)					
Guess from context only.					
Remember the word from the introduction.					
Apply a rule or rules.					
Sound out the word.					
Use context and consonant-sound associations.					

FIGURE 15-1　Evaluation of Reading Program: Kindergarten—Grade 2

From Robert L. Hillerich, "So You're Evaluating Reading Programs," *Elementary School Journal*, 1974, 75 (3), 179. Reprinted by permission of the University of Chicago Press.

4. *Content*—The specific changes intended in the knowledge, attitudes, and behavior of the students

5. *Instructional theory and teaching strategies*—The underlying learning theory and teaching strategies, and their relationship in the program

6. *Overall judgments*—Evaluative judgments about the materials

These broad categories are further broken down in subcategories for analysis. The category of *antecedent conditions,* for example, includes subcategories relating to pupil characteristics, teaching capabilities, and community requirements, school requirements, and the articulation of requirements (Stevens & Fetsko, 1968).

Information about educational programs can also be requested from the Educational Resources Information Centers (ERICs). These ERIC Centers, supported by the United States Office of Education, collect information about educational programs in a particular area. Although the information available might not be as systematically developed as the ones provided by SSEC, they still can be a useful resource. Current ERIC clearinghouses are listed below.

ERIC CLEARINGHOUSES

Adult, Career, and Vocational Education. Ohio State University, 1960 Kenny Road, Columbus, Ohio 43210

Counseling and Personnel Services. University of Michigan, 2108 School of Education Building, Ann Arbor, Michigan 48109

Educational Management. University of Oregon, Eugene, Oregon 97403

Elementary and Early Childhood. University of Illinois, College of Education, Urbana, Illinois 61801

Handicapped and Gifted Children. Council for Exceptional Children, 1920 Association Drive, Reston, Virginia 22091

Higher Education. George Washington University, One Dupont Circle, Suite 630, Washington, D.C. 20036

Information Resources. Syracuse University, School of Education, 130 Huntington Hall, Syracuse, New York 13210

Junior Colleges. University of California, 96 Powell Library Building, Los Angeles, California 90024

Languages and Linguistics. 3520 Prospect St., N.W., Washington, D.C. 20007

Reading and Communication Skills. National Council of Teachers of English, 1111 Kenyon Road, Urbana, Illinois 61801

Rural Education and Small Schools. New Mexico State University, Box 3AP, Las Cruces, New Mexico 88003

Science, Mathematics, and Environmental Education. Ohio State University, 1200 Chambers Road, Third Floor, Columbus, Ohio 43212

Social Studies/Social Science Education. 855 Broadway, Boulder, Colorado 80302

Teacher Education. American Association of Colleges for Teacher Education, One Dupont Circle, N.W., Suite 610, Washington, D.C. 20036

Tests, Measurement, and Evaluation. Educational Testing Service, Rosedale Road, Princeton, New Jersey 08540

Urban Education. Teachers College, Columbia University, Box 40, 525 West 120th Street, New York, New York 10027

Additional information about early childhood education can be sought from the following organizations:

Association for Childhood Education International. 11141 Georgia Avenue, Suite 200, Wheaton, Md. 20902

American Montessori Society, Inc. 175 Fifth Avenue, New York, N.Y. 10010

Black Child Development Institute, Inc. 1463 Rhode Island Avenue, N.W., Washington, D.C. 20005

Council for Exceptional Children. 1920 Association Drive, Reston, Va. 22091

Child Welfare League of America, Inc. 67 Irving Place, New York, N.Y. 10010

Day Care Council of America, Inc. 1602 17th Street, N.W., Washington, D.C. 20009.

National Association for the Education of Young Children. 1834 Connecticut Avenue, N.W., Washington, D.C. 20009

Parent Cooperative Preschool International. 20551 Lakeshore Rd., Baie D'Urfé, Quebec, Canada H9X IR3

Southern Association for Children Under Six. Box 5403 Brady Station, Little Rock, Ark. 72205

Teachers might also wish to communicate directly with schools and agencies developing innovative programs. Many of these are reported in various education journals and at educational conferences.

EVALUATING CLASSROOMS

A program is a promise of learning activities to be. The teacher must see that the promise is fulfilled. Program implementation can differ significantly from program intent. By assessing the classroom, the teacher will be able to judge the quality of implementation.

A number of observational schemes are available to monitor and assess classroom practices. Most of these are designed for research purposes and require an outside observer. However, there are some simple techniques that teachers can use to gather information about their own classrooms. They can provide limited but reliable information that can be used to improve educational opportunities for children. Two examples of such techniques follow.

Reference was made earlier to classroom dimensions identified by Elizabeth Jones (n.d.). Using the dimensions of hard/soft, open/closed, simple/complex, intrusion/seclusion, and high mobility/low mobility, a teacher can describe the physical dimensions of a classroom and determine if it approximates the setting the teacher desires to create for children. After recording the classroom dimensions, the teacher can modify the room systematically to make it closer to the ideal.

Harms and Clifford (1980) have developed the *Early Childhood Rating Scale,* useful for evaluating various preschool settings. Their scale is composed of seven separate subscales: personal care routines of children, furnishings and displays for children, language-reasoning experiences, fine and gross motor activities, creative activities, social development, and adult needs. The teacher can observe the setting, then rate each of the thirty-seven items on the scale, scoring them from 1 (inadequate) to 7 (excellent). Criteria and standards for each score are provided. Space is also provided on the scoring sheets for teachers to add comments. By summing the scores on all items in each of the seven subscales, the teacher can develop a profile of the setting. The identification of areas of strengths and weaknesses can suggest ways to modify the setting. Subsequent observations with the rating scale can help determine whether changes have led to improvements.

EVALUATING TEACHING

By evaluating programs and settings the teacher is evaluating the *preactive* aspects of teaching—that is, the planning and preparation activities. A teacher needs to evaluate the *interactive* aspects of teaching—the behavior that takes place in contact with the children as well.

A number of techniques have been used to analyze and assess teacher behavior. Generally, they require that observations be collected by an observer or through videotaping. The teacher can then analyze the records of these observations.

Probably most practical is some nonsystematic way of observing or recalling classroom incidents and analyzing them in relation to pupils' responses. A teacher might be able to sit alone at noon or at the end of the school day and write what can be recalled. For example, a teacher wishing to focus on a discussion session could try to write questions and comments as accurately as possible, analyzing those questions in a number of ways. Were they open-ended, requiring divergent responses from children, or closed, demanding a single convergent response? Did the questions elicit answers requiring higher-order thought processes, like analysis or criticism, or lower-order thought processes, like recall? Did responses to children tease out additional information or did they limit discussion? Were comments supportive of the children's contributions or did they "cut children?" Were responses personal or stereotyped?

With such an analysis, a teacher is in a better position to determine the consistency of behavior with intent. In such a way, a teacher can begin to develop self-awareness and analyze all areas of teaching and relationships with all the children. With continued self-reflection, teachers can become more sensitive to children's needs and more aware of how to serve them appropriately.

EVALUATING CHILDREN

We have two basic concerns in evaluating children: the *ability* of children to benefit from instructional experiences, and the *degree* to which they benefit. The former leads to a judgment about readiness for learning, the latter about learning outcomes. In either case, the teacher makes a judgment based upon observations of a child's behavior. If we want to judge what children can do, the best way is to observe everything they do.

Since teachers cannot observe everything that children do, they look for ways to sample their behavior and generalize from the samples collected. Teachers can use a variety of techniques to gather an adequate sample, including direct observation, checklists and rating scales, and formal and informal tests. The information gathered through these techniques must be judged, and both the information and the judgment recorded and communicated to others.

All evaluation involves some form of observation, either controlled as in a test or uncontrolled as in a natural setting. Each kind of information gathered offers teachers different insights into the child. Often information collected in different ways is combined in making an evaluation.

No matter what method teachers use to collect information about children, they need to be concerned with the validity, reliability, and practicality of the technique. *Validity* refers to the degree to which the evaluation technique assessed what it claims to assess. If an academic achievement test relies too heavily on the ability of the child to read and follow elaborate written directions, then the test may assess reading skills and mask the other academic abilities of children who have difficulty with reading.

Reliability refers to the consistency of a measure—the degree to which a child's score might vary from day to day on a test, or to which observations may vary depending on who is using an observation scale. *Practicality* refers to the ability of the teacher to use a specific technique under normal circumstances. Techniques that require high levels of training or a great deal of time to administer may be impractical for classroom teachers (Goodwin & Driscoll, 1980).

The evaluation of children often begins prior to their entrance into school. As preschool programs for handicapped children have been mandated, procedures to identify and screen them have been established. Such a screening procedure can utilize paraprofessionals and volunteers as well as trained professionals. Parents are invited to bring their children into centers for screening of visual and auditory acuity, speech articulation, and social-emotional, cognitive, and physical levels. As problems are identified, specific in-depth evaluations are made. The results of these procedures are discussed with parents, and services to help children are then offered. The goal of such early identification is to help handicapped children by providing early intervention and thus improve their chances of being successfully integrated into regular school classes later (Spodek, Saracho, & Lee, 1984).

Screening of handicapped children continues through the school years. Teachers in preschool, kindergarten, and primary classes need to be especially alert to possible handicapping conditions in their children, since not all children have gone through the screening process and some handicapping conditions only show up later in the child's life.

Observational checklists and rating scales are extremely useful in identifying handicapped children, as are screening tests. Among the screening instruments teachers might use are the following.

ABC Inventory. Muskegon, Mich.: Research Concepts, 1965.

Comprehensive Identification Process. Bensenville, Ill.: Scholastic Testing Service, 1970.

Cooperative Preschool Inventory. Princeton, N.J.: Educational Testing Service, 1970.

Denver Developmental Screening Test. Denver, Colo.: Ladoca Project and Publishing, Inc., 1970.

Developmental Indicators for the Assessment of Learning. Highland Park, Ill.: DIAL, Inc., 1975.

Metropolitan Readiness Test. Atlanta, Ga.: Psychological Corp., 1976.

TESTING YOUNG CHILDREN

In recent years there has been an emphasis on using formal tests with young children. Tests can be separated into two basic kinds: *norm-referenced tests* and *criterion-referenced tests*. Norm-referenced tests compare an individual's performance on a test with that of an external norm or reference group. A test of intelligence, for example, generates a score based on how well the individual performed in comparison to a representative group of children of the same age. Similarly, a norm-referenced achievement test compares an individual's performance on items related to academic learning in relation to others in the same school grade. Providing a norming group is useful in interpreting performance if the norming group is truly representative and if the comparison serves a legitimate purpose. Mentally retarded children, for example, are identified by scores on norm-referenced standardized tests of intelligence. These scores are useful in justifying the use of special educational services.

Criterion-referenced tests do not use a comparison group. The score on such a test is determined by a particular performance in relation to a standard of achievement. Spelling all the words on a list correctly could lead to a high score irrespective of how others might do in spelling those same words. Most teacher-made achievement tests that measure a child's success on an assigned learning task are criterion-referenced tests. While norm-referenced tests are standardized, with the identical test given to all in the same manner, criterion-referenced tests need not be standardized.

The tests usually given to children in the early years of schooling can be categorized into developmental, intelligence, readiness, and achievement tests.

Although readiness and achievement tests can be criterion referenced, the vast majority of all the tests used on young children are norm referenced. The fact that a norming group is used allows these tests to be developmentally appropriate.

Developmental Tests

Developmental tests are used to determine an individual's degree of maturation. Observation of a child's physical characteristics, such as body proportions or development of the wrist bone, can be used to assess maturation. Most tests, however, consist of items that require children's performance. Frances L. Ilg and Louise Bates Ames' book, *School Readiness* (1978), contains a series of tasks for children to perform. From an analysis of a child's performance on these tasks, a teacher might determine if the child is mature enough to profit from school instruction. The tasks described in many of Jean Piaget's studies may also be considered a series of developmental tests: these have been used primarily to determine level of intellectual development.

The information from developmental tests is useful in deciding whether a child is ready for a particular school experience. However, teachers should be careful not to exclude children from formal educational experiences because of lack of maturation. Human development is highly plastic and a child's experiences tend to modify his development. Rather than exclusion, what may be needed are differentiated educational opportunities.

Intelligence Tests

Intelligence tests contain sets of tasks that require using learned skills for adequate performance at specific levels. The assumption underlying them is that if all children have equal opportunities to learn these skills, the differences in levels of performance are the results of differences in inherent ability. Though all children do not have the same inherent abilities, many do not have the same opportunities to learn the skills sampled in intelligence tests. These tests generally seem to favor children of white, middle-class background and less adequately sample the inherent abilities of minority-group children.

Intelligence tests were originally designed to predict the academic achievement of children. Most intelligence tests can predict academic performance well when there is no significant change in the child's educational circumstances. Evidence suggests that when these circumstances are changed, predictive ability does not hold up as well. Moving children with low IQ levels from an educationally dull to an educationally stimulating environment may not only increase educational performance but also lead to increases in scores on intelligence tests.

Significant decisions about a child's education are often based upon intelligence test scores. Children can be penalized for not being able to score well because they have been denied the opportunity to learn those things sampled in the test. Although intelligence tests do not create discrimination, their careless use can perpetuate unequal educational practices in schools.

Readiness Tests

Most readiness tests assess the child's ability to profit from instruction. These tests are actually early achievement tests. They can also be used for diagnostic purposes.

In addition to using formal tests, teachers can also use a range of informal techniques for determining readiness. An informal assessment of reading readiness could collect information on the child's language ability and his desire to learn to read, as well as the information on the readiness checklist presented in chapter 5. Classroom observations can produce information about readiness since any information about a child's present achievement also provides information about his predisposition for further learning.

Achievement Tests

Achievement tests assess a child's or class's accomplishments in the areas of academic learning. Such tests are designed for administration at the primary grades or beyond. They are available for different curricular areas, and teachers may select a full battery of tests or administer only a single subtest.

Achievement tests do not sample the total curriculum offerings of the school, only academic skills. Teachers need to insure that inappropriate use of test results does not distort the program offerings.

Achievement tests, like intelligence tests, are standardized using a norm group including children from rural and urban areas, different socioeconomic levels, and different geographic areas. Since scores are averaged to create a grade-level norm, half the test scores fall above the norm and half below. Within the standardizing population, there are differences in average test scores of subgroups identifiable by geographic area, degree of urbanization, and socioeconomic status.

Grade-level norms are useful only to the degree that the population tested reflects the standardized population. If children differ from that population, the norms become less meaningful.

Norms are descriptive of a population at a particular time. They need not set expectation. It is possible for every group to exceed the norms on almost every achievement test under optimal learning conditions, assuming this achievement is the teacher's goal.

Although standardized tests are useful, many times nonstandardized criterion-referenced tests are more appropriate. Teachers should develop many formal and informal techniques to sample children's learning systematically. Nonstandardized methods can also provide process data that can be used to improve instruction. A number of children might get the same mathematics item wrong on a particular test. One child's error could result from faulty computation, another's because he did not understand the concept involved, while a third might simply have been careless. Analyzing test errors might suggest different activities for different children. If evaluation is used as a diagnostic tool in planning, this type of data collection becomes invaluable. Nonstandardized means of data collection include teacher-developed tests, observational techniques, checklists, rating scales, sociometric techniques, and collections of children's products.

Observational Techniques

Teachers may take time at the end of a day to record the significant occurrences. They can note what happened to individual children or individual problems that arose. Such anecdotal records are helpful in thinking through a school day and in planning for future activities, but memory is selective. It is the extraordinary, rather than the normal, that is remembered, and an unrepresentative picture of a child's behavior may result. The use of running records—on-the-spot observations of occurrences—is far superior in recreating a true picture of the day. Teachers should learn techniques for taking running records (see Cohen & Stern, 1978).

Direct observation of children's behavior has the advantage of giving teachers clues about the process of their learning. A careful recording of the interactions between a child and other children or between a child and a set of instructional materials can provide the basis for judgments about how a child is thinking or feeling. The results of such observations can be compared over time to judge changes in behavior for individual children.

Observing and recording children's actions is time consuming. One way to become more efficient in collecting this kind of information is systematically to sample behavior. Two approaches that have been used in early childhood education are *time sampling* and *event sampling* (Genishi, 1982).

In time sampling the teacher focuses on selected behaviors, noting their occurrence at uniform time intervals, which could range from several seconds to five or ten minutes or longer. If a category system is selected in which a tally mark or symbol is used to record the presence of a particular type of behavior on a special observation form, then little time is spent in recording. A teacher might be concerned with the type of social play in which children engage. Periodically the class would be scanned and a mark placed next to each child's name, *S* for solitary play, *P* for parallel play, and so forth.

Event sampling is used when teachers want to collect information on the frequency with which a particular behavior occurs. Such an observation system need not be time based. If a teacher is concerned with determining the amount of aggressive behavior manifested by a number of children, a tally mark might be placed next to each child's name each time aggressive behavior (hitting or pushing, for example) is noted for that child. At the end of the day, the tally marks can be added up for each child to get a sense of aggressiveness in each child's behavior.

Observational Scales and Checklists

Checklists and rating scales allow teachers to assess children's behavior or performance. While they do not provide descriptions of behavior, they allow a summary judgment, based upon continued observation, to be recorded simply.

Checklists generally include a series of descriptive statements about children's performance. The teacher checks those statements that characterize the child, ignoring those that do not. Using a reading checklist, for example, the teacher, after marking those items related to readiness that characterize a particular child, can judge the child to be ready to begin reading instruction, or determine whether particular readiness skills need to be taught first.

Rating scales also allow teachers to record judgments about children's characteristics or behaviors. The rating scale, however, also provides for a qualitative judgment to be made. The scale presented in Figure 15-2 allows the teacher to identify both the skills the child has and the degree of proficiency shown in each skill. In using such a scale care must be taken that the rating on each item is well thought out and does not result from a halo effect.

Sociometric Techniques

Teachers concerned with children's social behavior can use sociometric techniques to assess it. Each child can be asked a set of questions to elicit his choice of friends. Such questions as "Whom would you like to play with outside?" "Whom would you like to have sit near you at snack time?" or "Whom would you like to invite home after school?" might be used at the nursery or kindergarten levels. Appropriate questions for older children can be developed as well. The children's responses to the questions can be plotted on a chart, which will then show more and less popular children and what groupings of friendships exist in the class.

Sociometric techniques are less reliable for children than for adults; best friends can easily change from day to day. Teachers need to collect a number of such observations over a period of time, looking for evidence of stable relationships and shifts that might occur as a result of program changes.

Collecting Pupil Products

Another way of sampling children's learning is to systematically collect the products of their work: drawings and paintings, stories and mathematics work, and reports. Such a cumulative collection allows the teacher to review progress and judge their work at any point in time. The collection of children's products must be systematic; the great temptation is to allow them to carry each product home, leaving the teacher without an important data source. A painting or a story should be periodically selected to keep in school, and if children are told why materials are being collected they will usually not resist. Work with

Name of child _____ Date _____

	Rating	Comments
Self Care Skills		
Zippers clothes		
Matches shoes to feet		
Ties laces		
Puts on snowsuit alone		
Washes hands properly		
Cleanup Skills		
Washes paint brushes clean		
Sponges tables clean		
Puts materials back in proper order		
Sweeps floor if needed		
Puts apron away properly		
Social Skills		
Shows leadership		
Participates in group activities		
Takes turns		
Follows classroom rules		
Physical Skills		
Can walk a balance beam		
Can hop		
Can skip		
Climbs well		
Can draw a straight line		
Can use scissors well		
Can use a paint brush		
Can hammer a nail in straight		
Can saw a straight cut		

Rate each child on a scale from 1 to 5

1 Shows high level of performance consistently
2 Shows good performance, not consistent
3 Shows fair performance, inconsistent
4 Performs poorly, erratic
5 Cannot perform

FIGURE 15-2   Skills Checklist

name, date, and circumstance of production helps; if the teacher uses a portfolio for each child, storage problems are minimized.

Some products are hard to collect. A clay bowl will not store in a portfolio, and a child's block construction cannot be saved. A verbal production disappears immediately. Works of this kind can be described or collected on tape or film. These collections are invaluable in assessing children's progress throughout the year and demonstrating it to parents.

JUDGING CHILDREN

Collecting data is only one step in the process of evaluation. The teacher must interpret data and judge them. Finally, plans for action may result from these interpretations.

Teachers use evaluation data to make decisions about children's programs. If the children have achieved the goals of a study unit, they can confidently move on to new work. If they have not, then special activities should be planned or the program modified.

The information collected on each child can also provide the basis for differentiated educational activities. As the teacher becomes aware of each child's skills, abilities, interests, and behavior patterns, programming can become more meaningful and closer to the needs of particular children. Pacing may vary and other forms of programming tried.

The results of evaluation are often shared with others: future teachers, ancillary personnel, the school principal, and parents. The need for communication and for later reference requires that teachers use some record-keeping system. Many schools maintain cumulative record folders on children; teachers may supplement these with their own records. A good record-keeping system is one in which significant information may be found easily.

Maintaining Classroom Records

In addition to the cumulative record folder, teachers keep a variety of records on the children that may not follow them to later classes. Records of daily attendance are generally required, and new teachers should become familiar with the procedures in their schools. Some schools require that all absences be accounted for, or children may have to submit a release from a physician before entering school after certain illnesses. Even if the child is absent for a short time, it is wise for a teacher to contact the family. Such absences may signal family crisis. At times, families may even move from a community without notifying the school. Brief contact with the family helps the teacher understand the reasons for absence and may provide clues to help the child.

Teachers often have the children tally their participation in specific activities and may wish to transfer the results of the tally to a more compact form later. The results of teacher's observations are also an important record of the child's activities. Most observations are short and can easily fit on one or two five-by-eight-inch cards. Organizing these in a card file allows the teacher to leaf through quickly to review information on the child.

Because teaching is a public trust, teachers are being called upon more and more to justify their professional acts. Records are important not only for the teacher's decision making but also as a way of justifying their decisions to others. Demands may come from supervisors or from the parents and the community the school serves. The ability to document the sources of decisions and judgments is a requirement that the public can make on the professional, and teachers must be prepared to meet this requirement.

REPORTING TO PARENTS

Parents are interested in the progress of their children in school. Reports to parents represent only one part of the teacher's relationship, but they are important and require the utmost in care and honesty.

An ideal report should be easy to complete, yet be comprehensive. It should communicate clearly and unequivocally the child's behavior and learning in school without being burdensome to read or requiring the parent's comprehension of professional language.

However, it is difficult to communicate clearly when the teacher and the parent may have different referents for the same words. It is hard to be fully descriptive when thirty or more reports must be completed several times during the year. And it is difficult to pinpoint progress without seeming unnecessarily judgmental.

Most reporting systems are the result of compromise. They are not too difficult to administer and they communicate reasonably clearly. Teachers seem unsatisfied with almost all reporting systems; perhaps there is no ideal system. Most schools tend to use report cards, descriptive letters to parents, or parent conferences as ways of reporting; often these are used in some combination.

Report Cards

Report cards are relatively simple to complete and communicate fairly well to parents. A report card may contain lines representing various areas of pupil achievement, such as reading and writing. Schools sometimes also include certain behavior characteristics or study habits.

Symbols are often used to report a child's achievement, such as letter grades *A* to *D* or *E,* or *U* for unsatisfactory and *S* for satisfactory achievement. Additional symbols for improvement or high achievement can also be used.

Though it is simple to assign a letter grade, it is often difficult to determine exactly what it means. If grade level standards are used, then performance level is fairly well communicated by the report card. It is difficult to know, though, if a child is working at his expected capacity, above it, or below it. If children are graded according to the teacher's estimate of their capability, then the letter or symbol will mean something different for each child and the common base in communication breaks down.

Despite the limitations of report cards, both parents and teachers often state that they like to use them, possibly because of the security built by years of tradition. However, schools frequently find that they must augment this type of communication, sometimes with supplementary checklists.

Descriptive Letters

A report card communicates a child's level of performance; not the qualitative aspects of school work, however. Teachers may use descriptive letters to tell more about the quality and content of the child's work, providing a fuller picture for the parent. It might contain information about the child's learning style, about books read, materials used, or about interactions with others. Some teachers may write individual letters about each child; others duplicate a single letter telling the parents what the class as a whole has done during the year, supplementing this with individual reports through conferences.

Parent Conferences

The most communicative, but also the most time-consuming, means of reporting is the parent conference. In a conference, parent and teacher can sit face-to-face and discuss mutual concerns about the child. Any misunderstandings can be instantly corrected, and immediate feedback provided.

Parent conferences should be planned carefully. The teacher can make a list of concerns as an outline of items to be covered in the conference. Parents bring up their concerns as well. Teacher records are invaluable in the conference. Observations can be shared, test results, ratings and checklists can be referred to, and pupil products can be shown to parents to demonstrate growth over the school year. It is useful to keep a record of a parent conference, noting the topics discussed, the reactions of parents, and any procedures that should follow up the conference, such as additional observation or communication.

Parent conferences are often used at the nursery and kindergarten level because of the lack of grade-level standards upon which to base a grade symbol. This requires that descriptive reporting take place. Conferences can be equally useful at every level of education, however, and in many cases the best communication takes place through a combination of techniques.

Reporting is only one component of a system of evaluation. The major impact of the teacher's evaluation is in the improvement of the educational experience of each child. By knowing her children and the results of classroom activities of each individual, the teacher can continue activities that have proved successful, replace unsuccessful ones with new activities, and continue to extend the learning opportunities of the children. A realistic picture of classroom activities and their consequences can help provide continually richer educational opportunities to children during their early years in school.

REFERENCES

COHEN, D. H., and STERN, V. *Observing and recording the behavior of young children* (2nd ed.). New York: Teachers College Press, 1978.

EISNER, E. W. Instructional and expressive objectives: Their formulation and use in curriculum. In E. W. Eisner, H. J. Sullivan, and L. Tyler. *Instructional objectives.* Skokie, Ill.: Rand McNally, 1969.

Educational Products Information Exchange. *Report 42, Early childhood education: How to select and evaluate materials.* New York: EPIE, 1972.

GENISHI, C. Observational research methods for early childhood education. In B. Spodek (Ed.). *Handbook of research in early childhood education.* New York: Free Press, 1982.

GOODWIN, W. L., and DRISCOLL, L. A. *Handbook for measurement and evaluation in early childhood education.* San Francisco: Jossey-Bass, 1980.

HARMS, T., and CLIFFORD, R. *Early childhood environment rating scale.* New York: Teachers College Press, 1980.

HILLERICH, R. L. So you're evaluating reading programs. *Elementary School Journal, 1974, 75,* 172-182.

ILG, F. L., AMES, L. B., HAINES, J., and GILLESPIE, C. *School readiness* (Rev. ed.). New York: Harper & Row, Pub., 1978.

JONES, E. *Dimensions of teaching-learning environments.* Pasadena, Calif.: Pacific Oaks College, n.d.

LAZAR, I., and DARLINGTON, R. Lasting effects of early education: A report from the consortium for longitudal studies. *Monographs of the Society for Research in Child Development, 1982, 47,* (2–3, Serial No. 195).

MAGER, R. F. *Preparing instructional objectives* (Rev. ed.). Belmont, Calif.: Pitman Learning, 1975.

NICHOLS, A. S., and OCHOA, A. Evaluating textbooks for elementary social studies: Criteria for the seventies. *Social Education, 1971, 35,* 290ff.

STEVENS, W. W., and FETSKO, W. A curriculum analysis system. *Social Science Consortium Newsletter,* 1968, No. 4, 1–4.

SUGGESTED READING

ALMY, M., and GENISHI, C. *Ways of studying children* (Rev. ed.). New York: Columbia University Press, 1979.

BOEHM, A. E., and WEINBERG, R. M. *The classroom observer.* New York: Teachers College Press, 1977.

BUROS, O. K.   *Tests in print II.* Highland Park, N.J.: Gryphon Press, 1974.
COHEN, D., and STERN, V.   *Observing and recording the behavior of young children* (2nd ed.). New York: Teachers College Press, 1978.
DEAN, J.   *Recording children's progress.* New York: Citation Press, 1972.
GAGE, N. L.   (Ed.).   *Handbook of research on teaching.* Skokie, Ill.: Rand McNally, 1963.
IRWIN, D. M., and BUSHNELL, M. M.   *Observational strategies for child study.* New York: Holt, Rinehart & Winston, 1980.

Index